This second edition of *Feng Shui and Money* take:
Eric Shaffert's popular feng shui training courses
students report:

"Believe that something amazing is around the corner, and it has your name on it. That's what the feng shui course has shown me. Brilliant!"
—Dawn McKoy, credit counsellor, London

"This class is pure genius. The holistic approach has addressed abundance in all areas of my life and helped me heal my financial wounds. Eric's way of explaining these essential issues is both simple and profound."
—Lisa Lerner, teacher, New York City

"Eric is an intuitive teacher and an astute practitioner who understands people. He facilitates the group with incredible sensitivity and insightful knowing, both of which he shares with generosity of spirit. His work is life changing, and that is a rare gem."
—Fiona Moser, business owner, London

"Eric has brought to life how the home is an incredible metaphor for our own lives. His teaching tools are both intensively practical and refreshingly unique, enabling me to enhance my entire home life and pass this gift to so many others."
—Anusha Arulvel, naturopath, Essex, UK

"Just halfway through the course and already many areas of my life are responding. By applying these principles to my work as an artist, suddenly I am being paid outrageously well for what I love to do! Each week brings exciting new revelations."
—Isabel Thompson, artist, New York City

"Eric is such an inspiring teacher with a no-nonsense direct approach, yet he is full of compassion and humor. So far I have done two weekends and am already more calm and present and applying feng shui to turn my life around."
—Tara Jaff, musician, London

"Eric's spiritual connection combined with his practical experience entices his students into realms they never knew existed until they enrolled in his feng shui course. It is life changing."
—Jill Trelease, consultant in training, Bath, UK

"*Feng Shui and Money* gives you the tools to attain your heart's desire."
—Randi Lynn Ditman, Reiki master, New York City

Praise for *Feng Shui and Money*

"Eric Shaffert is the feng shui consultant I chose for my international coaching business. He is exceptionally gifted and intuitive, and his insightful recommendations quickly doubled our revenue. This book is the perfect combination of practical and mystical ideas that will turn your financial life around."

—Talane Miedaner, author of the bestseller *Coach Yourself to Success*

"In *Feng Shui and Money*, Eric Shaffert offers important keys for transforming our outer and inner worlds to help achieve true abundance. May his words awaken you to your own infinite worth!"

—Steven Post, author of *The Modern Book of Feng Shui*,
and first teacher of feng shui in the United States

"*Feng Shui and Money* is a design guide for the mind, home, and spirit. Step by step, it walks you through ancient methods for success, providing a healthy financial regimen that can rearrange your life."

—Thomas M. Kostigen, author of *What Money Really Means*

"I highly recommend for you to use Eric Shaffert's book as a wonderful reference for creating your abundant and prosperous livelihood. His practical and transcendental recommendations will help you go 'beyond the box' to enhance your quality of life. Enjoy the process!"

—R. D. Chin, author of *Feng Shui Revealed*

"Abundance is much more than money, and Eric Shaffert speaks to your heart and soul with this rich and insightful book. It is a great guide to a brighter future."

—Barbara Biziou, author of *The Joys of Everyday Ritual*

"With this book, Eric Shaffert has changed the way I view the world. No tool to accomplish our desires is more critical than money, and *Feng Shui and Money* shows you how to structure your daily life in ways to attract it. Heed the principles outlined in this book, stick to the nine-week plan, and you'll reach your financial goals. It's as simple as that."

—Jeff Olson, author of *Goal-Setting and Achievement* and *Cutting Costs*

FENG SHUI
AND
MONEY

A NINE-WEEK PROGRAM FOR
Creating Wealth
USING
Ancient Principles and Techniques

SECOND EDITION

ERIC SHAFFERT

ALLWORTH PRESS
NEW YORK

Allworth Press books may be purchased in bulk at special discounts for sales promotion, corporate gifts, fund-raising, or educational purposes. Special editions can also be created to specifications. For details, contact the Special Sales Department, Allworth Press, 307 West 36th Street, 11th Floor, New York, NY 10018 or info@skyhorsepublishing.com.

22 21 20 19 18   5 4 3 2 1

Published by Allworth Press, an imprint of Skyhorse Publishing, Inc. 307 West 36th Street, 11th Floor, New York, NY 10018. Allworth Press® is a registered trademark of Skyhorse Publishing, Inc.®, a Delaware corporation.

www.allworth.com

Cover design by Mary Ann Smith

Library of Congress Cataloging-in-Publication Data

Names: Shaffert, Eric, author.
Title: Feng shui and money : a nine-week program for creating wealth using
    ancient principles and techniques / Eric Shaffert.
Description: Second Edition. | New York, N.Y. : Allworth Press, an imprint of
    Skyhorse Publishing, Inc., [2018] | Revised edition of the author's Feng
    shui and money, c2002. | Includes bibliographical references and index.
Identifiers: LCCN 2018002592 (print) | LCCN 2018010078 (ebook) | ISBN
    9781621536437 (eBook) | ISBN 9781621536383 (pbk. : alk. paper)
Subjects: LCSH: Finance, Personal--Psychological aspects. | Feng shui. |
    Wealth--Psychological aspects.
Classification: LCC HG179 (ebook) | LCC HG179 .S4257 2018 (print) | DDC
    332.024/01--dc23
LC record available at https://lccn.loc.gov/2018002592

Print ISBN: 978-1-62153-638-3
eBook ISBN: 978-1-62153-643-7

Printed in the United States of America

Contents

Contents

Acknowledgments

This book would not have happened without the abundance of positive influences in my life:

His Holiness Professor Lin Yun and my feng shui teachers and mentors, Barry Gordon, Stephen Post, Edgar Sung, and Meihwa Lin; Sue Seel, my coach, who helped me clear the path for writing this book; my parents and the Shaffert/Reichle/Howden families, who enthusiastically supported my work in feng shui even before knowing what it was; my brother Kurt for diligently editing the first edition; my wife Monica, who followed the feng shui currents to my heart; my co-teachers R. D. Chin, Janus Welton, and Susie Shaw; and my many clients and students who have courageously shown me that feng shui really works by putting it into practice in their lives. Thank you!

Foreword

About sixteen years ago, I was enrolled in a feng shui training program in New York City and starting to consult for clients in their homes while working full-time at a job that I really didn't like. While I was excited about my new adventures with feng shui, I was also feeling deeply frustrated by a professional life that did not seem to develop. So, encouraged by what I was learning in my feng shui classes, I decided to implement a specific feng shui "cure" in my NYC apartment.

This "cure," which I now sometimes describe in detail in my classes, was intended to bring new opportunities via a mentor; this, I felt, was something that I had truly been missing. In fact, I would sometimes lament to friends, "If only I could meet someone who could help me move my career forward!" This had been, for many years, an unfulfilled wish.

A few weeks later, while sitting at my desk at work, I received an unsolicited phone call from a publisher, who eagerly suggested that we meet so he could refer some of his authors to the company where I was working. Despite his enthusiasm for meeting, I declined his invitation and suggested that we could easily cover all the details right then, on the phone. The publisher, however, did not relent, and so I grudgingly agreed to take the subway down to his office the following week.

When I arrived at the Allworth Press offices in midtown, I was warmly received by its founder, and yet I felt oddly uncomfortable. I was not sure why I couldn't relax, as he seemed to be a very easygoing fellow, so I decided to engage in some small talk to put my mind at ease. To start things off, I uttered the first thing that came to mind: "Oh, in addition to working at my current job, I also do feng shui . . . Do you happen to publish any feng shui books?"

The publisher, Tad Crawford, was quick to answer, "No . . . but if you were to write one, what would it be called?" Without thinking, I blurted out, *"Feng Shui and Money."* To which he quickly responded, "I like it—write me a proposal!" In that moment, I knew that this book would become a reality.

Sixteen years later, I look back at that conversation as if it just happened, but of course a lot has developed since then. This was my first book, and I truly had no idea what I was about to take on, but I left my full-time job a few months later and became devoted to putting on the page everything I had been learning about this incredible practice known as feng shui. The book was published a year later, and with the support of this new mentor and the opportunities that came along, my professional life changed in ways that I would never have predicted before doing that "cure."

Since that time, my professional life as a feng shui consultant and teacher has developed in ways that I could not have imagined. I have been featured on television and radio, conducted workshops with hundreds of people at a time, and created feng shui training programs in the US and the UK. I have consulted clients from the far corners of the globe, including a top fashion design company and a descendant of the French aristocracy.

I can see that the lives of many thousands of people have been impacted, all rippling out from that feng shui "cure" I implemented and which brought this book to print. And now, I invite you to learn the art of feng shui, to bring startling and invigorating changes to your life as well.

In all of my years of practicing this work, I have found that there is a special energy that surrounds what I call "a feng shui moment." Without wanting to sound too supernatural, it is truly as if the earth and stars come into a certain alignment, and there is a luxurious, timeless feeling that something very special is about to occur.

This was the energy I felt when I applied a relationship "cure" before meeting my wife, or when I shifted things in my apartment before receiving a very important contract. And this is what I felt as I sat on the sofa at Allworth Press in 2001, feeling a bit uneasy, just before the universe delivered the opportunity that became this book.

Before the book went to press, I was deeply honored to have a private meeting with His Holiness Professor Lin Yun, who brought this form of feng shui to the West, and who later passed away in 2010. I had sent a copy of the manuscript to him to review, and then traveled to his estate on Long Island, where I was very warmly received and offered a blessing ritual for the manuscript. Professor Lin also did a calligraphy to bring the blessing energy to all of its readers, which is included directly following this section.

I am excited to now offer the second edition, to update the ways that feng shui transformations can occur. The stories in this book are all true, and the methods have worked for me and my clients. If you are intrigued, read on!

This book covers extensive material that I offer in my classes, and a true degree of diligence may be required. While there might be books available on "instant feng shui," the benefits of this program will require a bit more of you. As with any field of study, if you regularly apply yourself, rewards for your efforts are certain to follow. Take your time, and allow the new opportunities to unfold.

I believe that there are no accidents. If you are holding this book in your hands, it is probably because you have the same yearning I had over sixteen years ago: to discover what new, unprecedented opportunities from the universe eagerly wait to be delivered to your doorstep.

May your feng shui bring you many blessings,
E. J. Shaffert
July 2017

財神

FENG SHUI and MONEY

越發越大

不敬不靈

二〇〇三年壬午端陽承佛門密宗黑教總持
朱筧立仁殷切之請碟書持無量咒以為

讀者　覽

作者　閬府祈福納財增慧保康寧

出版者　雲石精舍主人　林雲

Calligraphy Translation

The more money grows, the more wealth accumulates.
The more sincerely you worship a deity, the more you are blessed.

At the request of Crystal Chu Rinpoche, CEO of Black Sect Tantric Buddhism, H. H. Grandmaster Professor Lin Yun, owner of Yun Shih Jin She, wrote the calligraphy on the preceding page using cinnabar powder ink while chanting infinite mantras, to bless all readers, the book's author and publisher, and their whole families with good luck, prosperity, wisdom, and peace.

2002, Autumn Festival

> **Note:** The gray characters in the calligraphy are read from right to left. The first character means "wealth," and the second character means "deity." H. H. Grandmaster Lin Yun writes this calligraphy to encourage people who seek wealth to also pay respects to their deities.

Introduction

I must admit, I first became interested in feng shui for rather selfish and material-istic reasons. Not that there is anything necessarily wrong with selfish and materi-alistic motivations, as most of the world's great monuments are probably testimony to those aspirations.

But back in the 1990s, feng shui didn't occur to me as a spiritual or tran-scendental pursuit. Instead, I was drawn to it by one friend's particular story of how her financial and professional life changed dramatically, evidently due to this mystical practice.

At that time, I was a high school teacher in Brooklyn. One day, a colleague at the school pulled me aside to tell me she had been offered another job with a $10,000 raise. Then, with a hushed voice, she added that for her birthday, a friend had gifted her with a feng shui consultation for her apartment. Since that time, all sorts of weird and positive things had begun happening in her life, including this job offer.

Evidently, a few weeks after having her apartment "feng shui'd," my colleague was at a party and happened to mention in casual conversation that she was a music teacher. One new acquaintance mentioned that her school was looking for a new instructor for their music department, and soon to follow, the job was offered to my friend. Mere coincidence? She wondered . . . Upon hearing this, I raised one eyebrow and thought, "Hmm, interesting!"

My friend went on to say that she turned down the job offer, as she didn't really want to change jobs at that time. But an idea about the unexplainable power of feng shui had been planted in my mind.

There's more: That following summer, I saw my colleague again in pass-ing in my neighborhood in Brooklyn, and she excitedly told me that she had received another job offer, this time at *twice* her former salary. Again, she was at a party, casually mentioned that she was a music teacher, and once more, a new opportunity was presented to her rather effortlessly. This time, she decided to take the job.

With a look of slight bewilderment, she said in a reverent tone, "I think it has something to do with the feng shui." From that point forward, my interest in this particular form of mystical interior decorating was confirmed!

From there, my journey into this fascinating and often astonishing field of study began. After perusing a few books and becoming rather confused by the whole thing, I took a weekend feng shui workshop in New York City and was surprised how quickly it all began to make sense to me. I was very intrigued. The teacher told stories of how people's lives were dramatically changed merely by intentionally rearranging the furniture in their homes, and then went on to explain how it worked.

What I was coming to understand made very little sense at all from a Western perspective. How could it be that you move your bed in a different direction, or perhaps place a mirror over your stove, and happy "coincidences" start to happen in your life? That sounds like a lot of nonsense. But from the perspective of Eastern philosophy, it might make sense after all.

As I began to study feng shui, I realized that Eastern thought is based on a *non-dual perspective*, in which all things in life are connected on a deep energetic basis. In fact, the energy of thought is equally connected to the energy of all matter, and there is no distinct barrier between the "inner life" of our minds and the "outer" material world.

From this perspective, any shift we make, either in our minds or in our physical world, reverberates throughout reality; modern quantum physicists call this the "Butterfly Effect," suggesting that even the movement of a butterfly's wings on one side of the planet has a much larger effect throughout the world.

This concept, which has been common thought in Asia for thousands of years and is now supported by quantum research in the West, is the foundation of feng shui.

As I began to study feng shui (pronounced "fung shway," by the way), it was starting to take America by storm. I guess this is not surprising, considering the words in Chinese mean "wind and water." This ancient practice, which has been an essential part of life in Asia for thousands of years, was now becoming a highly desired feature of business and home life in the West. Suddenly, there were literally hundreds of books on the subject in stores.

Feng shui: "wind and water."

New York City is a particularly trendy place, and when something become popular, it becomes the "latest thing"; this was certainly the case with feng shui. After I took just one weekend workshop, and told friends what I was discovering about feng shui and how it works, people started asking me to come to their apartments and to see what their floorplans revealed. I willingly obliged, and was often a bit startled by the connections between what was going on in the person's space and how things were going in their lives. This was not just a connection between a messy house and a chaotic life, but rather deep, insightful connections between specific features in their homes and ongoing difficulties they were facing in their lives.

The good news was that, armed with just a few feng shui principles I had picked up in my first workshop, I was able to make some suggestions for the layout of their homes, which actually did seem to shift things in their lives in a positive way. I became quite excited by the impact of my initial studies.

Within weeks, the interest I received from friends increased to the degree that I started to have actual feng shui clients, and I was charging an hourly consulting fee, equipped only with the basic principles that I had picked up in a two-day workshop. I decided that for my own sake, and for that of new clients who were showing up at my door, I needed to increase my formal education in feng shui. I enrolled in a three-year formal training program to become a certified practitioner.

Now, hundreds of clients and students later, with a portfolio of fascinating client testimonials that support the impact of this work, I have put on the page some of the most essential principles that I have learned, which have benefited me and my clients in myriad ways.

DEFINING "FENG SHUI"

When asked to describe feng shui, I say that it is the Eastern art and science of living in harmony with your environment, for greater health, wealth, and well-being. Living in harmony does not just mean putting things in their proper or "right" place; it also means aligning your inner world with your outer environment.

It doesn't take a mystical book to teach you how to clean your house and find slipcovers that will match your drapes. Instead, the ancient teachings of feng shui will show you the direct relationship between what is happening in the energy of your environment and what is going on in your life. The connection is profound, and sometimes a bit spooky, but understanding and using these principles can give you a level of influence in your life like you've never had before.

Some people might say that it is all mere superstition, yet miraculous changes in my clients' lives have occurred after they did some simple feng shui "cures." Like a small pebble sending ripples across the surface of a lake, feng shui consultations can cause astounding things to happen, with very little exertion on the part of the clients. Here are some of my own clients' examples:

> I had wanted to sell my house for the longest time. After the feng shui consultation, I met a real estate agent "by accident" at the grocery store. She came over and looked at my place, and it sold in eight days!

and

> I hadn't been in a relationship for over ten years, but a few months after making necessary changes in the "relationship section" of my home, I met a man and fell in love!

Such stories are commonplace in feng shui circles, but the one thing that grabs everyone's attention is when people talk about making money using feng shui techniques.

> I had been working on a deal for months, and it looked like it was going nowhere. So, following your advice, I set up a "money altar" in my apartment—and the phone literally rang just as I was placing the last item. I made $4,000 just like that!

HOW TO USE THIS NINE-WEEK PROGRAM

You are about to embark on an exciting journey into your experience of money, exploring the ways that you can use ancient feng shui principles to increase your wealth, prosperity, and happiness. Time after time, clients have used these approaches to create miraculous changes in their lives. All that you need is an open mind, a willing spirit, and the intention to use the principles fully until you reach your desired goals.

This book is organized as a nine-week program in wealth consciousness and financial development. The approach is both mystical and practical, lighthearted and serious. In many ways, it reflects the manner and type of work that I do with my clients. It will be as if you have a feng shui consultant working right there with you in your home or business!

The approach that I use with clients to develop their prosperity has three parts: *environmental feng shui*, working directly with their environment (the space) and applying traditional feng shui approaches and techniques; *financial feng shui*, addressing and modifying the way they handle their money; and *inner feng shui*, working with the way the interior environments of their minds are constructed by their beliefs, attitudes, and expectations. When we combine all three of these approaches, the effects can be extraordinary.

Similar to a consultation, each chapter of this book is divided into three parts. We will examine each of these aspects of feng shui in each week of the program. Now is your chance to see what this marriage of East and West can produce for you.

Quotations from the *Tao Te Ching*

At the beginning each chapter, you will notice quotations from the ancient text, the *Tao Te Ching*. This is one of the most important works of Chinese culture, and the text created the foundation for the spiritual movement known as Taoism.

The *Tao Te Ching*, attributed to Lao Tzu, whose name means "Old Master," is a collection of poems and sayings that developed over a number of centuries in ancient China, from about the seventh century to the third century BC.

The first word, Tao (pronounced "dow," as in Dow Jones), means "The Way." Taoists believe that there is a specific current to the flow of life, and when we live in harmony with this Way, we experience success and happiness. But when we do not follow this innate flow, we start to have disturbances in our lives. This idea is central to the practice of feng shui.

The second word of the title is a bit more difficult to translate and has been the subject of arguments for thousands of years. The word "Te" (pronounced "duh," as in, "Duh, I don't know what this means") can signify a variety of things: character, life, courage, or propriety. I like translations that use the word "self-nature," which means the way that we really are on the inside, the core of our being. When we live according to our true inner nature, we are following the path of our true destiny. Since people usually pursue money for the fulfillment of their self-nature, we will refer to the *Tao Te Ching* for guidance on the path to wealth.

The third word in the title is "Ching" (as in "ca-CHING," the sound of a cash register). This word roughly translates as "classic text." When you combine all three words, you have a book that is titled *The Classic Text about the Path of Your True Self-Nature*. This is the inevitable path to wealth.

Committing Yourself to the Program

I have heard that 80 percent of the books that are purchased are never read from cover to cover. Looking at my own bookcase, I see that I've helped contribute to this horrifying statistic. However, your commitment to see this program through to the end is essential if you truly want to use it to develop a long-lasting and satisfying financial future.

The program is arranged according to a nine-week plan, but you can devote as much time as you need to fulfill the individual chapters. It could take you nine days, nine months, maybe even nine lifetimes to complete the program. Because feng shui deals with the evolution of an individual's consciousness, you need to accommodate the pace of your own personal growth. Do not skip over sections because you've run out of time or gotten flustered. Lack of time is usually an indication that you are having adverse reactions to the content, and you need to sort through your feelings before you move on.

Exercises, Activities, and "Cures"

The supplies you need for this program will depend on the feng shui situation in your home. All of the more esoteric items may available through the suppliers listed in appendix A. The only essential tools you will need, in addition to your own copy of this book, are a small notebook to record expenses, some graph paper, a pencil and pen, a calculator, and a large notebook that will be reserved for exercises, essays, doodling, and frequent journaling.

We will be referring to the large notebook as your *Prosperity Journal*. You will be using it often throughout the program, and you should have it with you whenever you are using this book; it will be your faithful companion through the ups and downs of your financial growth. Please choose a notebook that deserves this privileged status in your life.

You will probably need to put aside about an hour each day to read the essays and complete all of the feng shui applications in this book—treat this book as if it is a course you are taking. These approaches will eventually become so ingrained that they will support you for the rest of your life; I am often thinking about feng shui applications wherever I go. Making the various meditations part of your life will also take some time each morning or evening (or both), but the benefits can be profound.

Introduction

If this time commitment seems too heavy right now, give yourself extra time to complete the program. You can allot two or three weeks for each section, or even an entire month. Even if it takes you thirty days to complete each chapter, imagine that you can deeply transform your finances, your home, and your life in only nine months. It takes that long for an unborn child to come to term; isn't your financial life worth just as much time and effort?

Some of the exercises will be more difficult for you than others, and you do not need to do all of the feng shui "cures" or rituals in order to succeed. Do the ones that seem most relevant or interesting to you, and leave the others for another time. Do not, however, skip any of the financial assessments or projects; these are essential if you want to create monetary growth.

If there are certain essays or activities that give you a lot of problems, put a mark next to those sections and come back later. When you do return, you will probably find that the sections you skipped have the most "gold" in them for you.

Bring a Friend

To help bolster you through the difficult periods and make the process a lot more fun, you might involve a friend or relative with whom you can share this feng shui journey. Do the exercises and meditations together, and help each other analyze and "cure" feng shui problems in your homes. At the very least, you should have one supportive person with whom you can speak regularly about your progress. This program can also be a great activity for a group, perhaps with weekly meetings in a different person's home each week, so you can examine the feng shui issues of each house.

Get ready—your journey toward greater wealth and happiness is about to begin. Think about who you will be when you have gotten to the other side of this book and how different your life will be.

SIGN UP FOR WEALTH

To commit yourself to this journey, set your intention in writing. Open your new Prosperity Journal to the first page and write the following:

> I, _____, hereby commit to the intensive use of
> this program, *Feng Shui and Money*. I recognize this is a practi-
> cal, "hands-on" system that uses both inner and outer feng shui

methods for creating wealth, and I am dedicated to using these techniques to the best of my ability and with an open mind.

To help support me in the completion of this program, I am planning to check in at least once a week with [*write the name of supportive friend or relative*] to share my progress and insights.

I am committed to bringing greater wealth into my life, and I will share the benefits of this work with others, as it works for me.

Sincerely,   Date: _____

_____

Congratulations, you have made the first step toward greater wealth. Now, let's get started.

Establishing Your Foundation

A tower nine stories high
Starts with a single brick.
—The *Tao Te Ching*, Book 64

PRELUDE—YOUR RELATIONSHIP WITH MONEY

There are very few areas of our lives, if any, that are not affected by money. If you were born in a hospital, that first breath cost someone a bunch of cash. And if you plan to have the end of your life commemorated with a funeral service, you'd better start making your financial plans now. Though we spend a lot of time worrying about how much we're spending and how much more we need, few people take the time to think directly about their relationship with money.

By purchasing or even browsing through this book, you are evidently expressing an interest in transforming your relationship with money. So let's begin with some basics: What are we talking about? What exactly *is* wealth? Is there a fixed standard that determines if a person is wealthy?

PROSPERITY JOURNAL: "WHAT DOES 'WEALTH' MEAN TO ME?"

Take out your Prosperity Journal and write down some initial ideas about what "wealth" is for you. Don't worry about being right or wrong—the tax authorities will not be checking your answers. Write at least one paragraph: "Wealth is . . ."

Unless you are reading this book for entertainment purposes only, something about your relationship with money probably does not feel right. I make a similar type of assumption when I am asked to do a feng shui consultation. My clients are probably not hiring me because they are curious about feng shui or because they want to keep up with the neighbors who were recently "shui'd." Instead, something in their life is not satisfying to them, and they want to know if I can help.

Before conducting the consultation, I send forms that ask clients to rate their level of satisfaction in the nine areas of life addressed by feng shui (we will be reviewing these areas later in the book). They rate their satisfaction on a scale from one to ten, with ten being highest. Then, we prioritize consultation work based on these ratings.

Let's focus on your relationship with money. If you had to rate your satisfaction with money on a scale of one to ten, with ten being highest, how would it rate? Go ahead and try this now:

Low   1   2   3   4   5   6   7   8   9   10   High

If you scored your relationship with money as a ten, congratulations! Perhaps you can afford to use this book for entertainment purposes only. But if your rating was anything less, our work is ahead of us.

PROSPERITY JOURNAL: "MY RELATIONSHIP WITH MONEY"

Use your Prosperity Journal to explore your relationship with money. What's working, what feels good, and when and where do you feel frustrated, powerless, or "just not right"? Write one paragraph: "My present relationship with money is . . ."

Where Are We Going?

When planning a journey, you should know where you are leaving from and where you planning to go. Imagine getting on a plane and saying, "Take me someplace that I like—I don't know where it is, I just know I want to get there fast!" That would set you up for a tiresome and frustrating trip—and a big waste of time. It's unlikely that you will find a destination you like if you don't know where you're headed.

You may already have a vision of how you want your financial life to be. Maybe your best friend from high school is now living the way you always wanted. Or perhaps you skimmed the pages of one too many travel magazines to be satisfied with your present income. Whatever your dream life may be, it's time to get it out in the open—in as much detail as you can envision. This is not the time to question the propriety or reasonableness of your desires. As long as you keep them inside, they are not going to get you anywhere, and they will only get in your way.

PROSPERITY JOURNAL: "MY DREAM LIFE"

1. Write *at least* two pages about how you would live if you had unlimited finances: "If I had all the money that I wanted, I would . . ." This assignment alone requires more speculation than most lottery winners ever consider. What would you do? Purchase? Become? Dig deep into your aspirations. Your answers are probably the reasons you bought this book.

2. Now review the essay, and choose ten words or phrases that describe how you want your relationship with money to *feel*. Try to capture the essence of this seemingly elusive thing called "wealth." Write a new heading in your journal, "Top ten adjectives that describe my ideal state of wealth," and list the ten words or phrases. Allow yourself to brainstorm. Don't worry if the ideas seem irrational or bizarre; your aim is to connect to your subconscious. If you feel like writing "yellow" for some reason, then do so—you can always figure out what that means later.

3. Finally, review your list and mark the words or phrases that are most resonant for you, the ones where you felt yourself saying, "Yeah, *that's* it." Narrow the list down to your top three choices and put them in the place of honor, right here in this book. These will become your emblem of how you want your financial life to feel:

   a. _____

   b. _____

   c. _____

You can copy these words into your Prosperity Journal, as well.

By now, you should be getting a sense of your desired condition of wealth. Your lists are unique. The way that you handle money, and want to handle money, is directly tied to your experience of your own energy and to your connection to life itself. This is one of the most intimate relationships you will ever have. For this reason, books on personal finance tend to gather dust, since no two individuals' relationships with money will be identical.

Some people are highly conservative with their money and only feel comfortable when they know that it is in a secure account. Others are more adventurous and do not feel the power of their money until it is applied toward greater gains. It could be like asking an Amish farmer to live the life of an Italian soap opera star—the very idea is enough to make them run for the hills!

Your three key words or phrases are your guide to an ideal financial future. You will refer to them often as you do the exercises in this book, and you will see how their tone and energy reflect a deeper purpose for you. In many ways, they are keys not just to your relationship with money, but to your relationship to your whole life.

ENVIRONMENTAL FENG SHUI—THE INFLUENTIAL ENERGY OF YOUR HOME

Your home is not just the place where you sleep at night, it is the area on the planet most connected to who you are. Your home encases you like a bigger body: it affects how you feel, behave, and see yourself. Even when you leave the house each day, you carry the feeling of your home with you, wherever you go.

In each week of this program, we will focus on a different area of your house, and we will look at the ways it affects your financial potential. Most of the work will be in your home environment, but the techniques are also important in office and business settings. Adapt each technique to suit your needs, and you will be amazed by the transformations.

Before each consultation, I ask my clients to diagram their space. Whether they have a studio apartment or a ten-bedroom mansion, they need to become intimately familiar with the design of their house. This week, you will make a diagram of your floor plan, and you will use this drawing to assess and work with the feng shui of your home.

Most of our work will be on the ground floor of your home, but if there are rooms on other levels, you can address them as well. Do not include the basement in your drawing unless it contains residential space, and only add the garage if it is attached and considered part of the interior.

PROSPERITY JOURNAL: "MY FLOOR PLAN"

If you already have a blueprint of your living space, you can skip this activity and rejoice in your good fortune. If not, you need a large piece of graph paper, a thick pencil, and a long measuring tape.

1. Set aside a quiet time during the day and draw a basic floor plan of your home. Since you will use this diagram for the entire program, be sure that your drawing is clear and that the proportions are reasonably accurate.
2. Start at your front door and pace off the size of each room. Mark the entranceways, windows, and major pieces of furniture. Try to draw everything to approximate scale. Your diagram does not have to be overly artistic, but it should show the relative dimensions of the rooms.
3. When you are finished, you will have a road map for your feng shui journey to wealth. Tuck this diagram in a safe place in your Prosperity Journal, where you can access it often as you do this program.

Look at the Camera and Say "Chi!"

The basis of feng shui is an energy substance called *chi* (pronounced "chee"). This Chinese word means "life energy." In Eastern philosophy, chi energy is the component of everything we perceive. It took Western science thousands of years to catch up and discover that the ancient philosophers were on target.

Everything from the food we eat, to the chair you are sitting on, to the hair on the back of your neck is made of chi particles of energy that are conscious, alive, and have an intelligence of their own. These particles work together in a seamless fashion to bring us our daily dose of "reality," and they do this so effectively that we often forget there is any consciousness operating out there at all.

In the eighteenth century, the philosopher and mathematician Leibniz discovered that light vibration, which exists at both visible and invisible levels, is composed of units called photons. What is startling is that his research showed that each photon had the qualities of consciousness: intention and purpose—the very stuff that chi is made of!

This Eastern approach to reality applies to all aspects of life: food, environment, and how the body is treated. In Chinese acupuncture, ancient physicians were able to identify an invisible electrical structure that connects all the parts of the anatomy. This system of energy meridians, comprised of chi energy, runs throughout the body.

When the chi energy is flowing freely through a person's body, there is abundant health and vitality. You may have felt this after rigorous exercise, a pleasurable sexual experience, or even a day at the beach. Asian exercises like chi gong and t'ai chi open up this meridian structure so that energy can move more freely, leading to greater health and well-being.

If chi becomes blocked at any point in the body, health is affected not only in that area, but also in any points connected to it by the meridian structure. Anyone who has received acupuncture is familiar with this approach to diagnosing ailments. Have a headache? Try stimulating a point in your foot. Western doctors are now beginning to accept this alternative approach, which views the body as a collective of conscious parts in constant communication with the rest of the being.

Feng shui uses the same approach when treating the environment; it's like acupuncture for your home. Because chi energy is the basis of physical existence, problems occur when the energy becomes blocked or stagnant in the environment, just as they would in your body. An acupuncturist uses needles to promote energy flow in the body, while a feng shui consultant uses various objects and "cures" to move stuck energy and create a positive flow of chi in the space. With simple techniques, you will be able to create this flow in your own home or office for a healthy environment that is conducive to vitality and prosperity.

The Bagua: Ancient Map of Chi

Feng shui practitioners use an ancient model called the *bagua* to show how the chi moves through space and how this affects your life. The bagua is an eight-sided diagram that corresponds to various areas of daily experience. If the chi is ailing in part of your space, the corresponding area of your life is adversely affected. If you create positive-flowing chi in that area, however, you can expect marvelous, positive benefits.

In every consultation, I find a remarkable correlation between the events of a person's life and the areas of the bagua as it is applied to the person's home or office. Using the bagua as a guide, feng shui consultants "read" a person's space in much the same way that an astrologer reads a chart, or a tarot reader interprets the meaning of the cards. In a consultation, I can literally walk into a client's home and, without even exchanging any information, can often describe what is going on in the person's career, relationships, finances, and other aspects of the client's life, based on insights using the bagua "map."

The following diagram is the feng shui bagua. The symbol at the center represents the two opposites in life, the *yin* and the *yang*: positive/negative, male/

female, light/dark, and so on. By balancing the areas of our lives, we create a harmonious flow of the yin and yang, creating a sense of balance, grace, and health. This center area of the bagua is called the *t'ai chi*, which correlates with our general sense of health and well-being. In the outer ring of the bagua, we find eight areas of life activity that correlate with the feng shui of your space. Each area is called a *gua*. Starting at the bottom and going clockwise, they are as follows:

1. **Kan:** Career and personal mission
2. **Ken:** Self-knowledge and education
3. **Chen:** Family and household
4. **Hsun:** Wealth and prosperity
5. **Li:** Fame and social recognition
6. **Kun:** Relationships and marriage
7. **Dui:** Children and creativity
8. **Chyan:** Mentors and helpful people
9. **T'ai Chi:** The center of the diagram, where all of the other eight energies come together. It represents our general health and well-being.

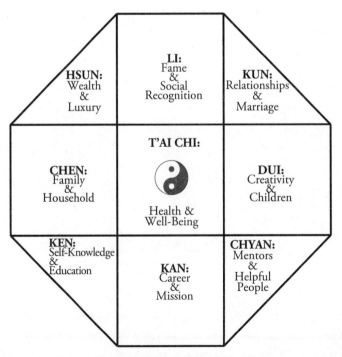

The feng shui bagua.

In each week of the program, we will examine, diagnose, and "cure" one of the feng shui areas of your home to promote a positive flow of energy and money.

Placing the Bagua over Your Floor Plan

Now that we have reviewed the meaning of the bagua areas, it's time to find out how they relate to your space. Take out the floor plan of your home and locate the front door. Put that side of the page at the bottom, so that it is closest to you.

When you apply the bagua to a floor plan, the front door will *always* be aligned with one of the three guas at the bottom: either Ken, Kan, or Chyan. For example, if your front door is at the bottom left, it is located in the Ken, or self-knowledge, area. If your entrance is at the bottom center, then your front door is in the Kan, or career position. If the front door is located at the bottom right side of the page, then it falls in the Chyan, or helpful people corner. Even if you do not use the front door of your home on a regular basis, and prefer to use a side or back entrance, the front door is always the determining factor in the alignment of the bagua, since this is how the space is designed.

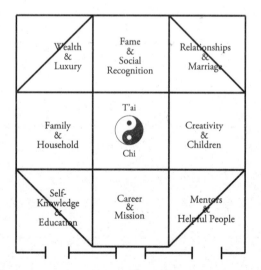

Align the front door of your home with one of these doorways.

No matter the actual design of the home, the bagua is always applied as a rectangle of nine equal parts. Since most floor plans are not a perfect square or rectangle, you will have areas in your home that extend beyond the symmetrical shape of the bagua. This does not mean the bagua does not fit your space; it simply means there are some irregularities in the design for which you must compensate.

Ideally, the shape of your home would be an even form that permits the open flow of energy. Rectangular and rounded shapes are preferable, since they avoid sharp interior corners and give a sense of a wholeness and stability. In contemporary architecture, however, a balanced shape is often hard to find; we are typically faced with designs that have strange angles and weird, protruding shapes. In those cases, some areas of the bagua may be directly associated with specific rooms, while other guas may not have any rooms associated with them at all.

Use a ruler to apply the rectangular bagua over the floor plan of your home, and divide the area of your home into the nine symmetrical areas. Don't worry if there are rooms that occupy two or more quadrants of the model. If you live in a one-room hut, that room will cover all nine areas of the bagua!

Now, label each sector according to both its Chinese name and its association with your life. For example, "Hsun/wealth" will be in the area that is at the top left corner of your diagram. Once you have filled in each of the boxes, you can start discovering the amazing correlation between your environment and your life.

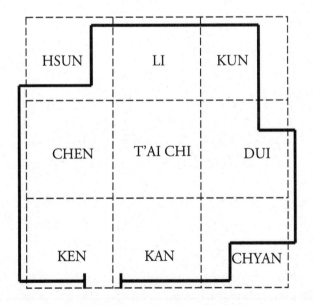

Applying the bagua over an irregular space.

Missing Sections and Extensions

One of your first tasks in feng shui is to compensate for architectural features that impede the flow of chi.

Notice in diagram A: the floor plan is missing rooms in the Kun section, in the upper right corner of the chart. When energy moves through the space, it does not flow in the Kun ("relationship") area at all, and this deficiency will affect that aspect of the person's life. On the floor plan, this is considered a "missing section." In a home with this design, the resident may have difficulty sustaining a satisfying relationship and may feel that there is "something missing" in his or her marriage or love life. But don't despair! There are specific feng shui cures used to address this problem.

Diagram A. Floor plan with a missing Kun section.

In diagram B, it *appears* that there is a similar problem in the Hsun area, associated with wealth and prosperity. But before you file for bankruptcy, you need to learn one technicality about feng shui: notice that the "missing" area does not correspond to just one area of the bagua, but also extends into the corresponding sector next to it, leaving only a small amount of space protruding at the top right corner. In this case, *because more than one-half of the space is lacking*, we do not think of this as a missing section; instead, the area on the top right is considered *an extension* of the interior space.

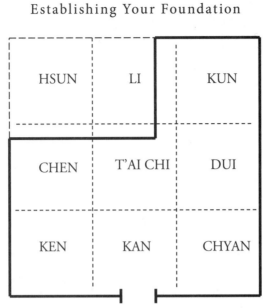

Diagram B. Floorplan that seems to be missing the Hsun section.

Extensions can actually be positive aspects of a design, since there is additional space for energy flow. Diagram C shows the correct way to apply the bagua to this space and designates the additional area as an extension in the Kun sector.

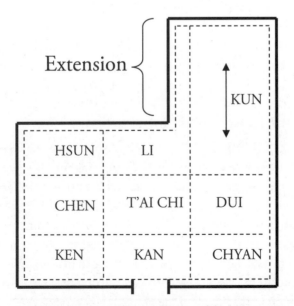

Diagram C. Correct application of the bagua.

One of my clients had a traditional colonial-style home with a rectangular shape. The Hsun sector occupied a portion of the living room, and it also over-lapped a small bathroom, which would not be conducive to wealth.

This client's family struggled financially for many years, until an inheritance enabled them to put an extension on their home. Without prior knowledge of feng shui, they wisely chose to add a sunroom porch in the Hsun corner. The new room was so inviting, they hardly used the living room at all and spent most of their time relaxing on this delightful new porch extension.

Corresponding with this addition in Hsun area of the home, the family's financial status became more comfortable. They invested the remaining portion of their inheritance, and their lives became as easy as the delightful sun porch they had constructed. They even were able to buy a second home in Florida, so that they could extend that sun porch feeling all year round!

If your home does not have a regular square or rectangular shape, you must discern whether the design has missing sections or extensions. You may even need to use a tape measure to find out if the metaphorical vessel of chi is "half empty or half full." But if you are missing a sector of the home, don't worry. There are many powerful feng shui techniques that can compensate for this inconsistency in the space.

If you had trouble applying the bagua to your space, review this section and carefully follow the guidelines. You will need this diagram throughout the program, so be sure your calculations are correct. You might get help from a friend who has feng shui experience, or you can contact me directly to verify your assessment of the space. Resources are listed in appendix A at the back of this book if you need help.

Bagua Sector of the Week: T'ai Chi

This week's feng shui focus is the t'ai chi area of your home, which is at the center of the bagua and is represented by the yin/yang diagram. If you are not feeling well, or your energy seems clogged, you may have a problem in this part of your environment.

Functioning as the heart of the home, this is the area from which all rooms diverge. In ancient architecture, this was typically the meeting area or banquet room. Lacking an adequate central space, people tend to feel fragmented or alien-ated. By opening up the t'ai chi area and centralizing the energy of the building, you create a union in the design of the home. If you want to balance your check-book, your first goal should be to balance your space!

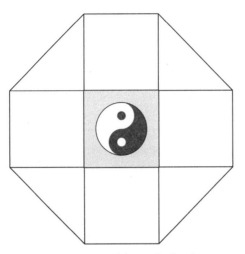

Bagua sector of the week: t'ai chi.

The nature and condition of the t'ai chi area tells a lot about the health of the inhabitants, the flow of energy in their lives, and the way they interact. If the architecture divides the area into two or more sections, this indicates a split in either the dynamics of the family, the individual personalities of the inhabitants, or both.

Think of it in practical terms. If you walk into a building and are immediately faced by two diverging hallways, you are hit by a choice: should you turn left or right? Either way grants access to an area of the home, but prevents you from entering others. Facing such a split causes confusion and anxiety, which can carry over into all areas of your life.

To find the t'ai chi position in your home, take out your floor plan. With a soft pencil, make an *X* from the four corners, and mark the point where the lines intersect. This will be the heart of your t'ai chi position. (See the following diagram.)

T'ai chi position in a rectangular space.

If your home is not a perfect rectangular shape, and it rarely is, finding the center can be a bit more difficult. If you have a "missing section" in your home, fill out this missing area first to make a regular rectangular shape, and then find the center area.

T'ai chi position in an irregular space.

If you have an extension in your space, however, do not include this in your determination of your center point.

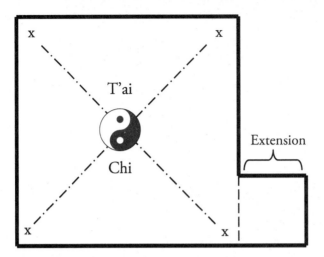

T'ai chi position in a space with an extension.

Now, walk to the t'ai chi position of your home, and notice how you feel. If this area is difficult to find or navigate, then you know that you have a problem. With a well-defined t'ai chi, you will probably feel rested, at ease, and connected to the rest of the house. But if the t'ai chi is occupied by a stairway, closet, or a convergence of obstructing walls, you may not know where to put yourself. If so, does that feeling seem familiar to you? Homes without a strong sense of center can imbalance you, making financial matters all the more difficult.

Without knocking down walls or moving to a new home, you can do a lot with the t'ai chi position to feel more centralized, integrated, and at peace. First, recognize the problem. Too often, we are soldiers in the face of adversity, never acknowledging how we feel—and are affected by—our environment. The feeling of fragmentation may seem normal, even exciting, but underneath, it prevents you from establishing a solid foundation in your life.

Case Study: The T'ai Chi Position

I did a consultation for a woman who had trouble choosing a career. She worked part-time in a dress shop and also had a number of little projects on the back burners. Whenever there was something she wanted to do, something else raised its head and called for her attention.

When I looked at the t'ai chi of her home, the energetic problem was clear. The center of her home consisted of a hallway that turned corners like a maze. To one side was the living room; to another, a set of stairs. At the end, the hallway hit a blank wall, then turned to face a different set of rooms. The whole arrangement felt complex, disturbing, and draining—exactly the way the woman felt in her life! With three avenues of chi splitting off in this way, there was a constant sense of anxiety about where to go and what to do.

Working with the T'ai Chi Area of Your Home

Before applying any specific remedies to your own t'ai chi, ask this question: "Do I feel centered and balanced? Are the areas of my life happily connected and integrated?"

The way you are feeling about your "centeredness" is connected to the t'ai chi of your environment. You can effect deep change on both inner and outer levels by making feng shui adjustments in this area.

Feng Shui Cures in the T'ai Chi Area

The first quality that you need in the t'ai chi position is space. If you can't find a place to stand in the center of your home, you are not going to feel in balance. Clear out any clutter or congesting furniture that clogs this area.

To further open the space, you might use mirrors to give a sense of expansion. For the client whose home had the diverging paths, I recommended a mirror for the blank wall at the end of the hallway, to give a sense of possibility. Beautiful pictures or photos also work, especially if they show pastoral scenes and calm, open spaces. Use accent lighting on the pictures to add focus, warmth, and illumination to this central space.

I often use rugs and carpets to integrate the t'ai chi area and connect any adjoining rooms. A circular rug is perfect, giving a sense of continuity, integration, and wholeness. A rug that incorporates the yin/yang design would be ideal, if you can find one.

Hanging a small wind chime in the t'ai chi area will integrate the flow of chi for the entire home. Since this area is associated with the number 5, a wind chime with five metal tubes is ideal. By hanging a chime in this position, you send a vibration that balances all of the areas of the bagua at one time.

The primal element associated with the t'ai chi area is earth, which reminds us that the planet Earth is our common ground. Use the color yellow, earthen tiles on the floor, and terra cotta planters to give a supportive and nurturing "earthy" tone to your center.

FINANCIAL FENG SHUI—ABILITIES AND ASSETS

The yin/yang at the center of the bagua represents the positive and negative cycles of life, exhibited in the active and receptive elements of human behavior. A person who is too yang can be a workaholic and always on the go. Continual activity, without time to enjoy the benefits, leads to exhaustion and resentment. This can make you feel impoverished, no matter how much money you are making.

People who emphasize only the yin energy may be highly imaginative and sensitive, but might not turn their dreams into reality, and can end up feeling unfulfilled and anxious. Being too yin makes one soft, lazy, or uninspired and eventually leads to dependency on others.

The yin/yang theory of consciousness parallels the left and right hemispheres of the human brain. The left hemisphere, which is more yang, is connected to analytical skills used in mathematical and linear thinking. The right hemisphere, which is more yin, deals with abstract reasoning and is related to creative and artistic activities. The two sides are interdependent, and we employ both orientations in our daily activities.

In Western culture, men are generally expected to be more yang, while women are considered more yin. Research on male and female hormones, as well as the general nature of male and female bodies, supports this definition to some degree, but men and women have both yin and yang aspects in their personalities.

Your financial development requires both yin and yang behavior. Many people—including most writers of financial guides—associate money management with yang functions: balancing accounts, defining financial goals, and evaluating investments. Certainly, these are essential aspects of financial management, and we will cover some of these fundamental issues in this book. But this is not the only approach that is important to your financial growth.

The yin aspects of financial development involve the creative, imaginative, and receptive sides of your personality. While the yang side tells you how much money you need to pay your bills, the yin side nurtures your intuition and gives you the inspiration to start a new career.

Years ago, I took an intensive goal-setting workshop in which we learned to prioritize our goals and outline the incremental steps. By the end, I felt immensely inspired and believed that I could accomplish anything—I just didn't know what I wanted!

Therein lies the split between the yin and yang aspects of personal development. While that workshop fueled the yang energy to manifest our goals, it didn't engage the yin energy for connecting to the inner self.

Quiz: What's My Yin/Yang?

Use following questions to identify your place in the yin/yang spectrum. Go ahead and check the boxes here on this page.

1. YES ☐ NO ☐   *I like spending time by myself, daydreaming.*
2. YES ☐ NO ☐   *When I meet people at a party, I usually introduce myself first.*
3. YES ☐ NO ☐   *My idea of a perfect vacation is to relax on an isolated beach.*
4. YES ☐ NO ☐   *I am bothered by a noisy environment.*
5. YES ☐ NO ☐   *I prefer an intimate conversation with one person to engaging with a large party.*
6. YES ☐ NO ☐   *To relax, I like to do crossword puzzles or other games.*
7. YES ☐ NO ☐   *I like to be "on the go" most of the time.*
8. YES ☐ NO ☐   *Nothing is better than relaxing in a hot tub.*
9. YES ☐ NO ☐   *I do not like to go to sleep at night until everything is in order.*
10. YES ☐ NO ☐   *When I travel, I like the itinerary laid out so I know exactly what I am doing each day.*
11. YES ☐ NO ☐   *My idea of a good time is to stay at home and listen to music.*
12. YES ☐ NO ☐   *People often tell me that I am very sensitive, maybe "too sensitive."*

Now, go back over your responses and give them the following points:

1. 1 point if YES, 0 if NO
2. 1 point if NO, 0 if YES
3. 1 point if YES, 0 if NO
4. 1 point if YES, 0 if NO
5. 1 point if YES, 0 if NO
6. 1 point if NO, 0 if YES

7. 1 point if NO, 0 if YES
8. 1 point if YES, 0 if NO
9. 1 point if NO, 0 if YES
10. 1 point if NO, 0 if YES
11. 1 point if YES, 0 if NO
12. 1 point if YES, 0 if NO

Add your total number of points, and put the total here: _____
Your total corresponds with its number on the following scale:

Yang 0 1 2 3 4 5 6 7 8 9 10 11 12 Yin

If you score high on the yang side of the scale, you are probably more oriented to linear and rational organization, and you will probably feel most comfortable with the objective, mathematical aspects of money management. Your challenge will be to embrace the abstract aspects of this work, such as meditation, visualization, and trusting your spontaneity.

If you rate more strongly on the yin side, you are probably most comfortable with the receptive and imaginative sides of yourself. It will be important for you to work consistently with the statistical aspects of your financial management (record keeping, time management, and so forth) in order to bring your dreams into reality.

If you scored in the middle range of this test, between the yin and yang poles of behavior, you possess aptitude and strengths on both sides of wealth creation. Your task is to integrate the intuitive and rational sides of your consciousness for the fullest benefit of your abilities.

Feng Shui of the Wallet

For an illustration of how you are handling money at this point in your life, start with your wallet. First of all, do you have one? Or are you somebody who prefers to let their bills roam freely at the bottom of their purse or pockets? You can tell a great deal about financial status by the way people handle their cash, so let's begin by looking at your wallet.

Right now, while you are reading this section, take out the cash that you are carrying with you and lay it on a table. Notice the condition of the bills. Were they sitting snugly within the sections of a billfold, or were they hiding in clumps in the deep recesses of your pockets? How do you feel when you handle these bills? Anxious? Excited? Depressed? Do you feel proud of your cash?

PROSPERITY JOURNAL: "THE QUALITY OF MY CASH"

Write a paragraph about the way you are handling your money. If your wallet or purse were a house, what would it be like to live there? Imagine you are a dollar bill, and write a brief account of what it is like to live in this temporary "home."

Since your wallet or purse is at the center of your daily financial life, you will notice a correlation between it and the t'ai chi area of your home. You are the center of your world, and your energetic tendencies express themselves on a big field much as they do on a smaller one. This is a daunting, but often enlightening realization. Once you change the way that you are on the inside, the feng shui flow of your life changes on many different levels.

Show Me the Money!

Now, notice the *amount* of money you are carrying. Was your wallet empty, or close to it? If so, there are specific feelings and beliefs, and not just financial circumstances, that make you refrain from carrying a lot of cash. Consider your beliefs about yourself and the world around you that make you limit the amount of cash you carry.

Or perhaps you are the type of person who only feels secure with a big wad of bills in your purse or pocket. A few years ago, I was having dinner with friends, and a group of men took out their money clips to show off (they were all basketball coaches, if that helps you understand this story). One fellow, who to my understanding was not making a higher salary than anyone else in the group, was carrying $800 in cash in his pocket, and evidently, this was typical for him. I'm sorry that I never asked why he felt compelled to carry this much in cash at one time. I imagine his answer would have illuminated how he felt about himself and about money.

Notice how much money you tend to carry with you and how that makes you feel. I habitually used to carry as little cash as possible, which I believe reflected an old belief that I would spend money wastefully. Beneath those ideas was a core belief that I shouldn't have any money at all, which I pieced together from early childhood experiences. The subconscious ways we handle money reveal our relationship to this very personal aspect of our lives.

PROSPERITY JOURNAL: "THE QUANTITY OF MY CASH"

Write a paragraph about what you learned by examining the amount of money that you are carrying. Consider your inner motives and list some of the subconscious beliefs that support this behavior.

Assessing Your Assets: Instant Wealth

This week, as you survey the shape of your home, you need to do a similar assessment of your finances. Every journey begins from where you are. If the foundation of your home is crumbling, you need to fix it. If your finances are in a shambles, you must recognize this in order to build a stronger financial foundation.

Let's begin with your material assets. If you have money problems, you are probably not even aware of the value of your assets. If you just said to yourself, "What assets?" read on! You may be surprised.

Beginning with your home, consider any item of negotiable resale value. Start with the building itself. Do you own, or do you rent? What is the resale value of your furniture, appliances, clothing, jewelry, and so on? Do you have any collections? Have you inherited any heirlooms or antiques? In this exercise, you are going to go from room to room, writing down anything that may have negotiable resale value. Remember, you do not need to know the dollar value before deciding it has resale potential.

Until you know the value of your assets, it is impossible to know how profitably you have managed your spending. This is the key to wealth: It does not matter how much income you have coming in; if the money is not spent in ways that fulfill you, you might as well not be making any at all.

I am not suggesting that you sell your children's toys without asking them or take the urn with your great-aunt's ashes to the nearest antique store. I am emphasizing, however, that everyone, from the multimillionaire with six homes to the college student in a cramped dorm room, often has more to their name than they realize.

I remember seeing a game show in which the contestant stood in a glass booth filled with circulating money and had to grab as many bills as he could before the time ran out. We are going to play a similar game with the assets in your home. You may want to get someone to help you, so you can call out items as quickly as possible while your helper writes them down. After you have finished, you can collapse amid all your wealth!

PROSPERITY JOURNAL: "SURVEYING MY WEALTH"

You can allocate ten minutes per room for this project. If you live in a one-room studio with a bathroom, you will have exactly twenty minutes. One bedroom with a living room, kitchen, and bath will get you forty. This may not sound like a lot of time, but remember, a smart burglar can do it in a lot less!

1. Put today's date at the top of the next blank page in your journal, and write the heading, "Material Assets." Using the outline below, go through every room and list the assets that you could sell for over $50. You do not need to know the exact resale value. If you believe that you can get more than fifty bucks for it from anyone who is not just a sympathetic friend or relative—write it down:
    - *The Home Itself:* If you own your home, put the house or condo on the list; if you don't own, consider the value of your doormat, but unfortunately, that's about all you can take with you.
    - *Living Room, Family Room, and Den:* Antiques, artwork, furniture, collections, and other items, including what's in the closets.
    - *Bedroom:* Furniture, jewelry, clothing, and so on.
    - *Children's Rooms:* Only those items that revert directly back to you when they move out.
    - *Kitchen:* Appliances you own, dishes, silverware, cookware, and so forth.
    - *Bathroom:* Small appliances, artwork, and so on.
    - *Home office:* Office equipment.
    - *Garage and Tool Shed:* Automobiles, boats, tools, lawn and garden equipment, camping gear, and stored items.
    - *Basement and Attic:* These can be treasure troves. As the expression goes, "There's gold in them thar hills!" Skip over the junk and write down the big-ticket items you are keeping in storage.
    - *Porch and Deck:* Outdoor furniture, grill, and so forth.

2. Now that you have a list of your material assets, are you surprised? Most people are shocked at the number of things of value that they have collected. For this reason, you may need to reevaluate the coverage in your homeowner's or renter's insurance.

(Continued)

---

3. Review your list, and write down your estimate of the resale value. This does not need to be a precise amount, but it should reflect what you could get within the next few months. Consider what your neighbor would be willing to pay if she saw it on eBay or a similar service. Don't put how much *you* would be willing to pay, since you may be biased. If you're still unsure, just call across the fence and ask! Cross off anything that does not measure up to the $50 minimum bid.

4. Next, total the value of all the assets. Put the value of your home on a separate line, since this is probably the largest item and is subject to other considerations. This list is almost like having cash in hand.

5. Now, circle any item that you have not used or enjoyed *within the past year,* and consider your options. What might you do with the money that is tied up in this asset? Material possessions are like potential energy, and your life could be greatly enriched by recirculating them in the great pool of commerce. Check out eBay, Craigslist, newspapers, antique stores, or tag sale options for ways to make this instant wealth available to you now.

In future weeks of this program, you will determine all your financial assets, as well as any debts and liabilities. As you assess the shape of your finances, you will get a sense of everything that is available to you. Your road to wealth has already begun.

Just the Facts: How to Use Your Spending Log

By reviewing your material assets, you can see how you have been investing your financial resources and whether or not this is fulfilling for you. Now, it's time to look at how you are using your financial chi every day. This may be one of the most difficult activities in the entire book, but it makes an enormous difference in your relationship with money.

All that you will need for this activity are the two tools carried by reporters in old movies: a pocket-sized notebook and a pen. Or, if you prefer, you might put notes in your smartphone or download an app specifically designed for recording expenses.

Open the notebook (or smartphone) and put today's date at the top of the page. Then wait. (It's okay; nothing is supposed to happen right away. Just keep waiting.) If you wait long enough, something will definitely happen: you will want to spend money. And that's okay. But when you make the purchase, whatever it is, act like a reporter and write down the name of the item and the amount paid. For example:

Caffe Latte	$3.65
Newspaper	$1.00
Big screen television	$2,000.00

For now, just observe. Your job is not to make judgments or to place any guidelines on your spending—just report the facts. By doing this conscientiously for a few days, you will start to notice a shift: you will become conscious of your spending like never before. And without much deliberation, you will begin to plug the leaks in your financial life. You will start to think twice before making a purchase, not because you have to, but because you want to. Studies have shown that just by listing daily expenses, an average person will automatically reduce their spending by at least 10 percent.

If writing down all of those digits for the big screen TV makes you queasy, you may change your mind about the purchase. Or you may not. But writing it down will give you a sense of empowerment, and you will realize that you have a choice about what you purchase and how much you spend. This sense of self-possession will transform your financial life.

INNER FENG SHUI—GATHERING YOUR POWER

Okay, it's time for a pop quiz. Based on the information in this book so far, and any additional background you have gotten from books, teachers, and the backs of herbal tea boxes, answer the following question:

> "What is the most important influence in the feng shui of your home?"

Your Answer   _____

Your Score   _____%

Go ahead. Fill in the blank right here on the page. Now, if you wrote "the television," "the air conditioner," or "my mother's picture," you are wrong on all counts; give yourself no points. If you wrote "my bed," "the stove," or "the front door," you are demonstrating some feng shui wisdom, but are still basically wrong. You can give yourself 50 percent, which is still a failing grade, but looks better than a zero.

The correct answer is *you*. That's right, *you* are the most important influence on the feng shui of your home. Your energy is the basis of the flow of chi, and the power of your mind, emotions, and intentions will ultimately determine what happens to you and your environment.

Most people think that feng shui only works with the external aspects of reality, but this is not the case. A person's consciousness is just as essential as, if not more important than, the way he or she arranges the objects in the home.

His Holiness, Professor Lin Yun, leader of the Black Sect feng shui tradition, stated that physical feng shui adjustments account for only 20 percent of the needed changes. The rest need to occur on the level of individual consciousness.

When people are first exposed to feng shui, they often focus on the external aspects of the practice. They may make a change in their home, like hanging a crystal in the "wealth corner" of the apartment, and—lo and behold—three days later, they get a raise at work or a surprise gift in the mail. But contact these people a year later, and you usually find that their lives have changed very little. Sure, they were happy to get the raise, but in the long run, the money just went to pay some bills or for an extra treat, and soon they are back where they started.

This explains why there are so many feng shui manuals on the shelves and so many people still looking for the right book! If you only do external remedies and do not focus on what's inside you, the changes are going to be superficial at best.

The Five Internal Components

We will be working with five components of your inner world: thoughts, beliefs, emotions, intentions, and plans. In subsequent weeks, we will use these to expedite the transformation of your financial life. The diagram below illustrates the relationship between these five influences.

During the first few weeks, we will define and reconsider our beliefs. Our beliefs dictate what seems possible for us in the world. What we believe we can have is what we will end up getting. If we could only master this principle, it would save us so much time.

As children, we were eager to figure out how the world worked and how to protect ourselves from threatening situations. We set up systems of ideas about how reality functioned, and unless those beliefs are questioned along the way, we continue to behave as if our childhood perceptions are true.

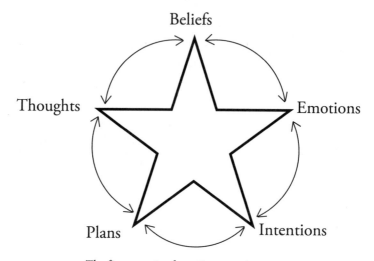

The five aspects of creative consciousness.

Anything perceived by a young mind is bound to have some distortions, so just imagine an entire lifetime based on childhood perceptions. We need to develop the aspect of our consciousness called the "Observer Self." This part of us perceives our beliefs, sees them in action, and does not automatically subscribe to them. Without questioning our beliefs, we may as well be stuffing fresh produce into a refrigerator filled with rotting fruits and vegetables. After a while, it's all going to stink.

Why Would Anyone Not Want to Have Money?

Having money is really great, and we would be crazy not to want it, right? Well, that seems reasonable, but if you are not satisfied with your finances, you are undoubtedly harboring some negative ideas that are limiting your capacity for wealth. Whether conscious of it or not, each of us has a part of our consciousness that staunchly resists bringing in, and keeping, more money. This position is based entirely on our beliefs.

Below is a list of common beliefs about money, wealth, and "rich people." Check off any that provoke a sense of agreement in you. Remember, your beliefs do not have to seem logical—that's why they are beliefs.

Establishing Your Foundation

When it comes to money, I believe that:

- ☐ Money corrupts.
- ☐ Money is the root of all evil.
- ☐ I would feel overwhelmed if I had a lot of money.
- ☐ There is never enough money.
- ☐ I don't deserve to have a lot of money.
- ☐ The rich get richer, and the poor get poorer.
- ☐ People only like rich people for their money.
- ☐ You have to work hard to make an honest dollar.
- ☐ Poor people have more soul.
- ☐ Blessed are the poor.
- ☐ Spiritual people don't care about money.
- ☐ Being concerned about material things is shallow.
- ☐ Money can't buy happiness.
- ☐ Women can't handle money.
- ☐ Men can't handle money.
- ☐ I can get by just fine without money.
- ☐ I am a poor-artist type.
- ☐ Nice guys and gals finish last.
- ☐ Thinking and talking about money is so crass.
- ☐ If you don't come from old money, it doesn't count.
- ☐ You can't trust rich people.
- ☐ If I had money, everyone would be jealous and hate me for it.
- ☐ I've got better things to do than think about money.
- ☐ There just aren't enough good jobs to go around.
- ☐ You have to be a workaholic to get ahead in this world.
- ☐ Rich people *only* care about money.
- ☐ If I were wealthy, I would always worry about people stealing from me.
- ☐ Money is hard to get and harder to keep.
- ☐ Nobody gets ahead in this world.
- ☐ You can't take it with you, so why think about money in the first place?
- ☐ I can't make more than my parents did.
- ☐ I was never meant to be wealthy.
- ☐ Nobody from my hometown could ever get wealthy.
- ☐ Life would be much better if I never had to think about money.

As you were going through the list, did any additional beliefs come to mind? If so, add them here:

_____

_____

_____

_____

_____

PROSPERITY JOURNAL: "MY TOP FIVE LIMITING BELIEFS ABOUT MONEY, WEALTH, AND RICH PEOPLE"

Now, go back over the list and choose the five beliefs that seem strongest to you. List them in your journal. How do you know which are strongest? They are probably the ones that you really believe are true! In fact, you may actually really like these ideas and not have any intention to change them. But beware: Any idea that limits your perception of money, wealth, and "rich people," for whatever reason, is negative and detrimental to your prosperity and happiness. You just don't have the luxury of holding onto them anymore.

Notice how it feels to look over your list. Consider the life vision created by these ideas. It probably looks a lot like your life right now! These ideas are actively preventing you from accumulating more wealth and satisfaction. They are like prison guards—they prevent you from getting out of your cage and prohibit any new opportunities from getting to you.

In the coming week, take time to notice your thoughts and reactions about wealth. Nothing will happen differently until you change your ideas about how reality operates.

The Meditative Millionaire

Meditation is a tool for developing the Observer Self. This is not the part of us that thinks, feels, reacts; this is the part that notices these things.

As you clear the clutter and obstructions from the t'ai chi of your home, you should also clear out your inner debris: anxieties, worries, distracting thoughts, and self-limiting beliefs. By meditating, we create an inner distance between what we are thinking and our sense of self. As the inner distance expands, we gain a greater feeling of receptivity. We see ourselves anew, becoming less attached to who we have already been.

The first step in awakening meditative consciousness is to realize that we are not our thoughts and feelings. We *have* thoughts and feelings, and they can be excellent representatives of what is going on in our lives, but they do not ultimately define us.

Consider the thought, *I am worthless.* This is an idea that most people have at one time or another. Sometimes I think that I am worthless, but that does not mean that I really am. It just means that I am thinking that about myself.

You can imagine that your thoughts and feelings are like articles of clothing. Most people collect a certain wardrobe to wear day in and day out. We go to our closet each morning (if we are neat enough to hang things up!) and see what's available. We consider the weather and what we are doing that day, decide what is appropriate, and then go about our day.

Our clothing affects us. It influences the way we feel and how we define ourselves. The same conditions apply to our thoughts and feelings. Unless we hit a crisis that makes us "change our minds," we tend to stick to the same thoughts and feelings, day in and day out.

When a person starts meditating, it's as if he is cleaning out his inner closet and seeing exactly what he has in his wardrobe. Just by opening the door of your consciousness, you will start to see why your life is operating the way it is. Then you can create the space for change.

Meditation Practice: Journaling

It may surprise you that the first form of meditation that you will be using is journal writing. That's right, your new companion, your Prosperity Journal, is going to be your meditation partner as well.

Since meditation is a practice that enables you to get in touch with your inner world, there are few tools more effective than journal writing. By facing a blank page each day, you can reflect on your thoughts, feelings, and beliefs. This perception gives you the perspective to create change.

On your journey toward wealth, the journal is an indispensable tool. Feeling tired with the same old job? Write about your feelings before you head off to work. This opportunity to express yourself will remind you that you have a job, but you are not your job. This can open your mind to new opportunities.

If you are tired of paying the same bills day in and day out, without any sense of relief, write about it in your journal. After a while, you may start to see a trend. "I hate paying so much for my phone bill," you may write. "I wish I could bring those costs down!" And because you planted the seeds in your journal, ideas may come to you throughout the week. Maybe a coworker will mention she just changed phone companies, and with a newly tuned ear, you discover a whole new set of options.

Your journal is a place to express your true self, no matter what you are feeling; in the area of business, nothing is more valuable. How else can you know where you stand and where you really want to go? Bit by bit, day by day, your journal shows you the way. By knowing where you have been, the path becomes clear.

Most of us associate journals with diaries, in which the details of the day are recorded in precious detail for posterity. But the function of the journal is quite different. Focus not on what you write, but on clearing your thoughts as fast possible so something new can come in. Do this as an experiment: if you clear your thoughts each morning, what might you do with this new openness?

Before working on sections of this book, I often wrote in my journal to clear out distracting thoughts and check in with my concerns. By doing this first, my mind was clearer, and my thoughts flowed much more easily. It's like working out at the gym in the morning: Your heart starts pumping and your chi starts flowing, and soon you are ready to face the challenges of the day.

Some people like to write in the evening, as a way to conclude their day. If that works best for you, so be it. I prefer to write first thing in the morning. While still in bed, I drag the journal onto my lap and follow all my thoughts as they flow out onto the page. I usually write three pages a day, and because I like to write fast— and this means messy—I use wide-ruled paper and even skip every other line. In this way, I write six pages of large script that would condense down to three pages of normal handwriting.

"But what if I still don't know what to write?" you ask. If that's the case, write: "I don't know what to write, I don't know what to write . . ." After a few pages of that, I am sure new ideas will come into your head! Remember, the purpose is not to figure out something deep or insightful to write; you're just clearing out the old thoughts to make room for new ones. Try writing three pages a day for at least three days this week, and see how this changes the outlook on your problems, your finances, and your life.

ACTION STEPS ON THE JOURNEY TO WEALTH:
WEEK 1 SYNOPSIS

During this first week of your journey, your commitment to the process will start to become clear. Is this just a passing fancy, or do you really want to benefit from these methods? The approaches in this book are cumulative, so try to finish all of this week's activities before starting on the next week.

Check the boxes as you complete these tasks:

- ☐ Review the goals you set for your t'ai chi area, and implement at least two this week.
- ☐ Play the asset game for Instant Wealth.
- ☐ Record, reporter-style, every penny in your spending log.
- ☐ Acknowledge your five most prominent beliefs about money, wealth, and "rich people."
- ☐ Write in your journal for twenty minutes each day, for at least three days, to clear your mind and settle on your prosperity goals.

Congratulations on finishing your first week!

Setting Your Sights

Tackle difficulties
By focusing on what is easy in them.
Achieve greatness
By attending to small details.
—The *Tao Te Ching*, Book 63

PRELUDE—WHAT'S MISSING IN YOUR LIFE?

"If only I were wealthy, I would . . ." Would what? How would you really like your life to be different? If you feel a need for money, something more than cash must be missing in your life. Becoming sensitive to that feeling, and figuring out exactly what you are longing for, is the key to financial fulfillment. Before writing a check for the future, think very seriously about what is missing and how you want to fill that hole.

When people say they want more money, I generally respond, "You're lying!" They look at me with a combination of shock and bewilderment. How could I accuse them of lying when this work is supposed to be about making more money?

I answer, "What good is money? It all looks about the same, and even if you are really hungry, you can't eat it. If you sew all the bills together, they won't keep you warm at night. So, what good is it?" To this, they usually respond with looks of total disdain, so I quickly add, "What you probably want is not money, but the things that money can buy. So let's be honest and talk about what you really want in your life."

Perhaps you hate your job, and more money would enable you to take time off. So, what's missing? Time to relax. But is that really the issue or is there something else? Maybe you are not respected at work. In that case, you are missing respect. Does time off give you a sense of respect? Ask the people who are checking off their days in retirement villages.

The next question follows: "Why do you feel disrespected at work?" Maybe you don't care about what you're selling, and you want to do something more meaningful with your life. You are lacking meaningful work. This is an important statement, which offers many avenues to be explored. With this realization, you can see that you are not just someone with insufficient funds; you are someone who wants to do something meaningful in the world. That's quite a shift of awareness in the space of only a few paragraphs.

Perhaps you love to make art and feel you missed your chance to become a great artist. Money, and even time off, will not necessarily give that to you. Maybe you want to help people in underprivileged areas. Whatever it is, your ideal future is not really about money. It's about the things that you want to do.

When we talk about wealth, we often refer to big-ticket items: expensive cars, luxurious homes, world-class travel. Sure, these things seem attractive. But is that what's really missing in your life?

PROSPERITY JOURNAL: "THE ESSENCE OF WEALTH"

Go back to your second Prosperity Journal exercise, where you defined three adjectives that describe your ideal relationship with money. List them on a new blank page. Then ask yourself, "How can I help myself feel this way right now?" If your ideal situation would be to feel relaxed, cared for, and luxurious, consider how can you bring these qualities into your life right away, instead of waiting until you achieve a prescribed quota for wealth. Come up with at least two or three ideas for each adjective, then circle one from each list that you can pursue this week. You are now on your way to the experience of true wealth.

The final goal is internal, not external. Putting a million dollars in the bank is not necessarily going to make you feel the way you want; in fact, an increase in financial responsibilities might actually take you away from feeling that way. Consider how you want to feel, instead of fixating on the package you have prescribed for it, and begin implementing the life you want.

Unlike the messages blared at us by advertisers, many of our desired conditions do not have to cost a lot of money. In fact, some of them would be hindered if we focused on finances and didn't go directly to what we want.

Wealth for one person could seem like misery to another. A home stuffed with antiques may be your dream, but don't expect the same response from adventure types who feel burdened with more than a sack on their backs and a song in their hearts. Before you dedicate your life to magazine-stand visions of wealth, take a closer look at what you want and what is really missing. It might not be as much as you imagine.

Back to the Bagua: Your Map of Fulfillment

As you'll recall from chapter 1, the bagua is the ancient model that outlines the areas of life as they connect to the chi in your environment. Like different notes on a scale, or the colors in the spectrum, each bagua sector has a different vibration. Constantly playing one note over and over is not very appealing, but when you engage all of them together, the musical possibilities are endless.

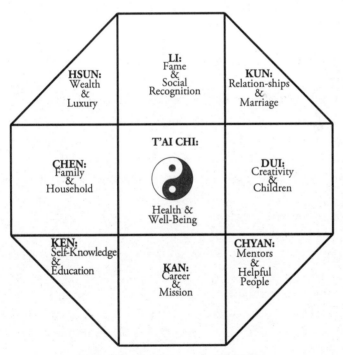

The feng shui bagua: a map of fulfillment.

Let's review each of the bagua areas, or guas. It's best to learn the Chinese name of each of the areas, and not just its reference. There is an area that directly relates to wealth, but you should learn its proper name, Hsun (pronounced "shoon"), instead of calling it your "money corner."

Starting at the bottom center of the diagram, the first gua is Kan (pronounced "kahn"). This area relates to career and life mission: the way you bring your talents into the world, which may or may not be directly related to your job or source of income.

Rate your level of satisfaction:

LOW 0 1 2 3 4 5 6 7 8 9 10 HIGH *(circle one)*

Now, write a few notes in your journal about your experience in this area of your life.

Going clockwise around the diagram, the next gua we encounter is called Ken (pronounced "ken"). This relates to self-knowledge and education. Spiritual pursuits, as well as practical training for a career or hobby, are all related to the energy of Ken.

Rate your level of satisfaction:

LOW 0 1 2 3 4 5 6 7 8 9 10 HIGH *(circle one)*

Write a few notes in your journal about your experience in this part of your life.

Continuing in a clockwise direction, the next gua is Chen ("chehn"). This is associated with family, whether it's your birth family or the family you are raising, and the running of a household.

Rate your level of satisfaction:

LOW 0 1 2 3 4 5 6 7 8 9 10 HIGH *(circle one)*

Add a few notes in your journal about your experiences.

The gua at the top left corner is called Hsun ("shoon") and this is the area associated with wealth and prosperity. Unlike the Chen area, which deals with basic housekeeping expenses, the Hsun gua relates to luxury and the finer things in life.

Rate your level of satisfaction:

LOW 0 1 2 3 4 5 6 7 8 9 10 HIGH (circle one)

Now, write detailed notes about your experience of wealth and prosperity.

The gua at the top center is called Li ("lee"), which relates to status in society, personal recognition, and fame. Do you feel recognized for your talents and the "real you"?

Rate your level of satisfaction:

LOW 0 1 2 3 4 5 6 7 8 9 10 HIGH (circle one)

Now, write a few notes in your journal about your experience of this in your life.

The next area is called Kun ("kuhn"), and it relates to marriage and relationships. If you are happily married or with a great partner, congratulations! Your relationship rating will be high. If not, don't worry. Even though this book is focused on money, it can help you with relationships as well.

Rate your level of satisfaction:

LOW 0 1 2 3 4 5 6 7 8 9 10 HIGH (circle one)

Now, write some notes in your journal about your current experiences with relationships.

The next area of the bagua is called Dui ("dway"). This energy relates to children and creativity. Raising children is one of life's most creative experiences, so it is connected to creativity in the bagua.

Rate your level of satisfaction:

LOW 0 1 2 3 4 5 6 7 8 9 10 HIGH (circle one)

Now, write a few notes in your experience with your children or creativity.

The last area, located at the bottom right of the bagua, is called Chyan (pronounced just as it is spelled). This area relates to mentors and helpful people in your life. It is also associated with travel, since we need people to guide us in unfamiliar territory.

Rate your level of satisfaction:

LOW   0   1   2   3   4   5   6   7   8   9   10   HIGH *(circle one)*

Write a few notes in your journal about your experiences in this aspect of your life.

PROSPERITY JOURNAL: "A PIE FULL OF CHI!"

The chart below is a new bagua, ready to be filled with your chi! For this exercise, you can copy the chart into your journal, or write directly on this page.

1. In each sector of the diagram, draw a line to fill each gua to the level that you feel fulfilled. For example, if you rated career satisfaction as an eight, draw a line at that level of the Kan gua, and shade in the area up to the line.

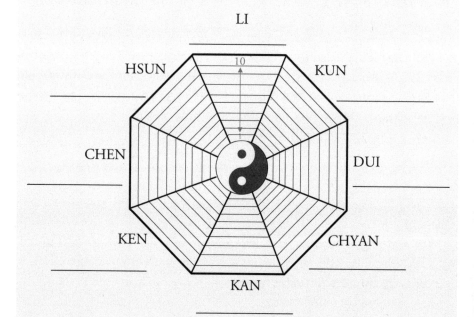

The bagua of personal fulfillment.

2. When finished, you will have a "pie diagram" that reflects your level of satisfaction in eight areas of your life. Perhaps you are more fulfilled in some areas than others. Notice how this looks on your diagram. What is missing in your life? Record your thoughts about this in your journal.

Filling in the Gaps: Your Dream Bagua

If it is money that you want, and only that, then your goal should not be difficult to follow. But if you want more than just paper currency, or numbers on a computer screen, then it is time to be more specific. You need to set your sights on what is most valuable to you and what you consider to be missing in your life.

One of the reasons why setting goals does not work for people is that they tend to list everything that appeals to them, without thinking about whether it is something they will use and enjoy. Everything that you have in your basement, attic, and closets that you now call "clutter" used to be something that you desired; now it's just getting in the way. Often, the reason that we acquire those things in the first place is not because we don't know what we want but because we are afraid of actually admitting what we want. We've settled for things that we thought we *should* want or thought we could afford, instead of the things that are most important to us.

It is much easier to want *everything* than to be specific and admit that we really do have specific needs and desires. Just as a sex addict is afraid of intimacy, a want-a-holic is afraid of desire. It makes us feel too vulnerable, too self-conscious, too afraid of not getting it after all. So we pin our dreams on big-ticket items that don't really mean very much to us and avoid the things that would really touch our hearts.

PROSPERITY JOURNAL: "MY DREAM BAGUA"

This is the time to really reveal your hidden desires to yourself. Devote at least one full sheet, front and back, to each of the eight feng shui areas of the bagua. During this week of the program, take note of what you really want in each area of your life. This is not the time to censor yourself. If you are watching a movie and the characters are living in a place you've always wanted to visit, put it down. You can always cross it off later, but if you don't write it down now, you will probably never pursue it.

At the end of the week, review your list, following these directions:

1. Is there anything on the list that you really want *right now*? Circle these things.
2. Which of these circled items would give you the most joy? Put a star next to them.
3. From the list of starred items, choose *one* thing from each gua that you want to pursue right now. Rate these as your #1 goals for each area of the bagua.

After selecting one main goal for each area of the bagua, write them on the line next to each gua in your pie diagram. This has now become your Dream Bagua. Make a few copies of this diagram and place it where you will notice it the most: at your desk, on the refrigerator, wherever. Every day, this will remind you to fill in the blank areas of your life with the objects of your desire. As you progress in your satisfaction levels, remember to increase the shading level of each gua. As you achieve a goal, take the next thing that you want from your list. These are the things that have been missing in your life. This is the direction of your dreams.

ENVIRONMENTAL FENG SHUI—BLACK SECT FENG SHUI

The feng shui methods in this book come from a particular practice, the Black Sect of Tibetan Tantric Buddhism, often referred to by the abbreviation BTB. Buddhism is not a religion but a collection of practices for increasing self-awareness. The final goal is a state of enlightenment, in which peace is achieved being totally present in the moment.

In ancient times, BTB feng shui assimilated Buddhist teachings from India with the preexisting practices of the Bon lineage in Tibet. As this hybrid developed, it moved into China and further mixed with various cultural influences, including Chinese feng shui, Taoism, Confucianism, ancient healing methods, and astrology. Though feng shui has been practiced in various forms throughout the world, it became particularly strong in China, where the BTB practices were integrated to become a cohesive discipline.

Black Sect feng shui was brought to the West primarily by one figure, His Holiness Professor Lin Yun. Born in China, Professor Lin's teachings connect this wisdom from India, Tibet, and China with the sensibilities of the modern world. Through the teachings of H. H. Professor Lin, contemporary BTB feng shui connects the ancient teachings to modern design theory, architecture, psychology, and ecology. The result is a unique blend of the ancient and the modern, the Eastern and the Western, and the spiritual and the material. Through H. H. Professor Lin's teaching, the wisdom of the ancients is directly applied to the needs and problems of the modern world.

Comparing the Black Sect Approach with the Compass School

In the West, there are two widespread approaches to feng shui. The distinction between these approaches is important, especially if you enjoy perusing the multitude of feng shui books on the shelves.

The BTB approach to feng shui emphasizes the way that chi, the life energy, flows through the space. The movement of this energy directly parallels the life conditions and the financial circumstances of the inhabitants. If the chi is flowing well, the site tends to attract positive experiences and good fortune. Plants grow well, children are healthier, and families tend to be happy. Even the finances seem to flow better—a point that brings us back to the subject of this book.

If the chi is blocked or impure, the health and fortune of the area seem to suffer. Plants die, people tend to be sick or bad-tempered, and businesses fail. There really are "happy places" and "unhappy places," characterized by the quality of the life energy that is flowing through the spaces.

As discussed in the first chapter, the BTB school of feng shui tracks the flow of chi as it enters the building at the front door. The first focus point when examining a building, therefore, is the main entrance. This is where both the people and the chi enter the dwelling. The areas of the bagua are aligned with the building according to the location of the front door, known as the "Mouth of Chi."

The other school of feng shui that is followed in the West is the Compass School. If you hear about a feng shui consultant who aligns the bagua with the use of a compass, or who instructs you to hang a crystal in the southeast corner of the home, you will know he is speaking from the perspective of the Compass School.

Unlike BTB feng shui, which emphasizes the way that the chi energy flows through the space, the Compass School is primarily interested in aligning the space with the compass points, believing that energy always flows according to these directions. This approach was important in ancient China, which was an agrarian society and dependent on the rhythms of the planet for survival. The needs of modern society are now quite different, in our cities that seem to never sleep, and so the energetic flow of the planet is no longer the determining factor for our feng shui outcomes.

Proficient feng shui practitioners may choose to use both of these methodologies to suit the circumstances of a particular client, but this book will focus on the Tibetan BTB approach as our foundation.

Looking for the Cure

For each feng shui problem, we apply a remedy, or "cure." There are two types of remedies: mundane and transcendental cures. The word "mundane" means "of this world," and these cures are practical and commonsensical, dealing with material problems in the environment. If the room is stuffy and smells of last week's fish dinner, open a window and haul out the air freshener. That is feng shui at its crudest and most practical level.

Transcendental cures relate to the spiritual or metaphysical aspects of life and are generally more mysterious and ritualized. The transcendental cures in this book are from BTB feng shui. Some of these cures have been used for thousands of years to create powerful influences—even veritable miracles.

Transcendental cures defy all rational explanations, which is why they are so powerful. The scope of our current scientific understanding, while helpful, is still fairly limited. Transcendental cures augment, and often defy, our current understanding of the universe and force us to admit the limitations of our rational minds.

In this program for financial feng shui, you will use both mundane and transcendental cures. Practical, mundane questions include "Did you balance your checkbook recently? Do you know how much you are spending each month? Do you have an income?" These are mundane concerns, yet obviously important. No matter how many crystals you hang over your desk or how many times you chant the ancient mantras, if you don't answer these basic questions, your finances will not do very well.

Transcendental approaches to financial development can also be very important. Creative visualization, affirmation, meditation, ritual, and prayer are all transcendental influences to empower your financial life.

The Calming Heart Sutra: Preparing for Meditation

In the Black Sect tradition, feng shui consultants begin every session with a chant and a brief period of meditation. If you feel distracted before investigating a dwelling, you need to take time to settle into yourself. The chant used in consultations is called the Calming Heart Sutra. This will help you release your distracting thoughts and settle into the intuitive wisdom of your heart.

The words of the chant translate into English as, "Take me to the other side." In ordinary waking consciousness, we perceive events from one side of reality. Things seem to happen around us—and to us. The chant asks for us to be taken to another perspective, to understand *why* things happen.

Begin by sitting comfortably, and relax into the pattern of your breathing. Become aware of your thoughts, and gradually let them go. If there is anything you need to attend to, do it now, before it infringes upon your session.

Be sure that your seating position is comfortable. You may need to change positions, or even move to another chair. Notice the way dogs and cats choose their resting places; it is always done with a great deal of experimenting and primping before they finally lie down. When conducting a consultation, I often spend a lot of time deciding on the best place to sit, and this helps get the session started from a good perspective.

Next, align your hands in the meditation *mudra*, which is a sacred hand gesture. Traditionally, men place the left hand over the right and women put the right hand over the left. Do this in a relaxed way, and connect the tips of your two thumbs; the shape looks something like an inverted heart. You may hold your hands at the lower part of your chest, so the mudra supports your heart, or rest your hands in your lap, so that they support your upper body like a cradle. Either way, make sure your arms feel relaxed and comfortable.

The words of the chant are as follows:

> *Gate, Gate, Para Gate*
> ("gah-tay, gah-tay, pah-rah gah-tay")
>
> *Para Sam Gate, Bodhi Svaha.*
> ("pah-rah sahm gah-tay, boh-dee svah-hah.")

The translation of the chant into English is:

> Gone, gone, gone across
> Gone completely across, to the Enlightened State, so it is!

Try saying it now as practice. If you relax as you say each word of the sutra, you may feel the vibration ringing through your body. You may want to write the words of the chant on a card, so you can practice it often in the next few days. Try to memorize it by the end of the week, so you can do the sutra at any time to feel more settled.

This chant is repeated nine times. The bagua has nine sections (including the t'ai chi at the center), and nine is considered a sacred feng shui number, representing wholeness. Many of the rituals are performed in sequences of nine steps.

Each time that you repeat the sutra, connect to the power within your heart. It can be done with eyes open or closed; experiment to find the way that works best for you. With practice, you can completely transform the way you are feeling by repeating this chant. It is a simple practice that has profound effects.

Bagua Sector of the Week: Chen

People who have done a little study of feng shui usually associate money and abundance with the Hsun corner of the bagua, at the top left. This gua is connected to wealth and prosperity, but the association can be misleading.

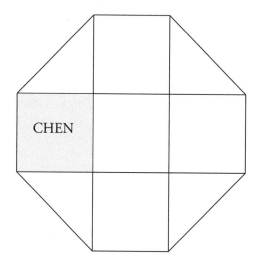

Bagua sector of the week: Chen.

The area of the bagua called Chen, which is the focus of our work this week, deals with the family and the daily running of the household. For many people, this is the center of financial concerns. I would be surprised if the only reason that you were reading this book was to find a way to finance a new luxury boat! Instead, like most people, you may be concerned about just keeping your daily lifestyle afloat.

Chen is the "meat and potatoes" of daily life, while Hsun is the "champagne and caviar." Just as you need both in your diet to be both nourished and tantalized, you need both the Chen and Hsun energies in your financial life to be completely fulfilled.

Even if you live alone, you are running a household, and you shouldn't wait until you have a spouse or family to think about how you manage your home. This is essential in order to move on to greater elegance and luxury. What's the use of a cruise around the world if you come home to a dysfunctional household?

If you are single, the Chen gua also relates to your birth family. This energy also relates to how you establish community and the way that you plant your personality in the world. Our financial lives are deeply rooted in the dynamics and experiences of our birth family, an important issue to be explored throughout this program.

PROSPERITY JOURNAL: "MY FAMILY LIFE"

1. Create a Chen section of your notebook, and write a few notes about your personal home life. Consider your daily expenses, the pace of your lifestyle, and the way you feel about coming home each day. Also, give some thought to your family and community structure, and write a few notes about this experience.

2. Now, go to the Chen corner of your home. By dividing the area of your home into nine equal sections, you'll find that the Chen is on the central left-hand side of the bagua.

3. Prepare your awareness by chanting the Calming Heart Sutra ("Gate, Gate. . ."), and quiet your mind. Then, in your journal, list four adjectives that describe how this area of your home feels to you.

4. Review your earlier notes about how this area of your life has been feeling, and compare these experiences to the condition of this part of your home. Consider any correlations between your inner experience and the nature of this sector of your space. You might write any observations about this parallel in your journal.

If your home life has been feeling good, the feng shui of this part of your home is probably in good condition as well. If the feng shui is not in proper alignment, however, you will need to do a few adjustments to create a positive experience. This is essential for establishing a better financial life.

Feng Shui Applications for Financial Development in Chen

Each area of the bagua is associated with a specific element and color. In this gua, the element is called "small wood," which relates to small trees and plants, like bamboo. As we weather the difficulties in our families and daily affairs, the energy of Chen is resilient, like bamboo that bends with the breeze. This Chen energy is developed by consistently planting seeds of new growth. By paying each bill on time and taking care of the issues that face the family, a strong household can withstand any storm.

Some of the best feng shui cures in Chen are live plants. If you care for plants on a regular basis, you can use that same diligence to manage your household and care for your expenses. Plants need daily attention, and so does your family and your bank account. If you ignore a plant for weeks, it withers; the same thing can happen to your family, your community, and your money.

Choose plants for this area that are small, leafy, and have sturdy roots. Each time you care for them, imagine you are nurturing the health of your household. Nine plants on a ledge or table is a perfect arrangement.

Objects representing the water element are also helpful, since the element of water feeds the element of wood. Glass mirrors, which represent water, can bring relief to a constricted home life and usher in new opportunities when placed in Chen. A small tabletop fountain in this area is also effective, especially if your finances have been "dry" recently and you have trouble paying your bills.

Are you having a difficulty with your family, or feeling haunted by a turbulent past? Make sure this area is light, airy, and full of soft textures and colors. Take out any abstract art or disturbing images that suggest chaos or conflict, and replace them with paintings or photos that show people enjoying each other's company. This is an ideal place to put photos of the people that you really love, but leave out any relatives or friends who make you feel uncomfortable or anxious. You do not need to invite the energy of anyone into your Chen gua who does not make you feel happy and content with your home life.

Review your Dream Bagua, and look at the personal goal you associated with this gua. Think of ways that you might embody the energy of that goal, in some visual way, in this section of your home. For example, if you have been dreaming of buying a new home, then put a picture of your dream house in this area, where you will see it every day. By making a veritable shrine to the feeling that this goal represents, you create the space for it to come into your life.

If you have any clutter or broken items in this area, you should replace them immediately. Their energy can disturb the solidity of your home life faster than you can say, "I'm home!"

If you are missing parts of the Chen gua from your home, place a large mirror on one of the walls and make sure that it is reflecting something beautiful. Also, you can use a row of nine plants or shrubs in the yard to offset the missing section.

PROSPERITY JOURNAL: "APPLYING FENG SHUI TO CHEN"

Review the feng shui cures listed for Chen, and list two or three changes you would like to make in this gua this week. Perform these changes in the spirit of improving your sense of family, home life, and community.

FINANCIAL FENG SHUI—INSTANT WEALTH, PART 2

Last week, we reviewed all of the "assets" accumulating in your home. Now it's time to go through the financial records. Do you really know your financial net worth? This is the foundation of your Chen energy. Though the thought may be intimidating, don't lose a moment before assessing your financial foundation.

PROSPERITY JOURNAL: "MY FINANCIAL STATUS"

Put aside an afternoon or evening, and lay out, in concrete figures, your financial status in these areas:

Banking
- Checking accounts
- Savings accounts
- Money market
- Retirement account
- CDs
- Stocks/mutual funds/ETFs
- Bonds
- Safety deposit box contents
- Debts owed to you
- Insurance reimbursement that has not been filed
- Gift certificates
- Other

Other Assets
- Property and real estate other than your home
- Business outside the home: office equipment, and so on
- Copyrights, domain names (yes, these have become very valuable), and logos
- Other

Write down the total of the amounts you have listed. Now, combine this total with the total you devised in the asset game in chapter 1.

Later in this program, you will be outlining your expenses, debts, and other influences on your finances. On your journey toward greater wealth, it's essential that you assess everything available to you. By knowing where you are, you have a better chance of getting where you want to go!

Watch Out! Incoming Chi: Charting Your Income

The only way to increase your assets is to increase your income. This simple fact has kept a lot of people in restrictive and even dehumanizing jobs, as they try to survive by supporting another person's dreams. This book will help you build a career that not only supports you, but helps you thrive.

Before falling into any despair about your earning potential, one thing needs to be emphasized: at some time in your life, you were, and possibly still are, earning some degree of income. This is a very important point, which shows that you have the skills and savvy necessary to bring in money. The only question now is, how much and for what?

PROSPERITY JOURNAL: "MY LIFETIME EARNINGS"

1. To establish yourself as someone who makes money, list every job you have ever had, from birth to the present. That twenty-five-cent allowance when you were a kid? Yep, it counts. Work-study in college? Absolutely, put it on the list. Be sure to include any self-employment and part-time jobs you have had.

2. Now, total the amount of money you have earned in your lifetime. You may be surprised by your wage-earning history! Meditate on this accomplishment, and consider how this shows the degree of social appreciation that you have received for your talents and skills.

3. Now *subtract* your total life earnings from the sum of all of your assets (as calculated in the final sequence of your previous journal entry). If your solvent assets exceed your gross lifetime earnings, you have obviously been investing your energy very wisely. But if your earnings are not reflected well in your assets, you need to start rethinking the way you use your energy.

Your Daily Bread

The assets you own are the materialization of the ways that you have invested your life energy. With wisdom, conviction, and care, you should be able to develop a garden of riches that can nourish you for the rest of your life. This will enable you to develop your assets even further. You must have a clear sense of these resources before charting the rest of your journey.

PROSPERITY JOURNAL: "ASSESSING MY FUTURE INCOME"

1. Review your current situation, and list all possible income coming to you. In your journal, outline these possible sources:
   - Current job
   - Part-time jobs
   - Miscellaneous freelancing (any ideas?)
   - Expected gifts
   - Debts owed to you
   - Interest and dividends from savings and investments
   - Tax refunds
   - Other
2. Set a date next to each amount when you can expect cash in hand.
3. Use these figures to estimate your monthly income for the next two months, which is the expected duration of this program. Beware: if you diligently apply the principles in this book, you may need to go back and increase these figures!

INNER FENG SHUI—THE WILLINGNESS TO BE WRONG

Our minds will justify our ideas at all costs, whether they contribute to our personal satisfaction or not. If a hypnotist tells us to be giant chickens, and we willingly comply, we'll do everything in our power to think, feel, and act like chickens, despite any evidence to the contrary. Similarly, if we believe we can't be wealthy, for whatever reason, we'll do everything in our power to justify that idea, even at the expense of the life we want.

For some, the true experience of wealth can be elusive. Because wealth is impossible? No. For whatever reason, we would rather keep it impossible than subscribe to a new set of beliefs. Time after time, we would rather be right than be happy. So we lie on our deathbeds, having suffered a lifetime of deprivation and lack, and a part of us exclaims with glee, "You see, I was right!"

"Blessed are the poor . . . Money corrupts . . . No one appreciates a genius/artist/honest person . . . I can't handle money . . . No feng shui technique could really help *my* situation . . ." Which would you rather take to your grave: your beliefs about money, or your memories of a prosperous life?

If you continue to think the way you've been thinking, you'll continue to get what you've already been getting. So far, everything in life has proven that your ideas are right. Now, the only question: are you willing to be wrong?

Are you willing to be wrong about the ways that money can come into your life? About the character of rich people? Are you willing to be wrong about the purported blessedness of poverty? About the level of financial reward you can receive and your ability to handle it when it comes in?

Just for this week, start using an important word: "Maybe." Whenever you are faced with a situation that you think will not work, toss in that word. "Maybe this really will work out okay . . . Maybe I can find a new job . . . Maybe I really can be wealthy . . ." Whatever it is, give it the benefit of the doubt, at least for right now. Maybe you will be right—or maybe you will be wrong. But if you are willing to be wrong, there are a lot of things that may turn out all right.

"What Do I Have to Lose?"

Self-limitation is about "either-or" thinking. I can either be spiritual or I can be wealthy. I can either have material possessions or I can have great relationships. I can either make a lot of money or I can do something that really interests me. *But I can't have both!* That type of reasoning is self-negating and it is also very childlike.

As children, we spent every waking moment trying to figure out how the world worked. The universe was a mystery, and also pretty intimidating, so we came to conclusions as quickly as possible.

If you were bitten by a dog at an early age, dogs became dangerous creatures you needed to avoid. If the first grade teacher was mean and scary one morning, perhaps you didn't want to learn anything ever again. That's a pretty hefty decision at the age of six!

The same process was happening in relationship to money. If your parents wouldn't raise your allowance, for whatever reason, you may have concluded you didn't deserve it and that your presence in the world was not so valuable after all. Wow—what a huge decision based on a twenty-five-cent weekly raise!

The beliefs held by parents infuse the child like intravenous drugs. It doesn't take long to form some pretty extreme views about money. These are some common childhood associations: "Money was scarce . . . something we didn't talk about . . . considered dirty . . . the subject of arguments . . ." The list of negative images goes on and on.

PROSPERITY JOURNAL:
"WHEN I WAS GROWING UP, MONEY WAS SOMETHING THAT . . ."

Take a moment to consider your childhood messages about money and wealth. Complete this phrase: "When I was growing up, money was something that . . ." List at least ten words or phrases that echo the financial environment of your youth.

As you identify negative messages from your past, remember the purpose is not to blame the adults or label them as bad; like you, they were deeply influenced by *their* parents and the culture in which they were raised. You can begin to see how limiting ideas have filtered down through generations, like a cognitive gene pool.

Out with the Old

In last week's chapter, we examined some of your favorite limiting beliefs. Those are the ones that you liked so much, you were hesitant to see them proven wrong. But now, you can't afford the luxury of self-limiting ideas. It's time to move on and start enjoying a life that really brings you benefits.

PROSPERITY JOURNAL: "REVAMPING MY BELIEFS"

1. On a new page, write two headings, side by side: "Column A" and "Column B." Go back to your journal entries from chapter 1 and review your top five beliefs about money, wealth, and rich people. Write them in column A of your new journal entry. Do they look as compelling as they did a week ago? From this week's work with family belief systems, you may start to see how you acquired these limiting perspectives.

2. Now, summon the courage to be wrong about these ideas. Take the first belief from column A and add it to the statement below:

   I *believe* that _____, but that idea is not necessarily true, even though I believe it. That is just an idea *about* reality and is not reality itself. From now on, I no longer accept this idea as my reality, and I am open to new possibilities.

3. Try saying this statement for each of the beliefs that you listed above in column A. Notice how it feels to actually reject your own ideas out loud. This may be one of the most liberating experiences about money that you ever have.

4. Now it's time for some new possibilities. In column B, write exactly the *opposite* of the limiting belief. For example, if you wrote in column A, "Rich people are selfish," you could now write, "Rich people are generous." Or "I can't handle money" becomes "I am very good at handling money." Whatever the belief, replace it with a positive one.

5. For the last step, you should substantiate at least one of your new possibilities. In feng shui, nothing is complete until it is materialized. Circle just one of your

(Continued)

new, positive beliefs and then set yourself this challenge: In the coming week, you must find some way to *prove* that this new belief is true! For instance, if your new belief declares, "Rich people are generous," you must find one example that substantiates this opinion beyond all doubt, whether in the newspapers, the media, history, or in person. And if you still don't believe it, get some better evidence. In the end, you will be not only wiser, but a lot richer as well.

Journaling Follow-Up

You have had about a week to commit your thoughts to your Prosperity Journal. How has this been? Have you been writing at least a few pages every day? Did you spring for the notebook at all, or did you decide that you can't afford it and that you will do the exercises "later"?

If you are seeking benefits from this book, you cannot afford to do without the journal. It is the lifeline to your thoughts. And why is this important? Well, where else are you going to get that one great idea (or two or three) that will make you a lot of money?

Journal writing has gotten me out of many confusing situations and taken me to a new level of comfort with my own thoughts. Without a journal, the thoughts just gallop wildly along, but writing gives us a rope to pull them in and use them for our benefit.

If you *have* been writing, congratulations! Keep it up. You may want to focus your writing this week on those nasty, limiting beliefs standing between you and your greater fortune. In any case, grab the pen at least a few times this week, and start writing your way to wealth.

ACTION STEPS ON THE JOURNEY TO WEALTH:

WEEK 2 SYNOPSIS

Now that you are dealing with the nitty-gritty of the program, this may be a challenging week. Take it one day at a time, and focus on the progress you are making with each step. Here is the work for this week.

Check the boxes as you complete the following activities:

- ☐ Learn the Calming Heart Sutra by heart, so that you can use it for meditation and feng shui work.
- ☐ Review your feng shui ideas for the Chen area, choosing at least two for this week, and make the intended changes.
- ☐ Count up all your assets.
- ☐ Make a complete analysis of all money coming in the next two months. You will need it for this journey!
- ☐ Make sure you are keeping up with your journal entries—they are very important. Be sure to do at least three this week.

WEEK 3

Energizing Your Life

He who possesses his self-nature
Is like a newborn babe . . .
He screams 'til the end of the day,
His harmony has achieved perfection.
—The *Tao Te Ching*, Book 55

PRELUDE—THE THREE FACES OF CHI

In the traditional, Western view of reality, the elements of life are distinct and separate. The energy of your home is one thing, your finances are another, and your spiritual life is something else. We try to cure the individual parts and hope it will all come together someday.

In the Asian perspective, however, these three aspects of life are not just connected—they are the same thing. The chi of your home doesn't just reflect your finances—it is a direct reflection of your financial energy. A lack in your spiritual life is automatically reflected in your financial and environmental chi, whether you are aware of it or not. These three aspects of life are constantly shifting together, creating your experience of life. When you affect one, it has an impact on the others, guaranteed.

The diagram below illustrates this relationship.

When sitting down to balance my accounts or pay my bills, I say to myself, "Okay, it's time to do my spiritual work." And that's exactly what it is. The way we give and receive energy is not just spiritual in intent—it is spirit, pure and simple. Spirituality is the flow of life, and everything we do that affects this flow is part of our daily religion.

Faces of chi.

Ask a child what is spiritual, and he will probably shrug his shoulders, give you a funny look, and then go off and play. But educate the child for a few years, fill his mind with all sorts of ideas, and what happens? You talk to him about spirituality, and he gets a very serious look on his face. "Oh, God is up there," he says, in a tone meant for a quiz at school. And then he stands there, waiting for approval. If you say, "Yes, that's good," then he will shrug his shoulders and go off and play.

Whoever created the idea that God and life are separate did the most destructive thing possible to all mankind. Absolve all the political tyrants of the world; we were vanquished the day we were separated from the source of life itself. Forget about all the religious practices we do and the creeds designed to make us "good." If we believe there is anything that is not spiritual, what should we do with that part? Throw it away? Ignore it? Take it out with the trash?

Even garbage has a purpose, which is more than can be said for religious ideas that condemn the daily holiness of life. To regain our spirit, to really know life, we need to let go of our ideas and return to the sacredness of our experience. This is what is called "Beginner's Mind."

Beginner's Mind

> *A simple man looks at the countryside and sees mountains and forests.*
> *A civilized man looks at the countryside and sees property values.*
> *An enlightened man looks at the countryside and sees mountains and forests.*

As adults, we have learned to distrust. We want to analyze, interrogate, and define everything before we are willing to receive. How do we know what we want to be when we grow up? Well, after a battery of aptitude tests, trips to an analyst, and a vote among our friends, perhaps then we will find our answer. But ask a child, and an enthusiastic response quickly follows: "a fireman," "a ballet dancer," "a race car driver," or maybe "just like my dad!" The child doesn't think about having to debate it; he recognizes the truth as it sits within him.

As a therapist, a large part of my job is to state the obvious. If clients come in and look angry, I say, "You look angry." You would be surprised at the shocked response I get from them. They look at me with disbelief. "Angry? Me? I never thought of that!"

The same approach is required of a feng shui consultant. If I walk into a home and the front door is obstructed by a bookcase, I say to the residents, "Move the books; the door doesn't open all the way." And they look at me like I'm a genius (which I may be, but that is another story). Now, I could have gotten a second grader to make the same observation, but all the children have to be in school from 8:00 A.M. to 3:00 P.M.—so I guess that leaves the adults who are trained as consultants to do the job.

We have learned to think with our heads, and not our hearts. We are trained to question, and distrust what we feel, instead of recognizing the wisdom within. Without this emotional foundation, we are dependent upon others to tell us how to live, what to wear, what sort of work to do, and yes, even how to decorate the interiors of our homes.

ENVIRONMENTAL FENG SHUI—CHANNELING THE CHI OF YOUR HOME

You may have visited some places on the planet that have very strong, positive energy. In such areas, the vegetation thrives abundantly and people are generally in very good health. Even a brief visit to one of these sites can leave you with that rigorous workout, great sex, day-at-the-beach kind of feeling!

On the other hand, you may have visited, or lived in, areas where the energy seems too low—crops don't grow well, and there is a sense of depression or lack of prosperity among the people. Here, for one reason or another, the chi is blocked, which has a dramatic effect on the health and vitality of the residents.

With feng shui, you can improve the movement of chi energy. By creating the right flow, you are literally able to empower a space in the same way that electricity illuminates a light bulb or music fills a room. The actual mechanics of the transformation are invisible, but the effect is profound. The atmosphere literally becomes magnetic with potential.

Originally, the word "enthusiasm" meant "filled with God." When our energy is high and we exude a sense of delight and wonder with the world, we are infused with the God energy that propels the universe. This is chi energy, which magnetically draws positive conditions and events into our lives.

The Mouth of Chi

The nature and condition of your front door affects the way that chi energy enters your space, thereby determining how financial energy enters your life. On a metaphorical level, your front door represents how you bring yourself into the world and how opportunities are able to greet you.

When I do a consultation, I spend a lot of time examining the front door. If you are reading this at home, go to your entranceway right now and examine the conditions we are discussing.

Start outside the door. Quiet your mind with a few deep breaths, and repeat the Calming Heart Sutra nine times ("Gate, Gate . . ."). Settle into your Beginner's Mind, and approach your entranceway as if for the first time. Notice: is the sidewalk clear and even, or do you feel uncertain as you approach? If you live in an apartment, notice the condition of the public areas. Are they welcoming and well lit?

One of the first things I installed at home was an attractive "Welcome" mat at my front door. This helps visitors enter the space with clean feet, but also gives them the feeling that their arrival is anticipated and important. Be sure to get a mat that conveys an enthusiastic greeting to life's opportunities. For an added invitation to prosperity, place nine Chinese coins, connected by a red ribbon, under the welcome mat, pointing in the direction of the Hsun/wealth area of your home.

I generally recommend that the client's name be featured prominently on the door just below eye level or by the door buzzer. A brass nameplate gives a special, commanding air to your entranceway. Take notice of the buzzer and door knocker as well. Does the sound of your doorbell make your heart sing, or does it give you heart palpitations? A small detail like the door buzzer profoundly affects the way you feel about contact with the outside world.

If your front door is made of glass, use curtain shades to prevent outsiders from looking in. A transparent door suggests a lack of boundaries, and you could start feeling out of control in your business affairs and unable to separate your personal life from your outside obligations.

Make sure the door opens to at least a ninety-degree angle. This is a very serious consideration. If the door is obstructed, it leads to feelings of limitation and frustration in business affairs. Clear all clutter away from the door, and remove any furniture that may be inhibiting the flow.

I often suggest an attractive, colorful rug for the entranceway. This excites the senses and makes the area more inviting and nurturing. Be sure to remove your cat's litter pan from this area, for the opposite reason! A bowl of potpourri, or a fresh orange studded with cloves, would be more enticing.

As you stand inside the front door, observe the interior view. If you face directly into a long hallway, the chi may gallop too quickly away from the door. If this is the case in your home, purchase a thirty-millimeter crystal and hang it from the ceiling about four or five feet into the hall, to spread energy as it enters. There are resources in appendix A at the back of this book for purchasing specialized feng shui supplies.

If there is a window or sliding glass door directly opposite an entranceway, the energy entering the building will often go right out through the exposure on the other side. Those sliding glass doors that were all the rage back in the Seventies can really wreak havoc with a family's income. (Perhaps you remember the recession?) To stop the chi—and the money associated with it—from disco dancing out as quickly as it comes in, use one of the multifaceted crystals, which should be hung about one to two feet above head level.

If your entranceway leads directly into a wall, you may feel that your horizons are constricted and new opportunities may be repelled from the space. Install a mirror opposite the door, or hang a beautiful picture to engage the eye and give a sense of space.

You may also have a condition of "split vision": half of your vision is blocked by a wall, while the view from your other eye goes directly into a larger space. This is considered a dangerous condition in feng shui, because it confuses the senses and sends mixed signals about your depth of perception. In this case, hang a picture or mirror on the wall to fully engage your view. H. H. Professor Lin has also suggested hanging nine $100 bills at the corner of the offending wall; each time you enter, your attention will be focused on counting the money to make sure that it's all there!

If your front door enters into your kitchen and directly faces your stove, this is considered very negative financial feng shui. Your opportunities will be burned up before you have a chance to benefit from them. If that's the case in your home, make sure that you pay particular attention to the section on the kitchen, and be sure to implement the cures that are listed.

Clutter (That's a Dirty Word)

Fifty years ago, if someone used the word "clutter" in a conversation, it would not have had the same sort of emotional charge that it does today. But currently, it is met with eyes rolled up and a sense of hopelessness. Clutter now occupies the ranks as one of the top ten causes of human distress: "I would have a lovely home, if I could only manage my clutter." "I'm ready to move on in my career, but I just can't get through the clutter." "I would love to elope, but I can't find my passport in all this clutter." "I *think* I have three children, but the little one hasn't been seen for months because of all of this clutter!" Ah yes, clutter has become the number one excuse for many of our ailments, but what exactly is this insidious condition, and how can we release the powerful hold it seems to have over our lives?

In feng shui, clutter refers to any condition that blocks the flow of chi energy. Often, these blockages start fairly harmlessly. Why spend time washing the dishes, when the pile of dirty laundry is calling and the heap of unpaid bills glares at you from the desk? You want to clean everything up, you really do . . . but it feels so overwhelming, the most you can do is stagger to the sofa and use your last bit of energy to search through yesterday's take-out containers for the remote control!

This can be a difficult truth to accept: one of the reasons that clutter is difficult to erase is because we actually like it. What? Did you read that correctly? Yes. Underneath all our grumblings about the mess and our complaints about not finding what we need, most of us have a subconscious attraction to clutter. Throwing things around gives us a sense of freedom. Especially after a demanding day at work, who wants to worry about putting things neatly away? I don't! Then, when the accumulation becomes a problem, we set ourselves up with an impressive New Year's resolution, which usually takes us as far as January 2.

There's another reason why we are so attached to clutter: it's exhausting. That's the reason we like it? Absolutely. The easiest way to avoid doing the things we fear is to find something that distracts us and soaks up all our energy. Clutter fits the avoidance bill, every time. With all this mess around, who has time to deal with the big problems, like being in a relationship or finding a challenging job?

Remember that old joke? A man went into the doctor's office and complained, "Doc, I've had a splitting headache for three days straight, and I just can't ignore it. Can you help me?" The doctor picked up a hammer and slammed it against the man's foot. The patient screamed in pain and cried, "What did you do that for?" to which the doctor replied, "Did you forget about your headache?"

This principle also applies to people who *seemingly* do not have any clutter at all. They are the model of good housekeeping, spending every moment ensuring everything is spotless and in its right place. They are so consumed by their house-keeping, they have little time for anything else. Which is exactly how they planned it.

PROSPERITY JOURNAL: "MY LIFE WITHOUT CLUTTER"

Make a list of ten things you would do if you did not have to deal with clutter. Now, start dealing with these things directly, so you don't need to live in a smokescreen!

When you are actually ready to do it, there are a number of helpful techniques to move the old energy out and bring the new energy in. The best thing I can recommend is to deal with the most annoying messes first. If the overflowing garbage pail is taking your attention, it doesn't make sense to clean the attic first. Handle the situations that are draining you the  most, and you will build a storehouse of internal chi for tackling the larger problems.

I call this the "80/20 Rule." There is a business principle that states that we get 80 percent of the total value from 20 percent of the work; the trick is to figure which is the most important 20 percent and attack it first.

This approach has been extremely effective with messy rooms and other tasks that seem overwhelming at the start. Whenever I face a daunting task, I tell myself, "I only need to do 20 percent to make a difference," and then quickly figure out where the prime 20 percent of the problem is located. If the idea still seems over-whelming, I usually give myself a time boundary, such as twenty minutes, but once I get going, I usually want to keep working until the entire mess is cleaned up.

From the feng shui perspective, the location of the clutter can tell you a lot about the condition of various areas of your life. Clutter in the bedroom suggests problems (or the avoidance of problems) in relationships, while the same condition in the living room suggests difficulty with your role in society. Clutter in the kitchen and bathroom usually relates to problems of nurturance and self-care.

The Mount Vernon Technique

Unfortunately, for many of us, getting in control of "the stuff" can seem like an endless battle, and taking on bits at a time might not take care of it. I, too, have struggled with this at times, and thankfully have found some other approaches that really work.

Here is a great one. It's called the Mount Vernon technique because it is actu-ally the approach that is used by the staff at the home of George Washington, the first president of the United States.

They start the process at the front door and begin cleaning in a clockwise direction. As they clean, the staff goes through every nook, cranny, closet, drawer, etc., and doesn't move on until that area is organized and spotless.

Interestingly, this is exactly how energy seems to flow in feng shui: entering at the front door and moving in a clockwise direction. So, George's maids must have been in the know!

Once they have gotten through that first room, the staff enters the next room, and moves on in a clockwise direction again. At the end of the day, they make a mental note of where they stopped and then start up at that point the next day.

Working in this way may seem slow, but it is certainly thorough. And once the entire house has been cleaned in this way the first time, the clockwise cleaning of the rooms goes much faster the next time.

Personally, I have used this method on occasions when I feel that the entire place needs a thorough cleaning, and it really makes a difference. It also gives me a great sense of accomplishment as I move in a systematic rotation through the entire home.

If your situation is extreme, however, and moving clockwise around a room gets impeded within the first few feet of the door, here is an even more extreme suggestion: Choose a particular room for your focus, and take *everything* out of that room except the furniture. That's right—*everything*, include the contents of drawers, cabinets, etc. Haul every item except the furniture from the room and lay it out in another room, or even outside, in three piles: things you use every day, things you love or use occasionally but need to store, and things you can easily get rid of. Then, working in reverse piles, get rid of the things you can, find storage for the things you want to keep, and make the things you need for daily use readily available.

When you return the things to the room from which they came, make sure they go to a proper storage place. Strive to keep all surfaces free of objects (table tops, window sills, floors, etc.). If it is not art or a valued photograph, it should not be on display!

By being this stringent with your possessions, you are sure to create each area of your home as an open space with room to breathe.

Bagua Sector of the Week: Hsun

When people think of wealth, they often envision luxury cars, expensive clothes, gorgeous homes and glamorous vacations. Such is the stuff of dreams . . . but this is not real life, right? Well, in feng shui, not only is this considered an aspect of real life, it's an essential and important part of it. Of the areas in the bagua, the Hsun gua is concerned with how we develop and maintain prosperous splendor in our lives. Now that you are clearing through the clutter, you are making room for something luxurious to come in.

Energizing Your Life

The leaves in autumn are ablaze in brilliant colors, and birds of a feather fly in shimmering hues, yet for some reason, we may believe that human life should be drab, tedious, and boring. Not true, say the ancient texts of feng shui. Just like the colorful flowers of the field and the other wonders of nature, we may have to exert some creative energy to fill our lives with splendor, but the impulse is ours to follow, and it's a limitation of our spiritual power not to indulge this part of life.

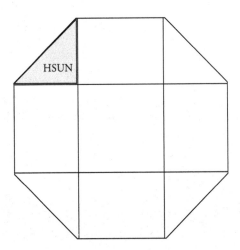

Bagua sector of the week: Hsun.

While the Chen sector of the bagua, which was the focus last week, is concerned with running the household and meeting the routine expenses, the Hsun sector of the bagua is concerned with luxury. By dividing the area of your home into nine equal sections, you'll find Hsun at the top left corner of your floor plan.

PROSPERITY JOURNAL: "MY SENSE OF WEALTH AND LUXURY"

1. Create a Hsun section of your notebook, and write a few notes about your experience of wealth and luxury in your life. Do you feel you have an abundance of the things that make life feel luxurious and comfortable?
2. Now, go to the Hsun corner of your home. By dividing the area of your home into nine equal sections, you'll find that the Hsun is on the top left-hand side of the bagua.

(Continued)

3. Prepare your awareness by chanting the Calming Heart Sutra ("Gate, Gate . . ."), and quiet your mind. Then, in your journal, list three or four adjectives that describe how this area of your home feels to you.
4. Review your answers to the first question about how this area of your life has been feeling, and compare these experiences to the condition of this part of your home. Consider any correlations between your inner experience and the nature of this sector of your space. You might write any observations about this parallel in your journal.

Feng Shui Applications for Financial Development in Hsun

The Hsun area is associated with the wood element, making it the perfect place for a greenhouse, indoor garden, or other houseplants. Look for strong, sturdy plants that will reflect a hardy bank account, and avoid timid or melancholy plants like the ficus that drop their leaves every time the stock market takes a dip! Chinese Jade plants, which have round, succulent leaves resembling Chinese coins, are considered especially auspicious.

The water element is often used in the Hsun gua, because water feeds wood, causing growth in this sector. Fountains are especially beneficial in this area, and I have used one with a jolly golden Buddha on the top ledge, with nine Chinese coins on the rocks under the cascading water. If the sound of running water always makes you want to run to the bathroom, you might consider instead a photo or poster of a large waterfall.

A model of a large boat, such as an antique merchant ship, is considered auspicious in this area, especially with golden coins and little treasure chests on its decks. Place one in your Hsun corner, facing into the home, to indicate that your ship is coming in!

Since mirrors represent the water element, they are especially favorable in Hsun. They are reported to double any prosperity they reflect, so be sure that only beautiful things are seen in the glass. The day that I hung a mirror over my fountain in Hsun, I received three new clients in one afternoon, which was a new record.

An aquarium in Hsun is ideal, especially when stocked with nine goldfish: eight of them should be red or gold, and one of them should be black. If any of the fish die while occupying this corner of your home, do not fear that your finances are in danger. When a fish dies, it is considered to have done a great service by absorbing the negative chi in the space; you can thank it, and then quickly replace it with a new fish.

This is also the perfect location for your prosperity shrine. Symbols of wealth, Chinese coins, golden Buddhas, and other luxurious items belong here. Start collecting pictures and objects that remind you of the luxurious life that you want to lead and place them here in a position of honor. Search colorful magazines for scenes of the wealthy experiences you desire. Travel agencies are great sources for free, full-color brochures about the places you want to visit.

If you have very large windows in Hsun, be careful that the energy does not leak out before you build a steady fortune. Hang a faceted crystal or wind chime in the window, and consider adding rich, luxurious draperies to soften the area and give a feeling of richness to the room.

The vibration of Hsun is represented by the color purple, and anything in a deep, vibrant shade of this color gives a charge to your Hsun energy. Amethyst crystals, live or silk flowers, rich purple curtains or upholstery . . . eggplants? Anything in this rich color that gives a feeling of luxury and wealth is perfect for this area of your home.

If you are missing parts of the Hsun gua in your home, do not despair. Compensate for this with mirrors, nine green plants in a row, or at the very least, a large, faceted crystal or wind chime. You can also augment this area from the outside of the home with nine trees or plants, a large outdoor fountain, or even a swimming pool. I have relatives who were missing the entire Hsun corner of their home, but had a lanai and outdoor swimming pool in its place; since they live in Florida, this seemed like part of the house. Their finances do not seem to have suffered since they moved in.

In the coming weeks, as we examine the other areas of the bagua, it's essential for you to continually return to your Hsun sector and address the condition and flow of energy in this area. Make it a daily ritual to add to your prosperity shrine, and continually bring new energy and intention to this area of your home and your life.

PROSPERITY JOURNAL: "APPLYING FENG SHUI TO HSUN"

Review the feng shui cures that are traditionally used in the Hsun area, and list two or three changes you would like to make in this gua this week. Be sure to do the Calming Heart Sutra before you apply any cures, to align your energy with the intention of your desires.

Return to your Dream Bagua and review the one thing you want to achieve in the Hsun area of your life. Now is the perfect time to put energy into achieving this goal, if you haven't already.

Three Secret Reinforcements: Making the Lucky Dollar

When we install a feng shui cure, we actually alter the vibration of our environment. Whether it is with color, sound, light, or physical mass, every cure changes the energetic field that we call "home." By making only one well-placed adjustment, amazing things can occur. It is like a session with a good chiropractor; if you know just which spot to hit, you can adjust the alignment and functioning of the whole.

The vibrational change is created not just by what we do, but by how we do it. Thoughts and feelings have substance just like physical objects, but their mass is on a much finer level than is apparent to the human eye. You may experience this when you cook a good meal. Food that is prepared with love not only looks better—it tastes better as well, because the ingredients are imbued with the energy with which they are assembled.

If you use a feng shui cure without really thinking about what it means, the vibrational effect in your environment will not be very profound. It's not just what you do, but also how you do it that changes the quality of your environment. For this reason, it is important not to make changes in the spirit of desperation and sacrifice.

In Black Sect feng shui, we recognize that the intention and the energy with which something is done determines the effectiveness of the cure. This is why many feng shui changes may seem to have limited effect. You may place something in a particular sector of your home and hope it brings results, but over time, it might seem like the object is gathering dust, instead of ushering in new possibilities. For this reason, be very clear about your intention for the cure and install it with a positive and contemplative attitude.

The Three Secret Reinforcements enable you to imbue each feng shui cure with positive energy in three ways: with thought, speech, and action. By combining all three levels of vibration in one approach, you are literally charging the cure with an energetic force that not only alters your perception of it, but alters its constitution as well. Once our scientific methods become more advanced, we will be able to see exactly how the energetic and even chemical composition of matter is affected by the energetic forces to which it is exposed.

The research of Dr. Masaru Emoto, which detailed how sound and thought vibration significantly affects the crystalline structure of water, is a remarkable demonstration of the direct impact we can have on physical matter. The photographs documenting his work are fascinating and can be seen in his book, *The Hidden Messages in Water.*

To practice the Three Secret Reinforcements, take a dollar bill out of your wallet or purse and place it on a table in front of you. You can use this blessing method to "charge" this bill with positive energy and intention. After the bill has been blessed, don't just put it back in your wallet and spend it. Instead, place it in a special section of your wallet, so that it will attract more money to you. You might also tape it to the front of your computer monitor, refrigerator, or bathroom mirror as a magnet for abundance.

Before blessing an object or cure, assume a meditative focus. Start by reciting the Calming Heart Sutra nine times, and allow yourself to settle into a deeper part of your being. Notice your thoughts and feelings, and allow them to pass through your consciousness like leaves floating on a river.

Once you have assumed a meditative perspective, you are ready to do the Three Secret Reinforcements. The first part involves speech. Sound vibration is very powerful, and it connects the life chi in your breath with the ritual object.

The chant that we use for these blessings is called "The Six True Words." Just as light is composed of the seven colors of the spectrum, it is believed that the vibration of truth is composed of these six words, or sounds. By reciting these six sounds, you are literally transmitting the frequency of truth. The words are as follows: "Om Ma Ni Pad Me Hum," and are pronounced "ome mah nee pad may hung." Translated to English, this means "All that Is, Shines like a Jewel in the Lotus."

Each time you recite the Six True Words, you should do a physical gesture that transmits your energy into the object. The gesture, or mudra, used in feng shui is as follows: men should use their left hand, and women should use their right hand. Extend all five fingers of the hand, and then draw in the middle and ring finger so that they touch the thumb. This gesture will look like the shape kids use to make the face of a fox in the light of a projection lamp. When your two fingers are touching your thumb, the mudra is in the ready position.

The blessing mudra, stage 1.

When you are performing the ritual, fling your two fingers outward so that all five fingers are again fully extended. This action pushes out your physical chi and imbues the ritual object with your energy.

The blessing mudra, stage 2.

The blessing cycle is done nine times, as follows: first, start with the vibration of your mental energy. Visualize the desired effect you want the cure to produce. For instance, since you are blessing this bill to make it into a Lucky Dollar, your intention may be to attract many dollars to you. If you want to place the Lucky Dollar on your computer monitor, maybe your intention is to gain a lot of wealth through writing or other work you do on the computer. If you plan to put the bill on your refrigerator, perhaps you want a larder full of expensive, delicious treats. Whatever it is, visualize your desired result in rich, full detail.

While the vision is burning brightly in your mind, say the Six True Words, "Om Ma Ni Pad Me Hum," and project your physical energy into the dollar with the hand gesture. That is the completion of one cycle.

Each time you do a blessing, you should perform the Three Secret Reinforcements nine times. Create a strong visual image of what you want to happen, recite the Six True Words, and express your physical chi with the hand gesture. Do this complete cycle with your Lucky Dollar, and then install it in the place that will give you the most benefit.

As a way of becoming more familiar with the Three Secret Reinforcements, try the technique on different cures at least once a day. Go back to any feng shui cures that you have already installed, and use this sacred method to set your intention.

FINANCIAL FENG SHUI—DETECTING FINANCIAL LEAKS

Just as a home full of clutter will drain your energy and distract you from your goals, there is a financial condition that creates the same problem: debt. This can start fairly harmlessly as a quick loan from friends or a shopping spree on the wings of a credit card. The accumulation of debt, however, can slowly start to nip at your heels like a pile of mess on the living room floor, until there is nowhere left to turn. In the end, you may spend all of your time and financial energy not to get ahead, but just trying to keep up with the debt.

Though difficult to imagine, at one time, credit cards were not even a glimmer in some banker's eye. If you wanted to make a purchase, but did not have the funds at hand, you would apply directly to a store for credit and then fulfill weekly payments until the amount was paid off. The credit business, however, has become big business, and for big reasons. At rates that can go over 20 percent annual interest, there are entire corporations making their living off our debt misery.

Credit companies are in the "risk business." Based on their evaluation of credit histories, they make loans to people who will pay back the amounts in full, *eventually*. But not too fast! The company is not going to get rich off the annual fees. They take the risk that we will be dumb enough, or weak enough, to succumb to temptation and spend more than we can afford to repay right away. By racking up exorbitant interest fees, we could have bought twice the goods that we set out to buy, or more, if only we had paid in cash.

We have become prey to a leeching that should be considered criminal. Cigarette advertisements are outlawed on television, yet we are beckoned to credit addiction every night of the week. And what sort of images do these ads portray? Desperate low-income families that need these cards to get through the month? Certainly not! Yet it's the people who can't afford their credit balances who are keeping these companies in business. Millions of people have given up on the pursuit of happiness and are living the penance for their lapse of wisdom with credit.

By falling behind on credit, you can sink into the quicksand of spiraling interest rates and fees, and you also endanger your ability to purchase a home. Are the credit card companies concerned about this? Of course not. They are betting their annual salaries on the hope that you can't handle your money, that you will lapse in your wisdom, and that you will end up paying them back two or three times what you originally borrowed. And they are probably right.

Can you actually remember all of the things you bought on credit? As a rule of thumb, never purchase anything with a card that you will not be able to remember easily when you finish paying for it. And if that rule sounds too difficult, here is another one: never buy anything on credit. Period. Pay as you go. If you can't afford it now, it's not the time to buy it. It doesn't matter what time the stores open. The wallet only opens when you can pay in cash.

To do feng shui of a credit card, all you need is a pair of scissors, a machete, a chainsaw, or any other demolition tool. Take the card in one hand, scissors in the other, and cut the umbilical cord. Remember: you are feeding it more than it is feeding you. If just the thought is throwing you into postpartum credit depression, I recommend Jerrold Mundis's book, *How to Get Out of Debt, Stay Out of Debt, and Live Prosperously*, which outlines a program for  ending the debt cycle and getting yourself on solid ground. But he is only going to offer you the same advice: a card in the hand is worth less than zero in the future.

If none of this inspires you to call the credit card companies now and accuse them of financial murder, consider this: would you trust anyone who borrowed a houseful of furniture every time they gave a party? Of course not. That would seem fraudulent. Well, that's exactly what you are doing every time you buy on credit. You are not really paying for the items. They don't really belong to you—they belong to the credit card company. You bought them with the *credit company's* money, not yours.

This perspective applies to informal debts as well. Whether you are borrowing from a credit company, a family member, or your best friend, the effect is the same: you are living to repay the past, instead of building for the future. Whether you are actively repaying the loans or not, this can leech your energy and drain your aspirations.

The Spiritual Meaning, and Healing, of Debt

Credit card use is credit card misuse. Even if you pay the balance at the end of each month, you deny yourself the opportunity to really exchange something of value. When you pay in cash, the gift is obvious. Each bill you count and hand to another person is an energetic exchange. But credit cards take away the pleasure of giving. It may seem powerful to whip out the card, but you are not really giving anything.

Psychologically, the reason that we are afraid of using cash—and this is about fear, you know—is because we are afraid of giving and receiving. We don't want to admit we really are dependent upon each other for our livelihood and that we work for a living. Really, we are afraid of money. So, we hide it, euthanize, it, and make it "virtual." But where is the pleasure in all that? "Happy Birthday! Let me give you a swipe of my credit card." "Congratulations (*swipe*)." "Thank you (*swipe*)." Out of sight, out of mind, and out of control.

In 1971, President Nixon took the United States off the gold standard when it became clear that our nation did not have the reserves to repay foreign debts. Before that time, every dollar in your wallet was a promissory note related to some bit of gold in a high-security vault. At least theoretically, you could take that note and exchange it for the hard stuff at any time. The gold really belonged to you, just as a lease on land declared your ownership of it, whether you lived on it or not.

When we left the gold standard, the bills were no longer deeds to anything of particular value. They simply became receipts that say you own pieces of paper. Kind of a downer, don't you think? Sure, it's better than just blips on a computer screen, but not by much.

This shift in the nature of our currency had a deep impact on our cultural psyche. We are no longer working for anything of value. We are working at best for pieces of paper, and at worst for numbers on a screen.

Credit card debt and cash earnings start to look a lot alike: just a bunch of numbers on a page. No wonder we are so prone to debt. The difference between wealth and poverty is a mere thought, a blink on a computer screen, and not a whole lot more.

With automatic deposits, internet banking, and credit/debit card use, the impact and importance of our work becomes lost. How many times has your boss handed over your salary and said, "Thank you"? Payment should be an expression of appreciation, but gratitude has become hidden behind electronic transfers, to such a degree that you may not feel you are being thanked at all. As money has become a numbers game, we too are reduced to feeling like numbers, without any intrinsic value or standard to substantiate us. Debt is a symptom of this dehumanization.

Clearing the Debt and Creating a Future

If you are already in a debt cycle and dependent upon credit just to get through the month, I can only recommend the motto of the Twelve Step Program, Debtors Anonymous: "Just for *today*, I will not debt." For the next twenty-four hours, find a way to get by without increasing the debt. Then, continue this practice every day for the rest of your life. Start applying the principles and methods in this book to get yourself on an even keel with your finances, your self-respect, and your life.

PROSPERITY JOURNAL: "DEBTS I OWE"

It's time to make a list of all the debts that you currently owe. Take heart: This may not be a pleasant experience, but the bout of unpleasantness will be shorter if you face it now. Like a bad smell in the kitchen, it won't go away by your ignoring it.

1. You do not need to include any debts for which you have supplied collateral, such as a mortgage or a car loan. These are called "secured loans," which means that the collateral will cover a default. If you gave your buddy in Las Vegas your gold Rolex in exchange for $20, that was a stupid agreement, but at least the loan is covered, and you don't have to put it on your list!

   Some of the debts you might want to consider on your list include:

   - Loans from friends
   - Loans from your family
   - Education loans
   - Store accounts
   - Any and all unpaid bills (were you expecting that one?)
   - Credit cards
   - Other

---

2. As you collect your papers and bills, put them all in one place where you will find them easily during the coming weeks of this program. You will be coming back to them soon.

3. Now, take the total amount of your debts and subtract this total from your monetary assets—your material assets only count in this equation if you already sold them for cash in the past two weeks! This final sum is considered your net worth. We all know that you personally are worth a lot more than that—this is just a statement of your funds as currently available. What you do with this figure is the subject of the rest of this book.

INNER FENG SHUI—DREAMS, THE INNER DEBT

When thinking of debt, we usually consider what we owe to other people: credit card bills, loans from family, perhaps the phone call we haven't returned.

But the debt that really runs us into the ground is much deeper. It's the debt that we owe ourselves—the things we never did, the words we never said. It's the promises we never made, and not the ones that we broke, that really seem to break our hearts.

Inside, there is a life unlived that has been waiting, first impatiently, then imploringly . . . and finally silently. This is the feeling of debt that will not go away, no matter how carefully we pay our bills, no matter how much we tithe to charity, no matter how responsible we become to the outside world. In our inside world, we are in debtor's prison. I believe that's the real reason that you bought this book.

It's the trip you wanted to take, but your parents said no; the person in your chemistry class you wanted to date, but couldn't find the nerve to ask; the art class that wouldn't fit into your schedule, so you let it go. Bit by bit, the desires of youth fall away, until we cease to recognize ourselves anymore. And without having a sense of ourselves, where do we turn? Usually, we seek to appeal to others.

No matter how ambitious, we knew in our hearts that our dreams were worth it. As kids, when we wanted something, the thought would consume us. It would be with us when we went to sleep and urge us out of bed in the morning. It put a glint in our eyes and warmed our hearts. Our dreams sustained us and reminded us of what was important in the world.

How do we know if we have abandoned that essential part of ourselves? Let me ask you this: do you wake up each morning, jump out of bed, and say, "Yes!"? The last time that you did that was the last time that you had a dream that really excited you. Do you hesitate to make a decision and agonize for days, maybe weeks, even years before choosing what you want? If so, this is a warning signal—your batteries are getting weak and may go out at any time. You need to be recharged, and *fast*!

Settling the Score

Let's do a bit of detective work. If you were paid to figure out the identity of some mysterious person in the big house down the block, what you would you do? Talk to their neighbors? Sift through the trash? Rummage in their closets? Sounds like a good plan. Try a similar endeavor with the next person we need to investigate: *you*.

PROSPERITY JOURNAL: "UNDERSTANDING MY MOTIVES"

Answer the following questions as quickly as possible. If you are hesitating and judging your thoughts, you already know that you have lost the scent!

1. When I was a kid, the job that I most wanted to have was _____
   _____

2. Three of my favorite toys were _____
   _____

3. I was always jealous of _____
   _____

4. I wish that my parents let me _____
   _____

5. The talent that I wanted to develop was _____
   _____

6. I remember going to sleep at night and wishing that _____
   _____

7. I loved it when my Mom _____
   _____

(Continued)

---

8. I loved it when my Dad _____

_____

9. I wish that we could have spent more time _____

_____

10. One thing I really regret about my childhood is _____

_____

11. I wish we had had more money growing up, so I could have _____

_____

12. The best experience I had as a kid was _____

_____

Now, take these answers and write a short essay on the person you really are inside.

The Meditative Millionaire, Part 2

In the not so distant past, meditation, in the broader sense of the word, was a natural part of life. Travel between points took much longer, and there was built-in downtime to reflect on thoughts and feelings. Before the use of electricity, natural cycles dictated our activities. In some seasons, more than half of the day was spent in darkness, or meditative time. This was the natural rhythm of the Tao, prescribed by the cycles of nature.

With the advent of virtually unlimited and relentless technology, however, the time and space given to self-reflection have practically vanished. We are urged to do more, accomplish more, and take less time to do it. In so doing, we've lost sight of our inner lives. The faster we go, the more dependent we become on the outside world to tell us who we are, what is true, and, of course, how to spend our money.

Meditation is actually quite simple. It does not require biofeedback equipment, incense, or even a guru's picture on the wall. It just requires *you*, which is the piece that has been missing in your life so far, the piece you need to bring back.

Find a place where you can be by yourself. Sit comfortably, with your spine straight and supported, and loosen any tight clothing. Close your eyes and begin to focus on your breath.

Feel yourself inhaling slowly through your nostrils, and exhaling gently through your mouth. You might choose to count each breath, up to perhaps ten, and then start again at one.

As you do this, your focus will undoubtedly be broken, at least momentarily, by an intruding thought or sensation. Notice the distraction, acknowledge it, and let it go. Imagine your thoughts are like leaves floating down a river. They may catch your attention for a moment, but let them pass through your consciousness, and return the focus to your breath.

At times, you may become aware of what is going on in your body. This may be the first time today, or the first time in weeks, that you became sensitive to what you are feeling. Notice any pain or tension, but do not fixate on it. Remember, you are building the awareness of your Observer Self. This is the part that notices, but does not intercede.

During meditation, it's okay to be interested, and even to remark to yourself, "Oh, I feel tight in my shoulders . . ." but then let the thought go, and continue to just observe. It's one thing to notice your tensions, and it is another thing to start planning your next visit with the chiropractor!

As you scan your body, you may find the tensions releasing on their own, and you may want to move or adjust your body. Feel free to do this and to let yourself respond to your body's impulses. But keep returning your awareness to your breath, and notice the natural rhythm of inhalation and exhalation. Your thoughts may seem to slow down, or even seem to be speeding up. In either case, notice how you react, and return your focus to your breath.

In time, this practice will deeply affect the way you relate to your thoughts, your feelings, and your life. Instead of rebounding from one issue to the next, or "flying off the handle" with your feelings, you will find a new perspective: you are owning your reactions, instead of allowing them to own you.

ACTION STEPS ON THE JOURNEY TO WEALTH:
WEEK 3 SYNOPSIS

This week, energize your home and your life with the simple methods outlined in this chapter. Things may be changing quickly now, so keep up with those journal entries to record your progress!

Check off the boxes when you complete these tasks:

☐ Survey your home for energy leaks and do the necessary cures.

☐ Start the clutter quell! Try the 20 percent method for twenty minutes to see what a difference it can make.

☐ Review your desires for the Hsun area of your life, and implement at least two cures this week.

☐ Make your dollar lucky—and learn the Three Secret Reinforcements. Have you applied this method to any cures you have implemented so far?

☐ Assess your debt, and make a plan to stop the debt cycle.

☐ Arrange with a credit agency to reduce your rates, if possible. Then cut the cards (literally!).

☐ Find some quiet time to do the breathing meditation at least three times this week, and consider how it changes your perspective on life.

WEEK 4

Possessing Your Life

Because I am unorthodox, I can become great;
Otherwise, I would already have become trivial.
—The *Tao Te Ching*, Book 67

PRELUDE—DROP OUT, AND DROP INTO YOURSELF

To achieve a true sense of fulfillment, we must "drop out" of any preconceived ideas of who we are, how we should earn money, and how we should spend it. I am not suggesting that we all need to grow our hair long, wear love beads, and move to some commune in the wilderness. That would just mean buying into another external vision of how we are supposed to be, instead of connecting to what is really true for us.

Being a savvy consumer does not just entail sniffing out the best bargains and clipping coupons for weekly sales. Rather, it depends upon knowing what you really want and investing the necessary time and energy into getting it.

I have heard that planning saves ten times the energy we would put into pursuing our goals, but I think that the ratio is actually much higher. Taking time for this essential introspection can save thousands, maybe even millions in returns on invested time and energy.

Consider this: most of us spend *at least* forty hours a week, or 50 percent of our waking hours, at our jobs. Since most people work at least forty-three years of their adult lives, this represents more than 86,000 total hours, not including overtime, devoted to commuting, prep time, education, and the time it takes us to recover from the whole ordeal.

Compare this figure with the time we devote to planning the careers we want. One hour a week? Probably not. Most people claim they "don't have the time" for that sort of introspection. Ten minutes? One minute? In our fast-food world of instant gratification, we rarely think about the things that matter the most. We devote over a hundred thousand hours of our lives to our jobs, and yet don't spend 10 percent of that time clarifying and defining what is most important to us.

I am thinking of a friend who was about to graduate from college. I asked what sort of career he was going to pursue, and he said, "Medical school . . . or law school. One of those." In that statement, he summarized the self-disconnection that would form the basis of his adult life. I estimate he spent about four thousand hours getting his undergraduate degree, and he probably spent less than 1 percent of that time planning the rest of his life.

But beware: the advertising world is much happier if we are *not* content in our jobs and relationships. If we were fulfilled in these areas of our lives, why would we urgently shop for the *latest thing*? The media wants us to forget what's important inside, so that we will busily try to be more, do more, and buy more on the outside. Their plan seems to be working, which keeps us working at jobs that may be less than fulfilling.

When we are busy, we waste the most money. Rushing on your way to an important meeting, you might not mind spending $10 for a sandwich. Need a quick pick-me-up to just get through the day? You may mindlessly spend $4.50 for a simple cappuccino. Exhausted after a long day at work? Grabbing a quick, hot meal to go for under $20 seems like a bargain, right?

There's nothing wrong with treating ourselves to a cappuccino, a nice lunch, or a take-out meal. But when these purchases are made in haste and desperation, the sense of fulfillment is usually low. The faster we go, the less stable we feel and the more dependent we become on outside goods and services. In this way, we can spend a lot of money and still feel poor.

The Hall of Shame and Other Emotions

Feelings are energy. They are the power of chi as it courses through our bodies. The more energy we have, the more feelings we experience. This is why people may stay stuck, disempowered, and impoverished in their lives; they are trying to avoid their real feelings.

Something happens in our life, and we react. Our body is poised to say something, do something, maybe hit something. And that can be scary. So instead, we suppress our feelings and act "nice." Our energy becomes constricted until we no longer recognize ourselves.

Shame, fear, humiliation, anger, hatred, jealousy, resentment. These are natural reactions to the events we encounter. But how do you feel about having these feelings?

Without our emotions, we don't know who we are and what we need to do. We become passive, listless, detached—and usually poor. The public relations side of us wants the world to think that everything is all right, when in fact we often feel the opposite. The problem with feelings is not that we have them, but that we don't listen to them.

Not only are our feelings a natural part of ourselves; they are indispensable. Without our emotions, what do we have to guide us through the world? Advertisements? TV evangelists? 1-900-PSYCHIC?

One of the main reasons we put aside our feelings is the belief that certain emotions are "bad." Angry? Not me! Jealous? Never. And hatred . . . that is something we never feel . . . right?

In the sections below, I have examined some of our least accepted feelings and explored how their messages can help on the daily journey toward wealth and fulfillment.

Shame

When we don't feel right about what we are contributing to the world, we feel ashamed. Unfortunately, many of us have been taught to feel ashamed of our most precious gifts: our sexuality, love, and generosity. Ironically, in our materialistic culture, we have even been taught to feel ashamed of our desire for money!

There is a natural shame, however, that shows us when we are not living according to our inner standards. If you bounce a check, admit it—don't you feel ashamed? If you arrive late for work and spend the rest of the day hiding from your boss, this avoidance is a sign of your shame. By differentiating between natural shame and the guilt placed upon us, we build an essential connection to our own standards.

PROSPERITY JOURNAL: "MY SHAME"

Make a list of ten times when have been ashamed of your relationship with money. The purpose is not to make you feel worse, but to highlight the lessons of your emotions, so you can create a life in line with your integrity. "Ten times when I felt ashamed of my dealings with money . . ."

Anger

Ah, anger. One of the favorite emotions in the therapy room. And for a good reason: anger is at the root of most of our disturbances. It might be expressed as frustration, resentment, hatred, or outright rage. Anger is the voice within that says, "No, this is not okay with me!" But when we silence that voice and tell ourselves we are not being "reasonable," or that no one will like us if we are angry, we start to lose our ground.

In my experience, strong anger is usually connected to deeper experiences in our emotional past. But that doesn't mean we should ignore the feelings in the present. By paying attention to our anger, our energy stays free and clear, and we can start to use it in a constructive way.

PROSPERITY JOURNAL: "MY ANGER"

List ten times when you felt angry in your financial history. Perhaps it was a job in which you felt underpaid or a client who did not pay on time. Anger at your boss, anger at your customers, anger at God or the IRS or our parents or our spouse . . . Recognize the feelings, and use the energy in a constructive way, or you will end up channeling it against yourself and your potential prosperity. "Ten times when I felt angry in regard to money . . ."

Jealousy

Jealousy is actually one of my favorite emotions, because it quickly leads us to a sense of who we want to become. Whenever you are jealous of someone else, you are seeing something that you want for yourself. The desire may be material ("I wish I had his car"), or it may be abstract ("I wish I were confident at parties like she is"). Whatever the projection may be, realize whom this jealousy is really about: you.

We have problems with jealousy because of limiting beliefs about what we think we can have. If we truly believed that we could achieve what other people have, we would not deny them the chance to have it too.

PROSPERITY JOURNAL: "MY JEALOUSY"

Describe the situations that make you boil with envy. Pour out your jealousy in detail. If you want to live like your favorite movie star, write it down, and describe what draws you to these feelings. You will have time to figure out what this identification is about and how to manifest it in your own life. "Ten people or situations that make me insanely jealous, and why I feel this way . . ."

ENVIRONMENTAL FENG SHUI—FAME, RECOGNITION, AND THE LIVING ROOM

The environmental feng shui work we will be doing this week is focused in the living room and the bagua area called "Li." The living room is the area of the home devoted to social activities, and it is a manifestation of the way we are perceived by the "outside world." By working in both of these areas this week, you can affirm your place in society and strengthen your capacity for creating wealth.

The Living Room

Each room in the house corresponds to a specific aspect of our personal and social life. Some rooms, such as the bedroom or a private master bathroom, lend themselves to the more personal aspects of a person's life. Others, such as the entranceway, the kitchen, and the living room, are associated with our more public activities.

A century ago, when social life was more formal, families would often have two different "living rooms." The public room at the front of the house was called the parlor and was reserved for entertaining guests. Children were not permitted to enter this room, except when guests were calling, and then only on their best behavior.

In the rear of the home, or on a different floor, households usually had an additional room for the everyday activities of the family. Away from the public eye, this area was more casual, and it may have included furniture formerly used in the parlor, now worn and considered unfit for public exposure.

In contemporary society, life has obviously become much more casual. Men and women walk down the streets in shorts, and stores often have to post signs to remind us that shirts and shoes are required! Instead of shielding themselves from public exposure, a lot of people seem anxious to air their dirty laundry in public, as they vie for spots on talk shows to discuss their tumors, their husbands' affairs with their sisters, and recent gender change operations.

As the parlor and living room merged, our sense of public space and private space also changed greatly. Imagine—people even install minicams in their homes, so their lives can be viewed twenty-four hours a day on the internet! Talk about the dissolution of boundaries between public and private spaces.

In feng shui, the living room represents the ways that we share ourselves with the public world. This is where we spend most of our time at home, where we interact with our families, and where we entertain friends and guests.

PROSPERITY JOURNAL:
"OBJECTIVE IMPRESSIONS OF MY LIVING ROOM"

Take a moment to look at your living room, and get a sense of this axis point between yourself and the world. If you like, you might even take a few photographs, so you can view the room even more objectively.

With your Beginner's Mind, ask yourself, "What sort of people live here? What are their interests? Are they happy in their life? How do they feel about their connection with the rest of society?" Write down your thoughts.

You might want to get friends or family members who do not live with you to answer these questions as outside observers. You may be surprised by their responses.

We often fall into a trance with the spaces we occupy and endure conditions that we don't like, simply because we see them every day. You may have this experience when returning from vacation. You can come back feeling renewed, only to look at your home with dismay and say, "Is this how I have been living? I can't believe it!"

Your Relationship to Relating

Studies in environmental psychology indicate that the level of comfort a stranger has in our home correlates with the degree that we have personalized our space. If you have imprinted your personality on the rooms, visitors will tend to feel welcomed and comfortable, whether they tend to like that style of décor or not.

If you are hesitant about personalizing your living room space, this indicates you do not feel comfortable presenting your real self in society. I have been in many New York apartments that have been professionally decorated. When a person abdicates interior space to the fancy of a designer, it can end up disguising the resident's true self. So now, notice the degree to which your living space presents your real self to the world.

The seating arrangement says a lot about how the person or family feels about relating. One client was a woman who complained she could not find a romantic relationship. According to her, she had tried everything, and there were "just no decent men out there." (This is a phrase I hear a lot from my female clients, which makes me wonder if I should introduce them to my male clients who say the same thing about women!)

When I went into her living room, I instantly saw a telltale sign: the only seating that she had in the room were two large gray leather chairs. The chairs were separated by a square, bulky table, and they both faced straight ahead at a mammoth large-screen television. If this woman invited any men into her place, the furniture would not even permit them to look at each other! I told her that if she was really serious about finding a mate, she needed to get rid of those ugly chairs and find a comfy sofa that was big enough for two.

If the major focus in your living room is your television, this says a lot about your relationship with society. You may have become a passive observer of life, putting in more airtime hours than you spend with actual people. In feng shui, televisions do not have a very positive reputation, and this is not only because TVs were not invented by the ancient Chinese! Television viewing is a passive activity that can become an addictive way to deplete our energy and potential. Bored? Watch TV. Can't sleep? Turn on the tube. Restless? Exhausted? Angry? TV land beckons to you. Without television, what would you do?

Consider putting the television in an armoire or other sort of cabinet, so it will not dominate the room when not in use. In feng shui, blank TV screens are considered just as negative as the ones that are blaring their media-hyped messages; they absorb your energy and create a metaphorical hole in the room. By putting it in a cabinet, you may forget that you have a TV at all and move on to doing something more prosperous with your time.

What's Your Style?

Feng shui is not the art of making things *right*; it is the art of making things *yours*. Your sense of style is essential if you are going to make your house into a home. I can't tell you how many luxury homes I have consulted that have been "designed"—which often means that the occupant is living within another person's vision of how his life should look. I know that this is not usually the intention

of a good designer, but unfortunately, this is what often happens. Would you want another person to pick out all your clothes for you? Having a home not filled by your own choices can have a similar effect.

The first step to creating your interior style is to realize that you have one. Anything that strikes your fancy is part of your style; you do not need to go to school to figure it out or even read interior design books to know what you like. Sometimes these outside influences can just complicate matters.

PROSPERITY JOURNAL: "WHAT'S MY STYLE?"

There are the following basic questions I use to help my clients define their sense of style:

1. If you could spend six months anywhere in the world, where would you go, and how would you live? Jot down some details about your dream destination in your journal.

2. Where have you already been in the world that gives you really fond memories? Make a brief list, then choose your favorite and describe it fully in your journal, even down to the predominant colors, smells, and textures. Make sure that the location is different from your answer to the first question in this exercise.

3. Next, what do you love about where you already live? Your first reaction may be "Nothing!" but cast your net a little wider. Look at the things you already own, and focus on the ones you like. Then, consider the building and your neighborhood. Think of the people in your life and the things that you like to do. Expand your vision even further to include your city or town, the countryside, your state, and even your country. Write a few lines that describe what you love about your current locale.

4. You have probably realized how much I like diagrams, especially ones that involve triangles, so here goes: draw a giant triangle on the next blank page of your journal. At the top point, write the name of the place you'd most like to live for six months. At the bottom left point, record the place from your past that brings you the fondest memories. And at the bottom right point, name the place where you live now. (See the illustration below.)

1. Dream Home

_____

Theme: _____

2. Past Visit   3. Where You Live Now

_____   _____

5. Now, ask yourself, "What is the common essence of these three places?" Consider the qualities that they have in common and what they remind you of. Also, compare this essence with the three adjectives that you chose in chapter 1 for your essence of wealth. Write a description of this central theme in the middle of the triangle.

6. Finally, make a list of three or more things you would like to do to implement your personal sense of style in your living room, and circle at least two that you can do this week. These are the qualities that you love, and you owe it to yourself to bring them into your life in every way that you can.

Bagua Sector of the Week: Li

Your reputation can either make or break your career, which determines your financial future. It's the way a product or service is perceived, and not what it actually does, that determines its value in the market. For this reason, the gua called Li, which is located at the top center of the bagua, stands like a central jewel in the crown of your financial future.

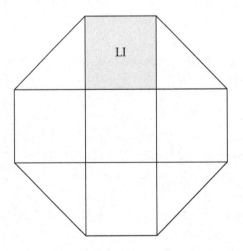

Bagua sector of the week: Li.

PROSPERITY JOURNAL: "MY FAME FACTOR"

1. Create a Li section in your journal, and write a few notes in about your experience of being recognized and achieving fame for your gifts and talents. Consider if you feel that people truly see you for your innermost self.

2. Now, go to the Li area of your home. By dividing the area of your home into nine equal sections, you'll find that the Li area is on the top central area of the bagua.

3. Prepare your awareness by chanting the Calming Heart Sutra ("Gate, Gate. . ."), and quiet your mind. Then, in your journal, list three or four adjectives that describe how this area of your home feels to you.

4. Review your earlier notes about how this area of your life has been feeling, and compare these experiences to the condition of this part of your home. Consider any correlations between your inner experience and the nature of this sector of your space. You might write any observations about this parallel in your journal.

Feng Shui Applications for Financial Development in Li

The fire element and the color red are associated with the Li gua. A few years ago, when I was in the process of changing careers, I painted the entire wall in the Li position a deep shade of red . . . and I received two surprise job offers within a week!

If painting an entire wall seems drastic, consider hanging a beautiful red cloth in this area, putting red curtains on the windows, or at least highlighting the area with a set of red pillows.

Anything associated with fire is auspicious in this gua. I have placed nine lava rocks at the base of this wall in my home. Nine candles are perfect, and you can use red ones for an extra kick. A fireplace with a roaring blaze is ideal in this quadrant, but lacking that, a photo or poster of an active volcano will also get you noticed.

Increasing light in this area is an effective way to increase the Li energy. A red light bulb can really make things happen, whether your Li energy is in the bedroom or not! If you really need to stoke up this area, put a bright light on a timer, so that the area is lit during the most auspicious times, from 11:00 A.M. to 1:00 P.M. and 11:00 P.M. to 1:00 A.M. Bright lights inside or outside the home will help if you are missing any of the Li quadrant in your home.

In the Li gua, highlight the things for which you really want to be known. Clear out any clutter, especially anything that reminds you of negative periods in your life, and replace it with symbols of your accomplishments and talents. Your college degrees, trophies, awards, and photos of you shaking hands with international dignitaries all belong in this sector of your home.

Cactus is generally considered a terrible plant in feng shui because of its prickly thorns and unfriendly exterior. However, placing a cactus in Li is considered auspicious, because it represents the ability to endure difficult periods and undue criticism. I have a beautiful, well-rounded cactus in my Li sector at home, which has weathered hard times with me and still maintained its demeanor.

The worst things that you can put in Li are fountains and mirrors, since these represent the water element and can diminish fire. Adding plants or other woodsy things, on the other hand, can feed the fire of this gua.

Make this area a shrine to the ideal you with photos, drawings, and other references to your pursuit of fame. If you are planning to write a book, frame a sample of the cover and place it here. If you want to be known as a wealthy person, collect and display pictures of yourself that support this image.

PROSPERITY JOURNAL: "FENG SHUI FOR LI"

Ask yourself, "How can I light up this area of my home and get recognized for my true talents and gifts?" Go back to your Dream Bagua in chapter 2, and identify the goal that you chose for fame and recognition, and consider how you can represent this goal in this part of your home.

See if you can include at least one or two of the traditional feng shui cures in this area as well. It is time to get creative about bringing your inner character into your external environment. Be sure to use Three Secret Reinforcements as you put these changes in place.

FINANCIAL FENG SHUI—PETTY DEPRIVATIONS

Making more money will not necessarily cure your financial woes. In fact, the number of responsibilities usually increases with an elevation in financial status, which explains why so many rock stars go on tour long after the prime of their careers. (Did you really think that it was because they loved singing that one hit single from thirty years ago?)

The solution to our financial despair often lies in how we handle the money we have, not in how much we are making. Just as your home may have energetic drains, people with money problems usually leak out funds without control or conviction about their spending. This engenders a sense of despair, which leads to further waste, debt, and humiliation. As the cycle continues, the individual can spiral further and further into a sense of powerlessness about money and life in general.

Most people treat their pets better than they treat their money. Can you imagine not feeding your pet for days or refusing to think about its needs? That's exactly what a lot of us do with our money. I have nothing against animal companions, but our lives don't depend upon them. Our survival does depend upon our finances, however, and we need to look seriously at the way we treat this staff of life.

We regularly face decisions about how to make money, save it, and spend it. These choices are not arbitrary; they point to our relationship with ourself. When you are comfortable with yourself and your desires, you will financially empower your dreams. But any inner discomfort will ultimately become apparent in your cash flow.

One example is what I call "petty deprivations." These are like minor crimes that we commit against ourselves. Every time we avoid some small expense that could fulfill our needs, it is a form of self-neglect. When we start to feel the pinch of financial problems, these petty deprivations appear as a form of self-sacrifice. It is a way of saying, "Okay, maybe I am not handling my money very well right now, but please notice that I *am* making sacrifices, so I can't be blamed for any problems that I may be having."

We often confuse sacrifice with money management: "If I do without something, then I must be managing my money as well as I can." But petty deprivation is rarely accompanied by any real financial planning. We might blow $100 for dinner with friends, and then come home to a dark living room, because we may have neglected to buy spare light bulbs. Or we may eat junk food all week, which really adds up, but refuse to buy ourselves a new pair of socks.

Deprivation is never about money management. Financial planning involves goal setting, commitment, and finding creative ways to get what you want with the money you have. Deprivation is about punishment: intentionally neglecting yourself for reasons that have nothing to do with money. And so long as you are depriving yourself, you are not going to get rich, you are just going to get miserable; you can quickly see the root of that word, which is "miser."

Start to note the ways that you derail your ability to feel—and ultimately become—wealthy by committing petty deprivations. I often find myself "forgetting" to buy more shaving cream, or using those disposable contact lenses longer than I am supposed to, or putting off haircuts until I look like I am trying to invent a new style! I justify this by saying that I am saving money, but in fact, I am really just creating a sense of poverty.

Petty deprivations don't just apply to purchases. We inflict neglect on ourselves in many creative ways, all in the name of being stoic, or busy, or too important in the world to take time for ourselves. Sleeping too little, eating too quickly, inventing more ways to use our time than Superman could fulfill . . . if this is a sign of importance, I would rather be useless!

PROSPERITY JOURNAL:
"MY PENITENTIAL PURSE AND PETTY DEPRIVATIONS"

In the exercise below, answer the questions quickly and without too much thought. Write your answers directly on this page. You may be surprised by the ways your self-imposed masochism has been ruling your purse strings.

1. In terms of my personal needs, I always seem to be running out of _____

_____.

2. If I only had a little more money, I would treat myself by _____

_____.

3. I never seem to have enough _____

_____.

4. I have learned to do without _____

_____.

5. Something I enjoy that I won't let myself have is _____

_____.

6. Something I really need that costs less than $10 is _____

_____.

7. Something else I really need that costs less than $50 is _____

_____.

8. Something I enjoyed as a kid that I won't let myself have is _____

_____.

9. I never keep the cupboards stocked with enough _____

_____.

10. Something that would be good for my health that I won't buy myself is

_____.

You may notice that most, if not all, of the things on your list are inexpensive, yet dear to your heart. Would you deprive a child of the things that make him or her happy and healthy? Why, then, would you deprive yourself? A slogan you can adopt for the rest of this program is "Be kind to yourself." If you only knew how valuable you really were, you would treat yourself better.

If you are living in the spirit of self-deprivation, no amount of income will appease your cruelty toward yourself. You will always find a way to feel punished, lacking, and neglected. Ask yourself for forgiveness, and then start to make amends. When you are ready to do that, choose something from the list above and give it to yourself as a gift this week. You will be amazed at how this can change your life.

Saving Your Life

Taking care of your immediate needs is not the only way to feel comforted and loved. Your savings account is a statement of the degree to which you are invested in yourself. If you are not saving, it is an indication that you are not committed to the long-term needs of your soul. And that hurts, on many levels.

Surprisingly, the period in my life when I had the easiest time saving was when I was in graduate school. Even though I had tuition bills, I was excited to be preparing for a lifelong career, and saving money was a natural response to this optimism. Since then, my dedication to my future has waxed and waned, and so has my savings account.

Few things will make you feel more secure than money in the bank. It doesn't have to be a lot, but it has to be enough so you can sleep soundly at night. What good is feng shui in the bedroom if you are so scared for the future you cannot fall asleep?

The banks do not make saving money seem desirable. They typically offer savings accounts with no interest, which can make us feel that we shouldn't be interested in saving at all! But it's not the banks' job to make you feel secure; it is your job. Anything you do to ensure a better future will make you feel more comfortable.

"But how can I consider saving when I owe all this money on credit cards?" you may ask. "That doesn't make financial sense, does it?" Though this is common reasoning, I haven't seen it help people pay off their credit bills any faster. If you run your accounts on empty until the bills are paid, you may not feel secure for a very long time.

You need to have a savings account in case of emergencies, unemployment, or other risky circumstances. Most financial planners recommend the equivalent of at least six months' net salary in an interest-bearing account. You probably won't be making much interest on it, but you need to know this amount is available when necessary.

If saving money seems improbable or impossible in the near future, here is a profitable exercise to try. First, go to your bank this week and open a savings account. If you can shop around for a modicum of interest, that's great, but do not be disheartened if the rates are not that welcoming.

You can start the account with a "loan" from your checking account. Most savings accounts can be started for $25 or less, and if you follow the procedure below, I can guarantee you will produce that amount. Then at the end of the month, you can return your "loan" to checking, if you like, and start filling the savings account directly.

Change Happens

Are you familiar with all those "nasty" nickels, pennies, dimes, and other coins that crawl around the crevices of your home? They climb into the cracks of the sofa, cluster at the bottom of a purse, or pile up on bureaus and tabletops. What's to be done with this financial clutter? Here is a simple trick to feel healthy, wealthy, and wise.

At the end of each day, empty your pockets and purse of all your change and put it in a large jar, vase, or piggy bank, preferably situated in your Hsun position. Then, during the day, whenever you make a purchase, pay only with paper money, and keep the change in a special pocket or purse for that evening's "deposit." If the bill is $1.01, give two dollars and pocket the change. This is now your savings account. You will be surprised at how quickly it grows.

An average consumer will accumulate $4 to $5 each day, which can easily become $100 a month, or over $1,000 in a year. Not bad for a pocketful of change! Sometimes, I enjoy this ritual so much, I go out and make tiny little purchases just so I can add to my savings account. It seems like cheating, but it's still fun.

You can decorate the area around your savings bank with pictures of the things you want: a beautiful house, a vacation, or any larger item on your wish list. Just be sure to gather the coins every day, and you can even do the Three Secret Reinforcements each time you drop them in the bank.

If you are afraid you will be tempted to dip into this account, try using a large juice can with a tiny slit cut into the top. I bought a grape juice can and put it in my "money corner," because purple is associated with the vibration of Hsun.

At the end of each month, gather all of your coin-filled juice cans and deposit the contents into your new bank account. If you accumulate over $50, you might invest in a mutual fund!

The only difficult part of saving this way is that most banks will not count your change for you. This is a big bummer, and something I rail against in bank after bank. I would gladly open an account in a bank that would take the twenty-pound juice cans off my hands! If your bank refuses, you can roll the coins yourself or get someone to do it for you. Alternatively, there are now machines in malls and grocery stores that will count the coins for a small fee. In any case, your savings account will be much bigger than if you never were to use this approach at all, and it is a fun way to invest in your future and yourself.

INNER FENG SHUI—RECOGNITION AND AFFIRMATION

If you have felt battered by various humiliations in your life, one of the quickest paths to revenge is by inspiring jealousy. Want to impress the gang at the high school reunion? Try driving up in a new Ferrari. The desire for revenge is one of the greatest inspirations for accumulating wealth, but also one of the biggest distractions.

If you are living to avenge the emotional injuries done by others, you will forever live in their shadow. This does not mean that past hurts should be ignored. It means you should reconsider abandoning your own life for the sake of revenge. Living to impress others makes you their slave and just reinforces the hurt that started long ago.

PROSPERITY JOURNAL: "SUFFERING DISRESPECT"

List ten times you felt disrespected by others. Note your age, the event, who was involved, and how you were affected. Then, mark the ones that seem to be directly affecting your financial behavior, and decide how to bring closure in a different way: by discussing it with the person, writing a letter you may or may not send, or working it out in therapy. Whatever way you choose, separate your past hurts from your future direction, so your life can really be your own.

As an addendum to this list, there is one additional culprit we need to address: you. Whoever hurt us continues to live inside, as a messenger of how we believe we should be treated. Though the original person may not be around to hurt us anymore, we continue to enact similar defeats against ourselves. This is a twisted way of trying to get ourselves to learn the lesson, once and for all. Look back over the list above and ask yourself: "Do I do this to myself as well?" Chances are, you are as guilty of your defeat as the bad guys from your past.

PROSPERITY JOURNAL: "DISRESPECTING MYSELF"

Make a list of ten ways you disrespect yourself: the ways you deprive yourself, open yourself to humiliation, and tarnish your own reputation. Then, if you like, confront the present culprit (you), and find ways to restore the treatment that you deserve.

Writing the New Script

Affirmations allow you to decide how you want to think about your life, versus following the same old script. Instead of "I can't do this job, it's too much for me," try saying, "This job is just right for me. I can do it well and really enjoy it." Truly let yourself have the pleasure of this positive view.

Try out your beliefs like a new set of clothes. In the beginning, you may not feel you deserve to be so positive, but remember, "deserving" is about old experiences and lies; it is not about the truth.

Back in the 1980s, there was a popular expression: "Question Authority." Each of us needs to question the real authority in our life. And do you know who that is? If you answered "My spouse," think again! It's your own mind. There is really only one voice that has a final say in your life, and that is the one that is constantly saying its piece in your head.

This voice cannot necessarily tell you what is true, but it can tell you what you learned to *think* is true. It's up to you to decide if you agree with those thoughts and beliefs. Your thoughts are about the past and the assumption that your future will be exactly like it. This makes them outdated ideas already—yesterday's news, that's all.

Perhaps you were in a demanding job, and you got fired or did not like the pressure. Can you be sure that your next job will be exactly like that old one? Take a law from natural science classes: nature never repeats itself. Once you have an experience, it is *impossible* to have exactly the same experience again.

If you don't believe me, try to duplicate something. It can't be done. Have you ever made love exactly the same way twice? Maybe you wish you could, but it's just not possible. Ever breathed in exactly the same batch of air? Again, not possible.

Try as you may, you will never repeat an experience you have had, so give up thinking you will. You can never step in the same river twice; nothing will ever be the same. It just can't. Once you realize this, you are free to see your future as an endless stream of new opportunities.

The Power to Affirm

If you cannot pay your bills, try using this affirmation: "I have a lot of money, and I can afford to pay all my bills on time." Really get into the feeling. Maybe it has been a long time, maybe never, since you felt this way. Commit yourself to the feeling of what you want, instead of what you don't want, and reality will follow.

Plan to put aside ten minutes every day to sit quietly, review your current thoughts about wealth and abundance, and "bust through" a major limiting idea with this affirmation process. In the beginning, it is helpful to write down the limiting situation and its opposite affirmation, so you are clear about what you want and how you are working with your ideas. After a while, the process will become second nature, and you will probably find yourself inverting negativity at every turn.

Reduce your affirmation to one sentence that you can repeat over and over in your mind, so that you can really get into the feeling of it. Here is one of my favorites: "I am financially secure, and I am really good at managing money." That phrase completely changed the way I felt and dealt with money. Whatever sentence you choose, play with the wording until you get it right, and then, when the ten minutes are over, let it go.

Don't try to affirm your new beliefs constantly for twenty-four hours a day. Not only will this prevent you from getting any other work done, but your fixation on the process is a way of affirming that you really don't think that it will work.

You might add a summarizing statement at the end of the affirmation session, such as, "The conditions I described, or something even better, are now coming into my life in ways that are best for me and everyone else." Think of your affirmation as a prayer that is seeding the cosmic clouds, so they will rain down new opportunities. I recommend that you use affirmations ten minutes each day, for the duration of this program, and see what miracles they produce for you.

Physical Affirmations

At some point in your day, after you have done your mental affirmation, choose *one* physical action to confirm that you have already accomplished the thing that you have affirmed. This gesture is symbolic and can be very simple.

You are training your subconscious, and the rest of the universe, to believe that you can have what you want, and the best way to show it is by example. If you want to prove that you can pay your bills, define one small action step to validate this idea. Perhaps you could write a check for $1 and send it to the electric company. Do it and affirm, "I enjoy the utilities in my home and pay my bills on time." You may want to enclose a note that says, "I am intent on paying my bills, and here is the first installment."

As another tack, you could turn on more lights, to show you trust that the money will come and that you can afford to live it up a little. Whatever you choose, it's *essential* that you physically manifest your positive beliefs in a way that is meaningful to you. Otherwise, the affirmations could stay in your head and never materialize in the world around you.

The Internal Flow of Chi

The degree to which we feel nurtured and fulfilled, which is the goal of wealth, is the quality of the chi inside of us. It's no wonder that we say that we "feel like a million bucks" after a good night's sleep and a fortifying meal. If we are feeling tired and drained, making more money is going to be difficult, if not impossible.

The feng shui of the home mirrors the flow of chi within our own bodies. When we are feeling happy and full of vigor, we naturally extend this energy into our environments. When we are feeling depressed or low in our energy, our homes reflect this as an accumulation of clutter, mess, and stagnant chi. Our internal *despair* translates into external *disrepair*.

Our financial energy also becomes a mirror of our own life chi. If we are emotionally and spiritually inspired, this affects the way that we pursue and treat our money. This is the reason why a lot of people like to exercise before they go to work. By getting their energy moving before they step into the workplace, they have a momentum and energy level that will carry them through the day.

As part of your daily meditation process, consider including various energetic exercises that will clarify and improve the flow of chi within your physical and spiritual structure. Just making changes in your environment, and not dealing directly with the energetic blockages in your own energetic field, is like washing your hair in dirty water!

The air that we breathe is a major source of the chi in our bodies, and many chi development exercises focus on the breath as a way to expand the energetic flow. In ancient times, the air was evidently so pure and filled with chi, it was not even necessary to eat food to fulfill energetic needs. In modern times, however, we must create a balanced regimen of food, breathing exercises, meditation, and proper feng shui to compensate for the quality of our air.

The entire universe is composed of chi energy, and your part in this cosmic dance either facilitates or constricts its flow. Working with your feng shui, meditation, and breathing, you make yourself a channel of this sacred life energy and become part of the positive expansion of the universe.

Breathe and Grow Rich: The Inhale/Exhale Method

The way that we breathe is a metaphor for how we relate to money. Money is like oxygen: if you don't take in enough on a regular basis, you could die! Your personal power is in your breath. Literally, the more you breathe, the better you feel, and the more money you can make. So let's start breathing!

The inhale/exhale method is an ancient meditation that expels negative chi from your body and fills you up with new life. Whenever you are feeling deprived, impoverished, or just plain "down," this is the perfect exercise to perform. Follow it with a positive affirmation, and you are back on the path to wealth!

Start by reciting the Calming Heart Sutra nine times, and settle into a meditative state. Next, tilt your head and upper body back a few inches, so that you are leaning backward a bit. Now, slowly inhale through your mouth, and visualize that you are taking in pure chi in the form of bright, clear sunlight. If you like, you can imagine that this light is streaming off of a spiritual figure, such as the Buddha, Jesus, or your Higher Power. Imagine this light filling your lungs and then extending to all parts of your body, until your entire being is glowing with the pure light of this chi. Imagine that this light is absorbing any negative feelings, disease, ill fortune, and feelings of deprivation and impoverishment.

Now, exhale this breath in nine short puffs, slowly bringing your body to its regular upright position. Imagine that the air you are exhaling has become dark and smoky from all of the negative chi you've absorbed, and that with each of the nine staccato puffs of air, you are expelling the old energy. You should do this breathing exercise in cycles of nine.

Each day this week, try to do this exercise at least nine times. If you have been feeling low in energy or depressed about your finances, you should do three cycles of nine breaths, for a total of twenty-seven breaths. If you practice this every day, it will dramatically change the quantity and quality of your chi, which will greatly affect your relationship with money.

ACTION STEPS ON THE JOURNEY TO WEALTH:
WEEK 4 SYNOPSIS

This is a busy week, so set aside some time and prepare for great progress. Be sure to check the boxes as you complete these tasks:

- ☐ Notice how you are feeling through the week and how this influences your spending habits. Write about this in your Prosperity Journal.
- ☐ Review your definition of your personal style, and implement at least three changes in your living room this week.
- ☐ Review the goals you set for the Li section of your home, and do at least two this week.
- ☐ Complete the journal entry on your petty deprivations, and spoil yourself a little this week with at least two loving pleasures.
- ☐ Arrange your sacred canister, and start your savings account with all that change.
- ☐ Try the verbal affirmations for ten minutes a day, at least three days this week. Do at least one physical affirmation on each of these days to help materialize your new beliefs.
- ☐ Use the inhale/exhale method to improve the quality of your chi. Breathe, and grow rich!

Finding Comfort

Perceiving what is small
Is called insight.
Residing in softness
Is called strength.
—The *Tao Te Ching*, Book 52

PRELUDE—STARTING EACH DAY

Connecting with your inner self and what really fulfills you is the most important key to feeling wealthy. What good is a lot of money if it doesn't contribute to who you are and what makes you happy? Money cannot buy happiness, but it certainly helps once you figure out what you like to do.

But who has time to think about happiness when they're struggling just to make ends meet? The answer: you do. All you need is fifteen minutes, so set your alarm clock a quarter of an hour earlier in the morning, and let's get started.

Supposedly, everyone is entitled to fifteen minutes of fame in their lifetime. I believe we are also entitled to fifteen minutes of happiness—every day. All it takes is an inquisitive mind and the willingness to be creative.

After going through an early period of racking up credit card bills, living in major cities, and traveling to far corners of the world, I discovered one major thing: wherever I went, there was always one common denominator—me. No matter how much I spent, the inside of me always turned up pretty much the same. If I was unhappy, I could be unhappy in Paris or Peoria; it didn't matter. If I felt like complaining, I could find something wrong in Rome or in Roanoke. It all came down to the same person.

Despite the insistence of the advertisers, happiness doesn't need to come in large packages. Look at children, and notice what makes them happy: a smiling glance, a butterfly, a chance to do whatever they please. As adults, we're not all that different. Our tastes may change, but we still like to follow our heart's desire, wherever that leads us. And when we allow ourselves to do that, we feel happy.

The surest path back to ourselves is to start listening again to our inner leanings: what we are feeling, what we desire, what we want to do. I have a colleague who posted a large sign in his bedroom that asks, WHAT IS MY DESIRE? By meditating on this question, all sorts of possibilities open up.

The technique is very simple and very effective: each morning, when you first awaken, ask yourself, "What do I really feel like doing today?" You can do this either before or after you write in your journal. Do not be satisfied with a negative response, such as, "I don't want to go to work" or "Nothing." Stay with your feelings until you get a glimmer of what would feel really satisfying to you.

Then, whatever it is you decide, figure out how you can spend ten minutes pursuing this activity, in whatever way you can. If you say that you want to go skydiving, ask yourself, "What's the closest I can get to the essence of that activity for the next ten minutes?" Perhaps it is a quick trip up to the roof of your apartment building (but don't jump!) to observe the fresh morning view. Or perhaps you just feel like jumping around in general; turn on your favorite tunes and do some aerobics. Whatever it is, that activity is your soul's theme for the day, and you need to hop on board before it is out of sight.

Your desired activity will set the tone for the day. Even if you cannot live that way all day, you will maintain a sense of who you really are and what you want in your life. Over time, this will make a difference.

That's it. That's the whole technique. Set your alarm!

ENVIRONMENTAL FENG SHUI—LOVE, SEX, MONEY, AND THE BEDROOM

In feng shui, the most important thing in your home is not the desk or the stove or even the front door; it's your bed. You spend more time there than anywhere else. This is where you restore your energy and communicate with your subconscious by dreaming. If your bed is not properly aligned or does not support your rejuvenation at night, you are starting each day at a disadvantage.

Finding Comfort

During a consultation, people often seem most concerned with the more public rooms in their homes, but the bedroom is the sanctuary—or at least, it should be. This room carries your vibration in its purest form and has the strongest influence on your feng shui. For this reason, many of the feng shui rituals for money are done in the bedroom. It is your private area, where you can be your most creative (and procreative).

Too often, the bedroom is considered a place to "crash." We may wheel madly through the traumas and circumstances of the day and then fall exhausted into bed at night. This must change if a person wants to feel more grounded and secure in life.

In the whirlwind of modern times, in which conspicuous consumption and achievement is rated above development of an inner life, private space has become suspect. We have ceased to see the bedroom as a place of nurturance. It has become almost like closet space, where we hang up our lives for a few hours before returning to work the next day. In New York, some apartment dwellers have actually made a closet into their bedroom, which says a lot about our perspective in the big city.

Feng Shui Techniques for the Bedroom (Ooh-La-La!)

Feng shui and interior design are interrelated, and the bedroom is one area where a few nice features can make a big difference. Make sure that you have attractive pictures on the walls that present a splendid world of possibility when you first open your eyes. This is definitely not the place for harsh, abstract art or disturbing images of any kind. This could disturb your sleep and set you off on the wrong emotional tone for your day.

A beautiful view from your bedroom window is a delight, but if that is not the case in your neighborhood, consider a luxurious set of drapes in warm, rich colors. This will help you feel snug and well cared for when you lie in bed. Key features to emphasize in the bedroom are luxury, warmth, comfort, and care. Setting this tone will help you feel wealthy when you close your eyes at night and open them in the morning.

Personalize the bedroom with enjoyable and loving details. Fond memorabilia of youth, photos of people and places that you love, artwork that soothes your senses . . . all of these contribute profoundly to your soulful sanctuary. If you share this room with your spouse or partner, celebrate what is special about your relationship with photos of romantic moments, souvenirs, and other items with sentimental value. Be sure that both people in the relationship contribute to the design and feeling of the room, to make each detail an affirmation of your loving partnership.

Feng Shui under the Covers

Go to your bedroom and consider your experience when you first wake up. What are the cues that inform your self-worth and importance in the world? Do you awaken to luxury and comfort, or do you look out on deprivation and despair? This is the first environment that affects you in the morning and the last one you experience when you go to sleep at night.

Lie on your bed, close your eyes, and notice how it feels: do you feel safe, secure, and loved? These are key elements in feeling wealthy. If not, this will affect your mindset for the rest of the day. Open your eyes, and notice what you perceive when you first look out to the world each morning.

Your bedroom is like a welcome mat into physical reality. What sort of message does it give? Does it say "Welcome to a Happy and Abundant Life" or "Land of Despair—Enter at Your Own Risk"?

PROSPERITY JOURNAL: "MY BEDROOM"

Write a few notes about how your bedroom reflects your current feelings about comfort and security. The external environment is a manifestation of your inner world. Use this opportunity to gain insight into the feelings being manifested.

Now, consider the three adjectives that you listed in chapter 1 as your essence of wealth, and decide how you can implement these qualities in the private world of your bedroom.

Sweet Dreams . . .

The bed is your most important piece of furniture, and it has the biggest effect upon how you feel about yourself, your work, and your life. It's amazing: people spend a year's salary on an automobile, and then skimp on their bed frame and mattress. Not only does this influence how you feel, it also has a strong impact on your health. Skimping on the condition of your bed is like eating poor-quality food. After a while, it affects you in ways that you wouldn't even imagine.

For a solid foundation in your life, you need a bed with a strong, supportive structure. Futons and mattresses that lie directly on the floor are a definite "no-no" in feng shui. First of all, they cause health problems by not allowing an adequate flow of energy under your body while you are sleeping. Pockets of stagnant energy accumulate, which affect glands and cause disease.

Bed frames with built-in drawers cause similar problems, which are made worse if you store junk or any sort of clutter in the drawers. Be sure the area under the bed is clear and free of any storage items. This will ensure that you feel supported in your life and that you have a flow of clear energy beneath you at all times.

The head of the bed represents feelings of support. Without a headboard, it is difficult to feel a strong backing for your life endeavors. If your bed already has a headboard, make sure it is firmly attached to the bed and that the shape feels comfortable and supportive. If there is not a headboard, purchase one or have one made that attaches directly to the frame.

A footboard is not essential for the feng shui of the bed. This makes the bed into a container of energy, which can feel cozy but may also seem restrictive. If you are starting a new career or business venture, or if you are single and looking for a mate, the containing quality of a footboard may inhibit you from reaching your goals.

Notice the linens and blankets on your bed. There is a connection between the quality of a person's bed linens and the clothing he wears. If you have trouble sleeping, indulge in linens that you really love, and change them frequently. Our bodies are sensitive to these conditions and restlessness in bed can be a reaction to poor treatment, which is a feeling that we carry throughout our day. The bed is one place where you should not skimp on quality.

Make sure the floor by your bed has a soft and comfortable carpet or rug, especially if you live in a cold climate; your first step into the world each morning should be a pleasant one. If your alarm clock awakens you without dignity, invest in one that has a firm but soothing sound, or get an alarm that gradually increases, so that it does not awaken you with a jump. By establishing your bedroom as a cozy, luxurious sanctuary, you will be on your way to wealth before you even leave the house.

The Command Position

Mention the Command Position for the bedroom, and certain images come to mind . . . But don't limit yourself; this is something that you can do in the living room, the kitchen, and even in your office at work!

The proper location of the bed, as well as the desk, stove, and other major furniture pieces, is called the Command Position. Proper placement of these essential elements helps you feel powerful and assertive, which influences the way you pursue and achieve wealth. If the location of these elements makes you feel weak, oppressed, or uncomfortable, however, this will adversely affect your entire life.

Many years ago, before studying feng shui, I was having dinner at a little Ethiopian restaurant, and as we were sitting down, I told my date that I wanted to sit against the wall, so that I was facing the entranceway. I hadn't really thought about why—that's just how I felt. My date thought it was interesting and didn't seem to mind. Then, the man next to us said that he felt the same way and always requested the same type of seating. We decided that it must be a "man thing," with references to mobsters who never sat with their back to the door.

Years later, I learned that I was referring to the Command Position, which has been recognized in China, and not just by gangsters, for thousands of years. In feng shui, it is always considered preferable to sit, or sleep, facing the entrance with a vantage point of the entire room.

If the head of your bed is along the same wall as the door to the room, the entrance is behind you, leading to a subconscious feeling that people can enter without your knowledge. This produces vague fears and suspicions, which can affect both your waking and sleeping hours.

Putting your bed on the other side of the room, directly across from the door, is problematic as well: you can only see the door if you sit up in bed. This is called the "Coffin Position" in China, because dead people are always taken out of the room feet-first. You want to sleep soundly at night, but not *that* soundly!

Deciding the best placement for the bed can be tricky, especially when you must consider windows, closets, and other architectural features. It is not best to have the head of the bed against a window, since the opening does not give a solid feeling of support behind your head.

The following diagram illustrates the advisability of various positions for the bed. Putting the bed on an angle in a corner may be highly satisfactory. This leads to a creative flow of energy, which is perfect for people who are initiating new beginnings or who want to do so. Fill the empty space behind the headboard with a large plant or tree, whether real or silk, or a decorative screen.

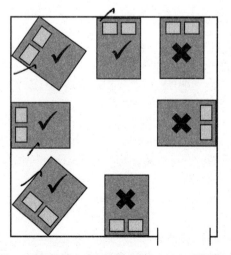

Favorable and unfavorable placement of the bed.

The Bagua of the Bedroom

If the room design supports more than one favorable Command Position, use the bagua to determine the best placement. To develop wealth or improve your career, place the bed in the Hsun or Kan areas. To receive more inner guidance, put the bed in the Chyan (mentor) or Ken (self-knowledge) areas, so that inspiration can infuse your dreams.

PROSPERITY JOURNAL: "FENG SHUI IN THE BEDROOM"

Make a list of feng shui applications you want to use in your bedroom *this week* to create greater comfort and luxury. Even a small change, like hanging a nice picture to greet you each morning, can have a deep impact on the way you feel about your life.

Make Money by Making the Bed!

Evidently, there are no extensive feng shui doctrines about bed making, even if your mother insinuated that ill luck befalls the person with an unmade bed. All the same, since the bed symbolically represents the doorway between the inner and outer worlds, not making the bed is a way of not closing the door behind us. It's like we are saying, "I am going out into the world, but I'm not sure I really want to!" We feel like we can always jump right back under the covers and pretend we never left.

If you habitually leave your bed unmade, try this experiment: for one week, make your bed every morning, and see how it affects you. By entering the world purposefully and with care each morning, you may start to feel more confident, more present, and more direct in your dealings. This will directly influence your finances.

Though it may seem trivial, when I undertook this one small assignment each morning, my energy level seemed to change. Instead of stepping back in social situations, as if wavering between reality and the world of sleep, I found myself more forthright, approaching people I didn't know and offering my hand and name with confidence. All from making my bed each morning? Maybe so. Try it, and see what happens.

Bagua Sector of the Week: Kun

Within the structure of the bagua, there is a triangular relationship between the areas of Kan (career), Hsun (wealth), and Kun (relationships). The connection

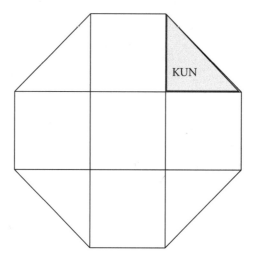

Bagua sector of the week: Kun.

between career and wealth is pretty clear; a successful job leads to financial gains. But why would the condition of your relationships have such a strong impact on your career and financial life? The reasons may surprise you.

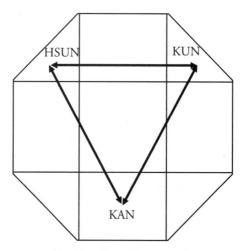

The Kan-Hsun-Kun triangle.

Behind Every Good Person . . .

A person's career often takes off once he or she enters a committed relationship or marriage. This is contrary to the fear of most single people, who believe that they will have to sacrifice their professional life if they are in a relationship.

Finding Comfort

A strong bond with another person offers a level of support, empathy, and enthusiasm for life, which automatically carries into the work setting. There is an old expression, "behind every good man is a good woman." We tend to underestimate the important role that a supportive and loving spouse can play in a person's success.

At the same time, career tracks are no longer limited to men; women, too, need faithful support and attention as they bring their gifts to the world. No one is exempt from the need for love and understanding. By fulfilling these needs in our personal relationships, we can break the expectation that our bosses, coworkers, and clients have to be the ones to give it to us. An understanding partner reminds us that we are loved and that there is someone there for us at the end of the day.

"Hey, Big Spender!"

There is also a direct parallel between the way we "spend" our sexual energy and the way we spend our money. Money, in its simplest form, is potential energy, and the way that we treat it is directly linked to the way that we feel about the energy in our own bodies.

If you are afraid of spending money, and you hoard whatever comes in, you are probably the type of person who also holds back on your sexual energy and is afraid to "let it loose." On the reverse, if you are someone who seems to leak out your money at every turn, you probably treat your sexual energy the same way and may be flirtatious and seductive, without having anything to show for it. The term "having holes in one's pockets" takes on a new meaning!

Healthy sexuality is akin to a healthy financial life: making heartfelt choices, committing to what you really want, and investing your energy in a life that is truly satisfying. You cannot cheat your sexuality. If you do not treat your energy with love, dignity, and respect, it will never lead you to happiness. Your financial life is asking for the same treatment.

If you feel loved and supported in a relationship, you won't be compelled to use money to compensate for emotional needs. Why spend $1,000 on a new suit, when your spouse already thinks you are adorable? Why take a two-week cruise, when you are happy walking in the park with the one you love?

Loneliness is one of the biggest cause of financial waste; we may try to fill emotional holes with material goods, and it never seems to work. Look at how advertisers use sexual allusions to sell a product. If only they could help us find satisfying relationships, we wouldn't need to think about the products they are trying to sell! With a mature relationship backing us up, we are empowered to use our money wisely and to build the kind of life that we really want.

Subconsciously, we may avoid wealth because it is the quickest justification for avoiding intimate contact. "Oh, I can't go out on a date—I have nothing to wear." "Get married? Not until I can afford it!" As long as there are money issues, we feel justified in shying away from deeper contact. Financial independence means security, and a lot of us run from the kind of security that would make us fully available to another person.

PROSPERITY JOURNAL:
"ESTABLISHING CHANGE IN THE KUN SECTOR OF MY HOME"

1. Write a few notes about the present condition of your intimate relationships. Consider how you are treating your sexuality and how this may parallel your relationship with money.
2. Settle into your Beginner's Mind and go to the Kun sector, at the top right corner of your home. Notice how this appears to you, and write down your impressions.
3. Next, define three or four adjectives that describe how you want your experience of personal relationships and sexuality to feel. Consider how you might bring these emotional tones to your bedroom.

Feng Shui Applications for Financial Development in Kun

Using the adjectives you chose, ask yourself, "How can I make this area of my home feel more like the energy I want in my relationships?" When people talk about the love life they desire, they often use words like "loving, fun, sexy, exciting, nurturing, adventurous, sensual." However you define it, you need to consciously and creatively bring these qualities into your Kun sector, into your bedroom, and into your life.

Since relationships connect two individuals, any pairs of objects that represent love and intimacy are perfect for the Kun sector. The colors for this gua are pink, red, and white, so a pair of red or pink candles in a beautiful set of candlesticks is perfect.

In Chinese culture, marriage is represented by a pair of carved wooden ducks. Place these on your nightstand, bureau, or anywhere in your Kun gua to bring the right energy, and do the Three Secret Reinforcements on them with a clear vision of what you want in a relationship.

Examine the artwork that you have in your home, especially in the Kun sector your home, and make sure that it depicts the positive, healthy relationships you are seeking. Be sure you have pictures of happy, loving couples, and hang them prominently in your Love Corner!

Opposites really do attract, and if you are seeking a partner of the opposite sex, you need to display your own sexuality in the décor of your home to send your vibration loud and clear. A number of single, female clients have told me how they mistakenly chose "masculine" things for their homes because they thought men would like them. One woman even had a gray bathroom, because she thought male guests would enjoy its conservative décor!

Most men want a woman to be feminine, just as most women are looking for a masculine man. Would you be attracted to a man who wears perfume, or a woman who smells of aftershave? By disguising our true natures in our homes, we confuse our guests and throw off their sense of us. Many of my female clients needed this vote of support from a male consultant to really indulge their femininity and bring it out in their environments.

The element associated with the Kun sector is earth, which suggests that relationships are like the supportive ground under our feet. Terracotta planters, beautiful vases, and statues of lovers in embrace are all perfect here. In Chinese philosophy, fire produces earth, so don't hold back on anything red and full of passion, like those ubiquitous red light bulbs!

If you are missing part of the Kun sector in your home, you can still find relationship bliss. Hang nine multifaceted crystals along the top of the wall, or place nine plants in terra cotta planters along the inside wall.

PROSPERITY JOURNAL: "APPLYING FENG SHUI TO KUN"

List three or four changes you would like to make in Kun this week to empower your relationships. Go to your Dream Bagua from chapter 2 and identify the goal that you chose for your relationships and sexuality, and consider how you can bring images of this goal into the bedroom. And don't forget to do the Three Secret Reinforcements for the cures you put in place for a satisfying love life.

The Fragrant Flower Method

If you want to bring fresh opportunities into your life, consider refreshing the chi in your home with a transcendental cure, the Fragrant Flower Method. A bouquet of flowers, whether elaborate or simple, can quickly change the energy inside a room. There's a reason why men bring flowers to women on a first date: they signify new beginnings and the flowering of all sorts of possibilities.

This traditional feng shui cure uses the vibrant chi of fresh flowers to excite the senses and enliven the chi in your environment. Over a period of nine days, you will be placing a bouquet of fresh flowers in each of three rooms: the bedroom, the kitchen, and the living room. This unites three important aspects of your financial  well-being: your security (bedroom), your nurturance (the kitchen), and your role in society (the living room).

On the first day you do this ritual, purchase or gather a large bunch of flowers. They do not need to be exotic or expensive, but you should have a total of at least nine stems. If cost is a concern, you should be able to find a large bouquet for under ten dollars at a grocery store or corner market.

Divide the flowers into three vases, and put one vase in each of the three rooms: bedroom, living room, and kitchen. When each bouquet is set in its place, do the Three Secret Reinforcements on each bunch, and visualize all the negative energy in the room being absorbed by the flowers.

After three days, dispose of all of the flowers, and bring in a new bunch that is distributed among the three vases. To affect the chi in new ways, try not to use the same type of flowers each time. Do the Three Secret Reinforcements again, and continue to visualize the negative energy being absorbed by the flowers.

After three more days, do this ritual cycle one more time, with three new bunches of flowers, while reinforcing the intention that any remaining negative chi is absorbed by the fragrant flowers. Again, dispose of these bunches after the third day they have been in your environment. Your home and your life should now be filled with fresh, vibrant chi that will grace your new path to wealth and prosperity.

FINANCIAL FENG SHUI—SIMPLE LUXURIES

Back in the 1980s, there was an annoyingly indulgent television show about the lifestyles of the rich and famous. The program depicted the outrageously hedonistic activities of various movie stars, while suggesting that such lifestyles were quite commonplace if you only knew the right people.

But how many viewers actually became millionaires by watching that show, or even increased the amount of luxury in their lives by one iota? Probably . . . no one. And why is that? Because watching TV shows about other people eating lobster on the beach at St. Tropez does not automatically make it happen to you. And why is that? Because it's hard to translate other people's visions of luxury into our own daily routine. Sure, it's nice to know that that your favorite movie star hangs out at a certain resort in St. Tropez (and I'll be sure to say "hello" next time we share a beach towel), but in the meantime, how can we translate what we have now into a life of wealth and luxury?

The first step is to realize that, even with feng shui bringing us as many possibilities as we can handle, we need to start translating what we have into what we want. The process is a bit like cooking: You start with a recipe, and then you make adjustments according to what you have on the shelf and what looks freshest at the market. Unlike a good cooking show, however, the *Lifestyles* program did not supply recipes for making it at home—so you were left feeling deprived and undeserving, while watching other people having the adventures of *their* lives.

We waste a lot of time, and let our ideal futures leak away, by waiting to have the whole package at one time, instead of putting it together piece by piece. The truth is, if everyone realized that luxury does not need to be all that expensive, programs like that would be out of business, and movie stars would have to find other ways to keep our interest (like acting, maybe?).

So let's start with the only thing we have: the present. If you are planning to get rich in the future . . . well, I don't know if you realize it, but the future never really happens. It's like trying to step on your shadow. You keep moving ahead, but you never seem to get there. So, instead, you need to realize you are standing on the future right now—"today is the day that is yesterday's tomorrow"—something like that. And if you keep putting off that life of luxury until that "someday" when you think you might afford it—chances are you are never, ever going to get it. Instead of waiting for the lottery to kick in and change your life, start creating your life of prosperity right now.

PROSPERITY JOURNAL: "MY SIMPLE LUXURIES"

Without thinking too much, answer the following question: "If I had *a bit* more money than I do now, I would treat myself by . . ." List ten things as fast as you can.

Did you notice that the instructions said "a *bit* more money," not "a million dollars"? The reason is that most of us have been conditioned to believe that luxury, and just about anything worthwhile at all, is going to cost a fortune, and this prevents us from getting even a little bit of what we want. Where did this message come from? The folks at the lottery office? Maybe. Programs like the *Lifestyles* show? Definitely. Or perhaps it's a childhood message. We asked for something when we were kids, and our parents responded, "What do you think we are, rich?" This most paralyzing idea prevents us from creating any goals at all.

Here are some examples of the things that I put on my own list:

> If I had a *bit* more money than I do now, these are some of the ways that I would treat myself:
> - Go horseback riding
> - Fresh berries
> - Hot croissants for breakfast
> - A set of crystal champagne glasses
> - A thick, plush bath towel

Perhaps something on my list gives you inspiration, or you might also pose this question to some of your friends and see what types of responses they provide.

Now that we have listed some "simple pleasures," let's take the process one step further. For each item on your list, raise the stakes a little, and ask yourself: Can I imagine this even better? If I really let myself really feel indulged, how might I enjoy having this?

For instance, take a look at the first item on my list: horseback riding. I am proud to say that when I first did this exercise, I indulged my fondness for riding and went for an hour's ride at a stable in the Bronx. Yes, such things exist. Total cost for one hour of luxury: $25. But what if I took this interest to the next level? In my greatest of fantasies, how can I imagine fulfilling my love of riding on a grander scale?

I could see myself taking lessons every weekend, and maybe purchasing a complete Western outfit with boots, spurs, a broad-brimmed hat . . . the whole look. And I might even consider working as a stable hand every Saturday, so I can fulfill my fantasy of life on a ranch—yes, jobs can be luxuries, if you really love them.

As I get on a roll with my fantasy about just one of my luxury items, the vision starts to get really exciting: vacations on horseback in Montana, owning my own horse, competing in riding shows, and maybe even running my own ranch some-day. That's a lot of vision from one afternoon of riding!

Are any of these ideas impossible? No. In fact, they seem a lot more possible than they did five minutes ago, before I started conjecturing about my interests. But none of this will probably happen if I don't start with that first, single hour on horseback. I can watch Westerns on TV all night and daydream about life in the saddle, but until I pick up the phone and reserve the first riding trip, it's all fantasy. So when my feng shui leaves me with an extra $25 and a friend who asks me if I want to go riding this week . . . I'll know that everything is working. But I have to take the first step.

However, once I actually show up at the ranch, all sorts of things can happen. Maybe I'll find that I don't really like horses at all, or that hanging onto that animal at full speed is just too terrifying, and I am much happier in a beach chair than in a saddle. Maybe. Or perhaps I will feel so much at home at that ranch that I won't want to leave; I'll start conversations with the stable hands and volunteer to pitch hay just so they let me stay. Who knows? The only way to decide your fantasies is to pursue them.

Once you begin the practice of feng shui, all sorts of things can happen in your life, and they do not have to be huge in order to be important. The universe will try to give you whatever you want and will probably start with small doses to make sure you want them. Show the universe what you want by taking advantage of the opportunities as they present themselves. "Don't step over God's miracles," as a friend once told me.

Go back to the list that you just made of simple luxuries, and make sure you get at least one of them this week. But remember: don't buy the ranch until you first get on a horse!

Make a Plan for Wealth

Say the word "budget," and what do you imagine? Living on rice and beans? Walking ten miles to work? Calling 1-800-FLOWERS and asking for a discount on last week's roses?

Budgets typically imply limits. Like the diets we impose when our weight seems out of control, these constrictive measures are rarely realistic, rarely satisfying, and rarely effective. Just the thought of being on a budget seems like punishment for bad spending habits. In this program, we will avoid these onerous implications altogether and consider your potential, not just your limitations.

Instead of talking about budgets and ways to inhibit your financial vision, we are going to focus on a plan: your Prosperity Plan. Where do you want to go, and how do you want to get there? The rest is really just details.

Anything you desire can go on your Prosperity Plan: fancy dinners, limousine rides, fresh bouquets at your door. That doesn't necessarily mean you can afford it right away, which is why you need a plan. Life is creative, and just because something isn't possible today doesn't mean it will be out of reach in the future.

Budgets have gotten a bad rap because of people who don't believe in the importance of what they want. As soon as they hit financial problems, they start tossing things off their budget faster than you can say, "How much?" Then, they adopt an ascetic lifestyle that is impossible to maintain, instead of creatively pursuing the lifestyle they want.

When making a budget, we often leave out the things that are most important to us and then wonder why we can't stick to it! If you are keeping, or have kept, a budget in the past, see if you included any of these items: clothing, evenings out with friends or dates, toiletries, gifts for yourself and others, snacks, "miscellaneous." Were you really expecting to live without these things for more than a week? In my experience, it's the "miscellaneous" things in life that often feel the most essential!

It's Time for a Plan

Your spending is dictated by your consciousness. If you are not conscious of what you are spending, you are probably going to run out of money. Period.

"But what if I just don't have enough for everything I want?" That common plea is the root of budgetary avoidance. If you believe you won't have enough and can't have enough, there is not much pleasure in making plans.

PROSPERITY JOURNAL: "MY PROSPERITY PLAN"

1. In the first week of this program, you were initiated into the use of your spending log. Using this as a guide, list all purchases you made in the past month, and the total spent for each. If you already recognize that a number of those expenses are not worth repeating, you can reduce your estimates, but do so cautiously. The quickest way to undermine your plan is to underestimate your costs.

2. Assign your purchases to categories, and total the amount spent in each category. Add any essential categories that may not have come up last month, and estimate their usual cost. Here is a list of things that you may need to consider: rent or mortgage; utilities; car expenses (payments, gas, insurance, maintenance); telephone; laundry and dry cleaning; groceries; dining out; clothing; furnishings and home care; education; cable TV; child support and alimony; books, magazines, and newspapers; entertainment; toiletries and personal care; gym fees; medical expenses; investments; savings; taxes; and (my

---

favorite) miscellany. If you are not anticipating any of these expenses, you do not need to put them in your plan, but be careful about glossing over anything that may come up soon.

3. Refer to the simple luxuries you defined earlier in this section, and put some of them at the top of your plan. List the luxuries by name—"running with the bulls in Spain" or "eating mangos on the beach"—whatever they may be. Then, make sure that you pay for these first!

Compare the income you defined in week 2 with the plan you just produced. If your income meets your current expenses, congratulations! *That* is the experience of true wealth. But if your expected needs exceed your income, that's the source of your financial agony and it's time to get creative. Don't just whittle away the things you know are "luxuries"; that's the quickest path to feeling deprived, which will make you resent your plans even before you start.

Go to appendix B at the back of this book and find a form called "Prosperity Plan." Make a number of copies of this chart, since you will use them every week.

Review the categories you created for your expenses, and ask about each one, "How important is this to me?" Prioritize the categories and assign them to your first "Prosperity Plan," with the top scorers at the head of the list.

In the second column of the plan, write the total dollar amount that you have been paying each month, and notice how this correlates with your priorities. For example, if docking and maintaining the family sailboat costs you $1,000 per month, but the old tub now sits at the bottom of your list, you may need to reconsider the expense. On the other hand, if movie night with your friends is the one thing you look forward to each week, and it rated just under rent and toothpaste, then make sure you maintain that expense at all costs!

Continue to record all purchases in your spending log, and transfer the totals to your Prosperity Plan at the end of each day. As you move through the week, keep tabs on how much you have left in each category. Try not to go over in any one area, but if you do, see how you can deduct from other areas, especially ones at the bottom of your list.

At the end of each week, figure your totals and balance for each category, and decide how you need to make changes in your estimates. If you went over in any area, consider the value of those expenses, and decide how to creatively minimize costs so you can develop the line items that are really important.

You might have envisioned wealth as a time when you will not need to think about money at all, and you can just bask in undisturbed bliss. This a throwback to your memories of the womb, and not a real reflection of a wealthy life! Consider yourself fortunate to be living in a period in history in which anyone can pursue real wealth—anyone who is willing to use their skills and creativity to make it happen.

When you can manage $1 with integrity and complete satisfaction, you are ready to move on to bigger sums as well. Whether figuring out how to pay for the next meal or how to fund the mortgage on your villa in Tuscany, the skills are the same. Creating your Prosperity Plan is an essential part of this process. Take care of the line items that you have, and you will be able to handle more.

The Great Wealth Accumulator

A powerful mystical technique for building wealth involves the use of a surprising tool: the piggy bank. You may have childhood memories of being given your first bank and taught to collect your coins and deposit them in a smiling porcelain pig. Now, these banks have a function that could greatly transform your financial life.

Hopefully, you have already realized the power of saving by augmenting the Change Happens system from Week 4. By collecting your change at the end of each day and saving it for your future, you are sending the powerful message that you are planning to be around for a while and want to invest in a fulfilling future.

The Great Wealth Accumulator Ritual, also known as the Piggy Bank Method, takes the power of saving to a new level. It creates a mystical vessel for your money, which actually attracts financial opportunities. This ritual is not meant to replace the savings you are doing each night with your spare change. The two activities complement each other thoroughly. One is mundane, and the other is transcendental; together, they can make you rich.

To set up this ritual, you need the following materials:

1. A new piggy bank, of a size that fits under your bed (if you sleep on a futon or mattress on the floor, note step 4 in the procedure below)
2. A new pen with black ink
3. A piece of red paper, cut into a circle three inches in diameter
4. Two round mirrors, three inches in diameter each
5. A red cloth large enough to fit under the piggy bank

Finding Comfort

It is best to do this ritual on a day considered especially auspicious for blessings and rituals. To find which days are best suited, consult *The Classic Chinese Almanac*, by Dr. Edgar Sung, or contact a practitioner of Chinese astrology or feng shui. Because of the powerful nature of this ritual, it is also recommended that the initial phase be done between the hours of 11:00 A.M. and 1:00 P.M., which is when the earth's vibrations are in their strongest cycle.

Once the materials are prepared, follow these steps:

1. Gather the materials around you in your bedroom, and do the Calming Heart Sutra nine times. Settle into a relaxed and focused state, and visualize your intention: establishing this Great Wealth Accumulator in your home will draw unlimited wealth and prosperity to you. Really get into the vision of this, and enjoy the details. Gain a sense of the sacred nature of this ritual and how it will contribute to your personal and spiritual journey toward abundance.

2. With the new black pen in your hand, take a deep breath and don't exhale. While holding your breath, write the words "Great Wealth Accumulator" on one side of the circle of red paper and then sign your name on the other side. Oh, and then exhale!

3. Attach the red circle of paper to either side of the piggy bank so your name is facing inward.

4. You now need to identify the side of your bed that corresponds with where your dominant hand rests when you are lying on your back. For most people, this is your right hand. Underneath the area where this hand lies, spread out the red cloth under your bed. If you sleep on a futon or mattress on the floor, you can still do this ritual. Place the ritual objects in the Hsun corner of your bedroom, but consider buying a new bed as soon as the new prosperity comes in!

5. Place one of the round mirrors on the center area of the cloth, and place the piggy bank over it. The bank is almost ready to start making bacon!

6. Take the second round mirror, and attach it to the underside of the bed so that it shines down on the piggy bank. It is as if you are making a piggy bank sandwich, with two mirrors and the bank between them.

7. Your Piggy Bank Ritual is now ready to go. To conclude the preparations, do the Three Secret Reinforcements, and visualize great prosperity coming to you with this method.

8. You now need to choose a denomination of coin you are going to collect and save in this bank for a period of either nine or twenty-seven days. It can be a penny, nickel, dime, quarter, fifty-cent piece, or dollar coin. You need to be prepared to collect *at least* one of these coins every day for the entire period that you are doing this ritual, so make your choice wisely. You should choose a denomination that has a sense of value for you.

9. Decide whether you are going to do this ritual for nine or twenty-seven days. If your money problems (or your aspirations) are quite large, you are best advised to do the complete twenty-seven-day cycle.

10. Starting on the day you set the bank in its position, you need to collect at least one coin of the chosen denomination to put in the ritual bank at the end of the day. Every time you make a purchase and receive some change, you must keep coins of this denomination separate from the rest; to keep these coins sacred, you may want to keep them in a special pocket or purse. You must collect at least one each day, and you may not spend any of the coins of that denomination for the duration of the ritual. If you do not make any purchases that day, you can make change so you have at least one coin to deposit. If you like, you can do the Three Secret Reinforcements each time you put money in this bank.

11. At the end of the nine or twenty-seven days, you may either leave the bank in its position under your bed or move the bank to the Hsun corner of your bedroom. Do not, however, spend any of the money you have accumulated. By contributing to this bank over this period of days, you have created an energetic container that is literally magnetic to money and opportunity, and you must safeguard this vessel so the vibration remains pure and active.

Here are a few additional notes about the conditions for performing this ritual:

1. If you forget to collect at least one coin in your chosen denomination during any day, you must start the ritual all over. Leave any coins in the bank that you have already accumulated, and start with a new nine or twenty-seven-day cycle.
2. If, due to a mistake or emergency, you spend one or more of the coins of your chosen denomination, do not despair. You do not need to start the ritual again, but you should note how many of the coins you spend, and replace them with nine additional coins for each one spent.
3. If you need to be away from home on any nights during the ritual cycle, you have two choices. Either you can *carefully* take the bank with you, or you can collect each day's coins in a special change purse until you return home.
4. This ritual is even more powerful when done by a husband and wife together. It is also a fun ritual for children, and will teach them a lot about the value of money, as well as invite great fortune to into their lives.

Before I had learned the Piggy Bank Ritual, I placed a bowl in the Hsun corner of my bedroom and deposited all the quarters I received each day into it. Within three days, I received an unsolicited check for $25 in the mail. But that was not all. I continued the coin ritual, and after another three days, I received an unsolicited check for $275! In less than a week, I turned a handful of quarters into $300—and didn't even have to travel to Atlantic City to do it.

Remain committed to your Piggy Bank Ritual, and you will probably have some amazing stories of your own. I look forward to hearing about your Great Wealth Accumulation!

INNER FENG SHUI—YOUR RIGHT TO ABUNDANCE

In this chapter, we are focusing on the comfort we get from relationships: with ourselves, with our homes, with money, and with our partner. But when we go to sleep at night, we are confronted with our most essential relationship: with God.

One of the ways we can connect with the abundance of the universe is with prayer. "What?!" you may exclaim. "*Pray* for money?" Exactly. If you do not believe that your prayers will be answered, you're not going to pray, are you? And if you don't pray, you must believe that the universe isn't interested in helping you.

The reality of prayer is really quite simple: it is a time when you communicate openly with the rest of the universe. Feng shui is a form of prayer. It is a way of making a statement, loud and clear, in three dimensions.

Sometimes when I talk about prayer, I get negative reactions from my clients. Images come to mind of six-year-old children on bended knee beside their beds, pleading to some faceless entity in the clouds while parents watch, making sure that it is done correctly. No wonder we don't want to pray. These images are the reason prayer is avoided and so ineffective.

Prayer is one the simplest acts we can accomplish, and most of us are involved in it many times a day, whether we define ourselves as atheists, agnostics, or born again Christians. It is a way of reflecting on our life experience, deciding what we want, and communicating this to the rest of existence. Unlike the plans we make each day, a prayer is a statement of desire, without knowing how these desires can be fulfilled. It is a revelation of our powerlessness, a statement of our vulnerability.

Without prayer, we live in a self-imposed cocoon of arrogance. We believe that we can handle everything, and if we can't handle it, then it's not worth handling. But inside, we know that we understand very little, if anything, about how the universe works, and we have little control over what happens in our lives. We are part of a bigger picture, of which we see only the smallest of specks. Feng shui is an ancient way of relating to the Great Unknown.

A client recently told me, "I can't do these feng shui rituals, I'm Jewish." And I wish I had said, "If you are Jewish, all the more reason for doing these rituals." I say that not because I think that she needs to supplement her practice of Judaism, but because her religion already gives her a strong format with which to use the feng shui treatments. Everything that we do in feng shui is really a connection to God.

If the title of "God" is uncomfortable for you, consider other options: You might say "Great Creator," "Higher Power," "Universe"—whatever helps you to relate to the power within the mystery of life. And if you prefer not to think about the mystery of life at all? Well, that's why they invented television.

When it comes to your financial life, you need to examine the question: does God want you to have money? If you don't believe it, you better not pray for it! Most of us in the West have a lot of kooky ideas about money, and a lot of it has come down through our religions. If you recall the limiting beliefs you outlined in chapter 1, many of them first came disguised as scripture.

Why would anybody want to limit our financial potential? The answer is obvious: Money begets power, which begets independence and free thought, going directly in the face of organized religion. Remember, Buddhism is not a religion; it is a system designed to help you discover your own inner path, wherever that may lead.

PROSPERITY JOURNAL: "SPEAKING WITH GOD"

Write a dialogue between yourself and God. The first line might go something like this:

You: Dear God, please help me get lots of money.
God: _____. (You fill in the blank.)

Keep writing this dialogue until you ascertain how your vision of God relates to financial prosperity. This exercise can give you insight into a great number of your limiting beliefs about money.

Prayer is communication. We don't need to speak only when we need something. Expressing gratitude is a natural response to feeling happy and fulfilled. Each morning, take five minutes and express gratitude to the universal source for whatever feels satisfying to you in your life.

You may have problems, perhaps very serious ones, but withholding your gratitude is not going to make you feel better—it just makes you miserable. There is time to address your dilemmas, and when you do, go feeling comforted in your heart. Let God know what you appreciate and you will get more of what you need.

Meditation for Borrowing the Buddha's Chi

We are put on this planet to give, not just to take. Our true nature is of unlimited light, love, and compassion. When we give our energy freely, we connect with our inner abundance and can circulate new possibilities in all areas of our lives.

Life circumstances may have made us afraid or angry. After decades of accumulated retreats and defeats, most of us have retreated from the natural flow of our energy and disconnected from the true abundance held inside. Financial difficulties exacerbate this feeling of energetic constriction. Feeling financially impoverished leads to further professional withdrawal, and the financial downward spiral begins.

The only way out of this negative cycle is to try to restore ourselves to a feeling of energetic abundance. This method of "Borrowing the Buddha's Chi" is an amazing meditation process that restores your energy and feelings of abundance. Practiced daily, it is an excellent antidote to stress, sickness, and worry.

To gain the benefits, practice it for a cycle of at least nine days. If you have been feeling notably weak, ill, or under stress, you may want to do it for twenty-seven days. Choose a quiet place to do the meditation, relax, and enjoy the benefits. You and your wallet will both be grateful for taking the time.

1. Sit quietly, close your eyes, and feel your breathing. Allow your breath to drop down into your belly and follow its flow. Imagine that your breath is dropping down into your feet and then into the ground, so that it feels as if your breath is ebbing and flowing from the earth itself.

2. As you follow your breath, imagine you are sitting on a large, pink lotus flower with a thousand petals, floating in the middle of space. Feel yourself resting on this blossom, feeling totally safe and secure.

3. Now imagine that there are an infinite number of Holy Figures and Buddhas surrounding you in space on all sides, to the furthest extension of the universe. Feel the comfort of the presence, and imagine that their holy light is radiating to you and filling every cell of your body.

4. As you are filled with this celestial energy, imagine that the light fills your heart and touches a beautiful closed lotus bud that is in your heart. As the light touches this bud, the flower starts to open, until it spreads a thousand tiny pink petals, and in the middle of the flower is a tiny Buddha, which is the essence of your own being.

5. This tiny Buddha in your Heart's Blossom is filled with its own light, and this light starts to fill your body. As the light expands, the Buddha starts to grow, until it entirely fills your form. Your hands are now the Buddha's hands, your legs are the Buddha's legs, and so on. Feel how completely your body and the Buddha's body have become one. As you move your fingers, you are moving the Buddha's fingers, and so forth.

6. Feel your Buddha light emanating out to all reaches of the universe. Send your light out to all the Buddhas and Holy Figures that surround you. Feel that they receive your light and then send their light back to you.

7. Now send your light out to all of your teachers (and feng shui consultants!) and other spiritual figures you have known. They receive your light and send their light back to you.
8. Now send your light out to all your friends and relatives. Visualize that they receive your light and send their own light back to you.
9. Now send your light to all children you have helped and to all children in the world that need your light. Feel the goodness of your light going out to these children. Feel them receiving your light and being nourished by it, and then feel their light coming back to you.
10. Now send your light out to any other people with whom you have contact: people who have helped you and people that you help. Feel them receiving your light, being nourished by it, and then sending their light back to you.
11. See yourself standing at the entranceway of your home. Feel yourself filling your home with your light, and then feel the home sending its own light back to you.
12. Now see yourself standing at the entranceway of your place of business. Fill this space with your light, giving it to all people who come there, and then receive the light emanating from this space.
13. Make a wish, and vocalize it softly to yourself. Imagine your wish coming to you in ways that are satisfying to you.
14. Finally, end this meditation with a short prayer of your choice, and feel the presence of the Divine within you.

ACTION STEPS ON THE JOURNEY TO WEALTH:
WEEK 5 SYNOPSIS

This week our focus is on relationships. Commit to the following activities, and discover how your life can be enriched. Check the boxes as you complete the following tasks:

- ☐ Review your notes on changes you would like to make to your bedroom, and implement at least two this week.
- ☐ Define the Command Position in your bedroom and see if you can move your bed to that area.
- ☐ Do you dare? Make your bed each day this week.
- ☐ Review the goals you set for the Kun sector of your home, and implement at least two this week.
- ☐ Consider employing the Fragrant Flower Method.
- ☐ Choose your simple luxuries, and indulge yourself by imagining them in detail.
- ☐ Support your vision of wealth with a wise and sound Prosperity Plan. Look at ways to reduce unnecessary spending to uphold your new vision.
- ☐ Make a plan to do the Great Wealth Accumulator Ritual—but only when you are ready to bring in serious money!
- ☐ Empower yourself with this week's meditation, Borrowing the Buddha's Chi.

Nurturing Yourself

Know contentment, and you shall not be dishonored.
Know your limits, and you will forever be safe.
—The *Tao Te Ching*, Book 44

PRELUDE—MONEY ADDICTION

In a chapter dedicated to the kitchen, it seems appropriate to discuss the problem of addictive spending. Overspending is like overeating; it's just one more way we try to fill the emotional holes inside.

The problem with overspending is that it leads to deprivation, the very feeling we are trying to heal. When we are in debt, we reinforce the belief that we are not enough and that we need to pretend to be more than we really are. Does this message sound familiar? For most of us, this is a message that has been thrown at us from all sides since birth, so it's no wonder we celebrate it in big letters once we can apply for credit.

Growing up, how often were we told that we were enough, just perfect the way we were, and we would be loved fully, no matter what? Once? Twice, maybe? Even three times may seem like a long shot.

Low self-esteem comes from low valuation in the family. For every grown-up who feels inadequate and unlikable, there was a parent who was critical and undermining of self-image. I am not trying to sell stock in psychotherapy by saying this; I am just making an observation that is supported by case after case. These criticisms lead children to develop negative beliefs about themselves and their behavior. The vicious cycle has begun.

We try to make ourselves feel better by any means possible. Some turn to alcohol or drugs, and others become addicted to material consumption. If you've ever gone shopping to make yourself feel better, you are part of that group. And if one shopping spree doesn't solve it, you'll be back for another, whether you can afford it or not.

"I am sure that he will like me better if I am wearing a new dress."

"A new suit would make me feel a lot more confident at my interview."

"I can't stand my life anymore. I am going to buy that new sofa before I think about how much I'm spending."

These are the thoughts of an active, or potential, money addict. All it takes is a credit card for the virus to set in.

If you see yourself in this description, you are certainly not alone. Anyone who has ever had trouble with money is probably addicted to overspending—and to the low self-esteem that goes with it.

Like any addiction, the difference between healthy spending and addictive consumption is connected to how much trouble it gets you into and whether or not you can stop it at any time. If you feel out of control with money and believe that the only way to happiness is by getting more, chances are that you are addicted.

Here are some questions you can ponder as you examine your relationship with money.

1. Do you tend to go shopping or buy yourself "treats" when you are upset, as a way to make yourself happy?
2. When you have cash available, do you spend it quickly, before you think rationally about how you are using it?
3. Do you ever lie about how much you have spent?
4. Do you put off paying bills, even when the money is available in your account?
5. Do you act "nice" with family or friends, to ensure that you can borrow from them if necessary?
6. Do you habitually avoid opening mail or answering the phone, for fear that it may be a creditor?
7. Do you avoid making financial plans because the idea makes you feel limited or depressed?
8. Do you feel more powerful or important when spending money?
9. Do you consistently overspend each month, without a plan to get yourself on track?
10. Do you avoid certain friends or family members because you owe them money?

Nurturing Yourself

If you answered "yes" to any of these questions, you have a money problem. If you answered "yes" to two or more, you probably have an addiction to overspending. If you answered "yes" to most or all of these questions, your addiction is certain and severe, and it must be handled before you have a chance to increase your wealth.

Money addiction does not necessarily mean that you are broke, just as being an alcoholic does not mean that you are always drunk. There are alcoholics who hold jobs and seem to function just fine, just as there are money addicts who stay employed and keep up most of their payments. Underneath, however, they know that there is something "funny" about the way they handle money.

I've had clients report that they feel uncomfortable when they are not buying something. Having money in their pocket is like a high. With any amount available on their credit cards, just the thought that they could walk into a store and buy something made them feel powerful, important, and bigger than life . . . until the bills arrived, like a hangover at the end of the month.

Talk to any recovering alcoholic, and he or she will all tell you the same thing: the only way to recovery is cold turkey. It is the same with debt: stop the spending. Use the tools in this program, get yourself on solid ground, and stay there. But first, you need to deal with the person who has been doing the spending: you.

The reason we have been overspending is not that the economy is down, or because we are underpaid for our talents, or even because our feng shui needs adjustment. Feng shui increases the flow in our lives, but we need to work with the problem on many levels. Inside, the addictive spender feels like that injured, angry, humiliated kid who didn't feel loved or recognized. And we would do anything in our power to never feel that way again. If buying something at the store or filling our time with some exciting and expensive activity makes us feel better, we will pay anything. No price seems too great, even if it puts us into debt we cannot conceive of repaying.

The only way out is to mourn the hurts and nurture a positive self-image. Most of us have done that to some degree, but probably not enough to dissuade the self-deprecating beliefs. As we separate the hurt that's been done to us from the original self that got hurt, we see past the attacks to the person we really are inside. And we begin to realize that *maybe* we really are enough the way we are, without needing any of the fancy packaging to make us seem better.

There is not a single purchase that can make you better than you already are. Yeah, sure, you may look better, or smell better, or have a nicer home, but underneath, you will still be the same person. The fear of this revelation has kept us in a buying frenzy, or in any other type of addiction.

Take a look at the accumulation in your basement or closets. At one point, you thought those things would make your life better! And maybe they did . . . for a while. But after a time, the limits of the crutch are revealed, and it's back to the mall or to online shopping, looking for the next fix.

Just as overeaters must examine the way they misuse food, overspenders need to look at the way that they misuse money. Diets are short-term solutions, and forcing yourself to maintain a restricted financial lifestyle only works for a short time. To really create change, you need to examine *why* you are doing the spending.

Try answering these questions:

1. I feel like overspending when _____

   _____.

2. I act "funny" with money when _____

   _____.

3. I use money to _____

   _____.

4. I want to impress other people that I _____

   _____.

5. I really don't feel that I deserve to have _____

   _____.

6. I can never have enough money for _____

   _____.

7. I use money to make myself feel better when _____

   _____.

8. I would feel ashamed if people knew that I use money to

   _____.

These ideas, connected to the injuries that caused low self-worth, are at the root of any overspending. Once you see how these ideas and the resulting misuse of money are causing you further injury, you can begin to make changes.

Continue to record each of your expenses, and later in this chapter, we will discover how your spending is either helping or hindering your sense of fulfillment. Your money is an expression of your soul in the world. What you do with it is very important.

ENVIRONMENTAL FENG SHUI—CREATIVITY AND THE KITCHEN

The environmental feng shui work for this week will be focused in the kitchen and the bagua area called Dui ("dway"). The kitchen is often the center of the home and family life; it represents the source of nourishment, which corresponds to wealth and the fruits of our labor. The Dui gua is connected to children and creativity, which are naturally associated with the hearth.

The Kitchen

This week, we will be taking the feng shui consultation into your kitchen to find out how you use your financial energy to nurture and "feed" yourself. This is often the most popular room in the home. This is where we nourish ourselves, connect with our families, do homework, and often celebrate birthday parties and other special events. It is the hearth, the "mother area" of the home.

In relation to money, the kitchen represents how we fill our larders, sustain ourselves, and save for the future. Every good cook knows that a successful menu relies on a careful spending plan, an understanding of the family's needs, and well-stocked cupboards. The way we fulfill these roles in the kitchen parallels how we manage our money and invest in our well-being. The word "salary," in  fact, comes from the Latin word for salt, since early Roman soldiers were paid in salt, which is an essential nutritional compound.

If clients tell me they have money problems, one of the first places I look is the kitchen. Even in New York City, where people practically live on take-out and restaurant food, the condition of the kitchen says a lot about a person's financial self-care. If you do not take time to stock your cupboards, you are probably not putting much foresight into your savings account. If your stove is generally cold and unused, you probably aren't feeling the benefits of your wealth and may feel malnourished, no matter how much money you are making.

It is distressing to note how the kitchen has dropped in importance in the family. With busy, conflicting schedules and the predominance of fast food and microwaved fare, cooking is seen more as a hobby than the pillar of daily life. And why should we spend time and energy at the stove, when our culture points to business and entertainment as our highest ideals?

All too often, I have walked into a luxurious Manhattan home and observed, "Wow, you have a lovely kitchen . . . do you use it?" The response is usually "No." Sure, there are cupboards full of vitamins and a refrigerator stocked with varieties of bottled water, but the connection to nurturance, the sense of warmth emanating from the central hearth, is missing.

Madison Avenue has succeeded; the advertising campaigns are working. Companies won't get rich by selling you the ingredients of a pot of soup, but they can make a bundle if they sell you the soup itself in a colorful can. Corporations won't get fat if you cook from scratch. Their job is to convince you that cooking at home is for losers, that what you really want is food that is quick, ready-made . . . and expensive.

The issue of self-nurturance is central to the development of your wealth. What is the point of bringing in more money if it does not "feed" you?

PROSPERITY JOURNAL: "THE HEARTH"

1. Take this book with you into your kitchen. Put on your private investigator hat, also known as your Beginner's Mind, and open the cupboards and refrigerator. Notice the condition and the content of the shelves. What sort of people do you imagine live here? How do they treat themselves, and how important do they make their nurturance?

2. Next, look at the general upkeep and character of the kitchen area. How does it feel to be in this part of the home? What adjectives come to mind that describe the feeling of this room? Write a few notes about your observations.

3. Consider how the quality of your kitchen reflects your self-care and how you handle your money.

Feng Shui for the Stove

In feng shui, the stove is one of the most important fixtures in the home. It represents wealth, bounty, and the fruits of your labor. If your stove is usually cold, your money situation is probably not very satisfying. You may make a lot of money, but you will never feel fulfilled if you aren't enjoying the fruits of your labor.

Your stove, and how it is used, is a clear symbol of how you receive and care for the bounty you bring into your life. Be sure to keep the top of your stove very clean to show your appreciation and receptivity to this wealth.

If your stove directly faces your front door, this is a big problem. The money may be used up as soon as it comes through the door! Since it's difficult to move the stove, the best thing is to hang a wind chime over the range top, so the chi is diffused before it hits the burners. Hang the chime low enough so the tassel brushes your head every time you work at the stove. Even if the burners do not face the door, this is still a beneficial cure, since the chime generates positive chi each time every time you pass the stove.

Ideally, you should see the door of the kitchen when you are standing at the stove. If this is not the case, hang a rectangular mirror above the range top to see behind you while cooking. The mirror gives the added benefit of reflecting the burners on the stove, which doubles the bounty of your hearth.

Ice Box, Bread Box, Cash Box

Look inside your refrigerator, and notice if it seems like a cornucopia of wealth. Prosperity in the kitchen means different things to different people. To some, it's having a few steaks in the freezer. To others, nothing says "luxury" like a pile of fresh organic vegetables. Whatever wealth means to you, the kitchen is a great place to make an edible statement that good times are at hand.

To augment your luxurious foodstuffs, roll up nine $1 bills, seal them in a ziplock bag, and place them at the back of your refrigerator as a symbol of "cold cash." Make sure that you do the Three Secret Reinforcements as you put them on the shelf. It may sound silly, but this can really change the feel of your fridge. Don't, however, put money in the freezer, since this can lead to "frozen assets"! You can also place this bag, or a red cloth bag with nine coins, in your bread box to signify that you have lots of "bread."

The Dining Table

The dining table, whether located in the kitchen, dining room, or living room, is the center of family life. If there is a problem in a family, the dining table is one of the first places I check. First of all, I check to see if there actually is a dining table. Believe it or not, I have done consultations in homes in which there is no particular place for eating. "Where do you eat?" I ask with a certain degree of trepidation in my voice. "Oh, anywhere," is usually the response. This seems all too common in our modern age.

Families seem to have forgotten the importance of eating meals together. Dinner at 6:00 has been overruled by soccer practice, club meetings, and a bloated workday. In our culture of rapid consumption, we have forgotten what all the consumption is for. It's a mad dash to see how fast we can go, while letting the very fabric of our lives deteriorate in the process.

When I go into a home where the table is missing or is covered in clutter or dust, I also know there is a problem with the finances. Even if the person is single, eating on the sofa, with the television as a dinner companion, is an indication that something is out of balance.

If you live alone and are afraid of feeling lonely, sitting down to a dinner table by yourself is an experience that you may try to avoid. Often, it feels less painful to avoid the experience altogether and squelch the hunger with a quick bite "on the go." If your dining room table is in the Hsun position, it is *essential* that you make it representative of bounty and abundance. A table that looks cold and barren can be covered with a luxurious tablecloth, with a giant bowl of fruit placed in the center. Fresh fruit is best, but even the plastic version can give the sense of abundance. Hanging a large mirror facing the table is very auspicious for wealth, since it doubles the bounty of your table.

Even if you live alone, the way you use your dining table will indicate how you reap the benefits of your money. If you don't like "reaping" alone, invite someone to dinner. There is an old expression: "Poverty is having only one slice of bread. Wealth is having a slice of bread, but having someone to share it with." The feeling of wealth is contagious, and the best way to develop that feeling is to share what you have with someone you love.

If you don't have that person in your life yet, set the table, and he or she will appear! Try putting two placemats, with two full place settings, on the table each day. Light the candles and do the Three Secret Reinforcements for that special person to arrive.

PROSPERITY JOURNAL: "THE WEALTH OF MY KITCHEN"

1. Refer to the three adjectives that you used to describe your essence of wealth, and decide how to bring these qualities into your kitchen and dining area.
2. List the feng shui changes you want to make in your kitchen, and prioritize the top two or three things to do this week.
3. In addition, make a short list of culinary luxuries you would love to have on hand. Then, at some point this week, put at least one of these items on your shopping list, and enjoy!

Bagua Sector of the Week: Dui

All it takes to make a fortune is one great idea—and the conviction to make it available to the world. But thinking is not enough—you need to take your creative ideas and turn them into reality.

Before becoming a feng shui consultant, I worked in theater, and all my years working in theater design showed me that you can make just about anything out of just about nothing. Want to do a show about ancient Egypt, and all you have on hand is a bunch of refrigerator boxes, your grandmother's dining room curtains, and a band of eager actors? No problem! With a little sweat, a dab of elbow grease, and some clever lighting, we can turn those ingredients into a show!

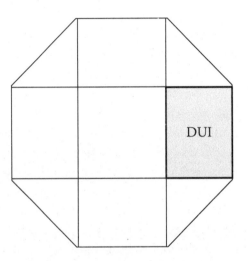

Bagua sector of the week: Dui.

The Dui sector of your home relates to creativity and children. Since raising children is the most creative thing anyone could possibly do, it seems appropriate that these two themes are combined. The term "children" also refers to any creative projects that you are developing.

If your kitchen is in the Dui sector of your home, this can boost your culinary abilities, but there is nothing wrong with creative energy in your living room, or bedroom for that matter. Wherever this sector falls in your home, boost this energy so it feeds the way you produce and invest your money.

If you are having problems with your children, this can be a drain on your energy and your finances. In wanting to provide the best for their kids, parents often get overwhelmed by demands. Help your children to express their own creativity, and teach them to develop financial well-being.

It is appropriate to discuss the Dui sector in the same chapter as the kitchen. People who do not usually consider themselves "creative" are often creating miracles at the stove—no kidding. Need to feed a family of three on a single mother's income? It's possible, with a little ingenious planning. Need a cocktail party for twelve for less than $50? I bet it can be done.

I remember a game show many years ago that offered a group of women the following challenge: produce a dinner for yourself and a date for under $5. And do you know what? They all did it! Unfortunately, one of the guests had to consume dried prunes for dessert, but the point is still made: if you really want to do something, no matter what your budget may be, it's possible.

When you want something, whatever it is, put it on your Prosperity Plan, and find a creative way to get the *essence* of what you want. As an example, let's say I want to go to France this summer. Nothing else matters, as long as I can sit in a café, drink red wine, and watch Paris unroll at my feet. Sounds like a good goal, right? Now, imagine I put it in my budget, and then find I get walloped with a bunch of unexpected expenses that year: my cat needs braces, my houseplants die and need proper burials, that kind of thing. So when July comes around and I'm ready for my trip, I find that I all I have is . . . $10. Yep, you read that correctly—there is only one zero after that digit. What is this forlorn Parisian wannabe supposed to do? Take my trip off the Prosperity Plan and throw those ten bucks into the slush fund? Certainly not.

It is the essence of what we want, and not necessarily the big picture, that is ultimately satisfying. Just getting a taste of what you want is better than going without. So, with that ten-dollar bill in hand, I go on my vacation . . . as far as I can go. Across the street from my apartment, I settle into my neighborhood French restaurant with a glass of house red and Hemingway's stories of Paris in the thirties. True, I didn't get all the way across the Atlantic this time, but I still got to spend an afternoon "away" . . . and that Gallic beauty at the bar may just have an apartment in Paris where I can stay during my *next* trip.

PROSPERITY JOURNAL: "CREATIVITY AND MY CHILDREN"

1. Consider how your experience of creativity and children has felt in your life recently, and put a few notes in your journal.

2. Now, stand in the Dui section on your home, which is at the central right side of the bagua. Next, go into your Beginner's Mind by chanting the Calming Heart

Sutra nine times. Get a feeling for the energy in this part of your home, and write down a few adjectives that describe how this feels to you.

3. Decide how you would like creativity and children to feel in your life, and choose three or four adjectives that describe this feeling.

4. Consider how you can apply these qualities in your Dui area, and put down a few notes.

Feng Shui Applications for Financial Development in Dui

The element that is associated with the creative Dui energy is metal, so anything shiny and bright is going to add to your creative output. Chinese philosophy states that metal produces water (which you can observe when metal pipes "sweat" in the summer), so anything that produces or depicts water, such as a picture of a waterfall or a tabletop fountain, can produce a flow of creative ideas. Metal fountains are especially appropriate here.

Mirrors, which represent the water element, work extremely well in this area, since they multiply your creative options. Metal wind chimes are practically essential in this area, as they ring in the vibration of new creativity.

If you are missing the Dui section in your home, this can adversely affect both your creativity and the well-being of your children. Use large mirrors to compensate or a row of nine faceted crystal globes hung along the inside wall.

The color associated with Dui is white, so this is one place you may want bright white walls, pure white slipcovers, or big bottles of Elmer's glue for all your creative projects!

PROSPERITY JOURNAL: "FENG SHUI FOR DUI"

Review the list of adjectives you chose for your desired essence of Dui, and list two or three ways that you can bring this energy to your life *this week*. See if you can include at least one of the traditional feng shui cures. Be sure to do the Three Secret Reinforcements with every change. If you get creative, the money will follow!

FINANCIAL FENG SHUI—EVALUATING EXPENSES

If you are not sure if you are throwing away your money needlessly, take a look at your spending log after the first month. You now have a report card of the value you are getting for your dollar.

If you have been unwilling to keep track of your expenses during this period, it tells you one thing: you would rather be in denial than admit that you are throwing away your money. If you have been unhappy with money, it's not just because you're not making enough; it's also because you are spending it on things that are not satisfying for you. You can never get enough of what you don't need.

There are two types of valuable expenses: the things we love and the things we need. Sometimes, purchases fit both categories: if you need clothes and you find a suit you love, you've made a valuable purchase.

The things we love are usually luxury items: clothes, vacations, entertainment, and so on. The things we need are necessities—food, a place to live, medical insurance, etc.

If your needs are met, but you lack luxury, your life will feel flat and not worth living. On the other hand, if you surround yourself with extravagances, but ignore your basic needs, you are not going to feel fulfilled. A diet of beans and rice may be healthy, but will it make you happy? At the same time, no one can live on just champagne and caviar.

Seek a balance between your basic needs and the things you love. By combining these two aspects in every way you can, you will build a satisfying life filled with both wonder and security.

Start by reviewing your spending log, and put a series of checks next to each expenditure: one check if you truly need it and one check if it is something you love. What if you need it *and* you love it? Then, put two checks.

Lastly, consider how much you paid. Maybe you did need a new electric toothbrush, but was it really necessary to spend $200? If you got the purchase for the best possible price and could not have gotten it for less without wasting a lot of time, then place another check next to it. I phrase it to myself this way: "Could I have spent significantly less by having an open mind and doing a little legwork?" If not, it was a wise purchase, and it gets another check.

At this point, you may exclaim, "I thought this program was about being wealthy. Why should I pinch pennies with every purchase?" The point is, *yes*, this program *is* about being wealthy, and you are checking to see if your spending patterns are helping or not. If you overspend on junk food, and then can't afford a nice dinner out, you need to take a second look at those expenses.

In the end, you may have a page full of expenses with three checks next to each item: you need it, you love it, and you got the best price for it. If so, congratulations! You are creating a strong sense of value for your dollars, and you are probably fairly happy with your financial situation.

If an item does not have any checks, it obviously should not be repeated. If it gets one check, it also probably doesn't belong in your spending program. Why buy something you need for more than it is worth? In addition, if you love it, but aren't getting it for a good price, that purchase needs to be reconsidered. Overspending is taking money away from better things, like your future.

If an item has two checks, you are headed in the right direction. You might wonder why you are buying things that you don't both love and need at the same time, or which you are still not buying at the best price, but the purchase is probably a good one overall.

Obviously, any purchase with three checks is a perfect buy; you should bring more things like that into your life. It might be the skiing sweater you need for winter, in your favorite color at 50 percent off. Or the lovely dinner you cooked for friends, for less than the cost of one entrée in a restaurant. If it gets three checks, it is a winner!

If your expenses still exceed your plans, you will need to keep reducing the spending. Were these things you needed or loved? If not, they are the first to go. Are you really getting the best price? As you build your ideal future, you do not have money to waste on unnecessary expenses.

If you are still having trouble balancing your Prosperity Plan, you might enlist a supportive friend to help you review your expenses and settle each line item. This may seem like a lot of work, but it is truly the only way to fulfill your dreams.

Tithing to Yourself

Tithing money is traditionally a way to support religious activities. By consistently bequeathing a certain portion of your income, you are ensuring the upkeep of the organization. But if you are not religious in the traditional sense, can you still have a higher purpose for your money?

In the larger scheme of things, nothing is separate from the spiritual nature of life. God is in the details, and anything that brings love and fulfillment into your life is part of your spiritual mission. But how does this influence your use of money?

By applying the concept of tithing, we acknowledge there are things that are important to us, and we commit our finances to supporting this on a consistent basis. Starting this week, make the decision that you will consciously put aside 10 percent of your net income toward those things that you want to have in your life. I call this Tithing to Yourself.

Tithing does not have to be religious to be meaningful and spiritual. If you love baseball, dedicate this money to your love of the game. If you value fine clothing, assign this money to those articles that catch your eye. Make the decision to create your ideal life in a very real, tangible way with tithing. This 10 percent for yourself will directly support your inner self-nature.

If 10 percent seems absolutely impossible right now, it's because you have not created a flow in the direction of your dreams. Review your expenses, and find out where you have been misusing your funds. Five dollars for fast food could instead go toward your tithing sum, and money spent on "just another movie" could be used to change your life.

Right now, while you are thinking about it, define 10 percent of your net weekly salary and put this line item at the *top* of your Prosperity Plan. This allocation directly supports your self-nature, and it should be the first one you pay. Then, figure out how you may need to tuck in any loose ends to make it happen.

If you conscientiously try to allocate the funds and still can't manage it yet, define the exact percentage you can afford (not less than 1 percent, please!), and begin this week. Plan to increase at least 1 percent each month until you have reached your goal. Tithing to yourself is the quickest path to feeling fulfilled, and it will save you a lot of money in the end because you will be directly fulfilling your true desires.

INNER FENG SHUI—CREATING WHAT YOU WANT

We try to impress others by acting as if everything is just fine. The mask of fulfillment goes very deep and is embedded in our culture: "How are you?" "Fine." It is as if we believe that if we are not totally satisfied with our lives, there must be something wrong with us.

Everyone wants and needs something. So why don't we admit it? Unless you are a mystic living in a cave, content with breathing the chi of the mountain air, your state of wanting is probably pretty pronounced. Better you should stand on the mountaintop and exclaim, "I am not satisfied, and there are things I really want in my life," than to retreat into a numb state of benign apathy.

If you purchased this book, you must want something, and I truly doubt that it is just a pile of paper money. Your job is not to figure out how reasonable it is, whether it is the "right thing," or if you are *supposed* to have it. Those questions are not relevant to your journey. Your task is to demand of life what it has planted in your heart and to make sure you find it. Only then will you fulfill your purpose on this planet.

The experience of wanting is energetic and visceral. To some people, it is a "gut feeling"; others "feel it in their bones." In whatever way you connect to yourself, really indulge in this feeling this week, especially as you complete this next assignment.

PROSPERITY JOURNAL: "WHAT I WANT"

Set aside at least three pages in your journal for the things you want. On the first page, write the word "BE." On the second page, write "DO." And on the third page, "HAVE." During this week of the program, record all your wants in each of these areas. Cast your net wide, and do not censor your responses. This is your chance to compile your biggest wish list ever! There will be time to prioritize later.

After you have compiled at least one page for each category, review your lists and consider which items you really want to pursue in the next six months. They do not have to be fully achievable in six months, but should be things in which you will invest your energy in the next 180 days.

If you want to be a rock star, can you see yourself pursuing this in the next few months? If not, perhaps this is something that you should leave for another time. The only question now is what you want to pursue in the next 180 days. No matter how exotic these things may seem, or how deprived your present condition appears, this is your focus.

Now, choose the top ten items from each of your BE, DO, and HAVE lists. These will be your focus goals for the rest of this program—and the months that follow. Lay them out as shown on page 140.

BE

1. _____
2. _____
3. _____
4. _____
5. _____
6. _____
7. _____
8. _____
9. _____
10. _____

DO

1. _____
2. _____
3. _____
4. _____
5. _____
6. _____
7. _____
8. _____
9. _____
10. _____

HAVE

1. _____
2. _____
3. _____
4. _____
5. _____
6. _____
7. _____
8. _____
9. _____
10. _____

The lists make a triangle for a reason: your next step is to draw connections between the items. Literally draw a line on the page between items that can be grouped together. For instance, if you wrote that you want to be a rock star, you want to move to New York, and you want new clothes, think about how you can combine these three desires into one vision. Go on Craigslist and search for New York bands looking for new members. While you are at it, check out the clothing styles popular in those music circles, and fill in your wardrobe with the clothes that fit your vision. Once you define the connections, every item you achieve will take you closer to your desired goal.

Now, assess which three clusters have the most connections, and write the top goals in the diagram below:

BE

_____

_____

_____

VISION

_____

DO   **HAVE**

_____ _____

_____ _____

_____ _____

Play with these pieces until you can create an integrated vision of your dream. Notice how the pieces relate to each other, and get a sense of why you felt they belonged together. Once you have a feeling for this integrated vision, choose a name or title for this meta-cluster. For instance, if you want to be a rock star in New York, you could call that one "New York Rock Star." If you made a connection between meditating every day, organic food, skiing in Colorado, and being financially independent, then you might put "Running a New Age Ski Lodge in Colorado." Here is an example:

BE

Ski bum

Entrepreneur

Enlightened

DO	VISION	HAVE
Ski	*Run an organic, New*	Organic meals
Meditate	*Age ski lodge in Colorado*	Girlfriend
Mountain climb	*with my girlfriend*	Cash in the bank
Travel in Colorado		

Remember, *anything* you do from these lists will take you closer to your central goal. You may not get the whole package in six months, but you can start pursuing your dream right away. If people ask why are you taking an organic cooking class, you can inform them, "I am getting ready to run my ski lodge in Colorado." And when composing your personal ad for the dating site, you'll know exactly what to write: "Seeking adventurous, spiritually minded partner who loves organic food, meditating, and hiking the Rockies." All the pieces form a package we call *You*.

The words "integration" and "integrity" have the same meaning: When you pull the aspects of your desires together, you define your soul on Earth, which is your integrity. By focusing on your Dream Clusters, every step you take draws you closer to your own self-nature. Remember to use your daily tools of affirmation and journal writing to focus on achieving this central vision. In addition, you will now develop one of your strongest inner abilities: visualization.

The Power of Visualization

"A picture is worth a thousand words." You can talk all you want and complain about how awful your life may be, but if you do not have a vision of your desires, you will probably never fulfill them.

There are three aspects to the Three Secret Reinforcements in feng shui. The first uses sound vibration to imprint your intention on the object or "cure." Earlier in the program, we set a procedure for using affirmations to imprint your goal with the power of a chosen phrase.

The second approach uses physical movement to affirm the direction of your desires. With the sacred mudra, you learned to project your chi energy into the ritual objects. You should also be doing one physical activity each day to substantiate the verbal affirmations you are creating.

The final aspect of creation is visualization. This part of the process is the roadmap for transformation. Most of us are trying to drive through life without a map, hoping we will bump into something we want if we just keep pushing the accelerator. Wouldn't it be nice to have a vision of where we're going and how to get there?

Though our needs and fears are similar, everyone is on a different journey, and we must construct our own maps as we go along. Your Dream Clusters establish a vision of what you want, but your work is not over; it has just begun. The visualization process will help you fill out the details of your dreams and organize your success.

Just Imagine . . .

In addition to the few minutes each day you spend with verbal affirmations, devote an additional ten minutes to visualize your dreams. Before you go to sleep each night, or when you have a bit of peaceful time (find some!), close your eyes and check in with your breath. Feel the energy flowing in and out of your lungs like the waves of life, constantly being replenished. This makes me feel relaxed just writing about it.

Now, imagine one object, just one small thing from your big Dream Cluster. Really enjoy your vision of the object: notice how it looks and how it feels to touch it. Does it have a smell, taste, or sound? See yourself using this object the way you want, and feel the satisfaction of having it in your life.

Now, allow the picture to expand a bit, and incorporate the other items from your Dream Cluster. Sense the desired circumstances around you. Where are you, and what are you doing there? Notice how you are dressed and how you behave in this place.

Are there other people in this vision? If so, what are they doing, and how do they respond to you? What do you talk about? Notice who these people are and what you enjoy doing with them.

Now, imagine this scene even better! By expanding it even more, you increase its chances of happening. By aiming just over the top of your dream, you are more apt to hit the bullseye.

Since this book is focused on wealth, you should use all the exercises to bring in more money. Each time you visualize, incorporate positive images of yourself *handling* actual money. Don't just include money in the picture; see yourself using it in important ways. For example, if you want more friends, see yourself buying a round of drinks. If you have been struggling at a low-paying job, see yourself cashing a bigger paycheck each week and getting value from it. In whatever way you envision an ideal life, see yourself blessed with an abundance of financial chi.

At the end of the ten minutes, there is one more essential step in the process: Ask yourself, "What do I need to learn and change about myself, so I can enable this desired life to happen?" We all have behaviors we must change in order to support a new life. Perhaps it is a feng shui adjustment, or maybe just a practical step in the direction of your dreams. Whatever it is, gain insight about this connecting step. Make a mental note, and get ready to receive your new reality.

Then, prepare to let go of the vision. Remember, you should only be doing this exercise for ten minutes each day. Doing it too often, and separating from the world around you, actually reinforces the problem and makes it harder for the new reality to come in.

Use a statement to affirm your new vision of reality. I like to use the following phrase: "This vision that I have just experienced, or something better, now materializes in ways that are totally harmonious to me and all others, for the good of everyone concerned." Imagine releasing this vision to the universe, and allow it to be integrated into the great cosmic scheme in ways that will benefit you.

As you open your eyes, your only responsibility is to go about your life and to look for the seeds of your dreams as they start to emerge. Your positive images will accumulate in the atmosphere, and then, bits and pieces of your dreams will start to rain on your path. Your job will be to pick up the pieces and put them together.

Be spontaneous, and follow your impulses. If you have a sudden desire for Japanese food, follow that clue; it may lead you to your dream. The last time I did that, I started talking to a person who worked in the restaurant, who turned out to be a budding costume designer. I ended up hiring him to do the designs for one of my plays, and he was the best designer I ever had.

The importance of every piece of the puzzle is often not clear until the journey's end. It often takes from three to twenty-seven days for the effects of visualization to manifest. Be patient, and nurture your dreams on a daily basis. You never know where they will lead you.

ACTION STEPS ON THE JOURNEY TO WEALTH:
WEEK 6 SYNOPSIS

This week, we are focused on the kitchen. Get creative and cook up some surprising new opportunities in your life! Check the boxes as you complete the following tasks:

☐ Review your goals for the kitchen, stove, and dining areas, and implement at least two feng shui cures this week.

☐ Review the goals you set for the Dui section of your home, and implement at least two this week.

☐ Get truthful about your spending so far, and rate each expense with one, two, or three checks. Make plans for how you will spend your wealth in the future.

☐ Set aside a physical or virtual place to store your tithe, and begin tithing to yourself this week. Use the money to start funding your new Dream Clusters.

☐ At least three times this week, add ten minutes of visualizing to your daily routine, and be sure to follow each session with a physical affirmation.

WEEK 7

Discovering
Your Mission

Only those who live not for the sake of life
Can know the true value of living.
—The *Tao Te Ching*, Book 75

PRELUDE—THE POWER OF PURPOSE

There are really only two ways to solve your money problems: spend less or make more. Usually, the path to wealth involves both. This chapter is focused on how you can make a contribution in the world and get paid for it. You need to ask yourself very seriously, "How do I want money to come to me?"

Money is given in exchange for what we contribute to the world. If you don't have enough money, you are probably not sharing your abilities to the degree you could. Just as we inhale oxygen and exhale carbon dioxide, money comes into our lives in return for what we express. It's a natural process: I give or do something for you, and in return, you give something to me.

No matter how you arrange the feng shui in your home, you still need to decide how you want the money to come to you. If you say, "I am a nobody, and I don't have anything to give," you are setting yourself up for a life of poverty. If see yourself only as someone who needs a job, of course, you are not going to feel very valuable. But when you consider the importance you could have in the world, and the contributions you might make, your financial potential starts to open up.

ENVIRONMENTAL FENG SHUI—MENTORS, HELPFUL PEOPLE, AND THE BATHROOM

This week, our environmental feng shui will take us into the bathroom and to the bagua area called Chyan. The energy of this gua corresponds to the mentors and "helpful people" in our lives, who are essential for financial growth. The bathroom can also be a place where we are restored and cared for, but it can pose some serious feng shui problems that must be examined.

The Bathroom

The bathroom is symbolic of the way we care for ourselves. But the bathroom also comes with a variety of feng shui problems that are detrimental to your wealth.

In traditional China, the toilet was located in a small building outside the main home. Toilets have an extremely bad reputation in traditional feng shui. Anyone who has visited rural China knows the toilets are easy to find—just follow the overwhelming smell! For some reason, despite the sanctified practice of feng shui, toilet cleanliness was never a major priority in traditional China, so the bathroom was kept separate from the home.

In modern China, the bathrooms are incorporated into the home in typical Western design, but the stigma attached to toilets continues. If you have perused other feng shui books, you may have noticed that terrible luck is associated with the location of the toilet, to a degree that you could become paranoid about having a bathroom in the home at all! Books about traditional feng shui do not keep in mind, however, that a modern bathroom is often the most luxurious room in the house.

Maintaining a luxurious bathroom within the confines of your home is not only acceptable, it can even be a feng shui advantage. It is a symbol of how we appreciate and take care of ourselves. The key issues are how the space is designed and maintained and where it is located in the floor plan.

The Toilet

While the sink and bath should bring fresh flow into the home (beware of faucets that do not work), the energy flow in the toilet quickly goes down the drain. If you have a bathroom located in Hsun, your wealth sector, the problem is obvious. Sinks and bathtubs are bad enough, but a toilet in Hsun—talk about flushing away your wealth! One of the simplest and easiest things you can do is keep the toilet seat lid down (except when you are using it, of course). This is not just proper etiquette—it signifies that the chi is not going down the drain.

Also, keep the bathroom door closed at all times. Initially, this was difficult for me, because I hate approaching a bathroom and not knowing whether it is occupied or not. You can also put a mirror on the outside of the bathroom door to deflect any energy moving toward it. In my former apartment in New York, the bathroom door was directly opposite the front door, which suggests that opportunities that "come knocking" may get flushed away.

The element associated with wealth is wood. If the toilet is located in the Hsun sector, plants are practically mandatory. They will symbolically draw the chi energy into their roots, instead of letting it flush down the drain. Place a leafy plant on the back of the toilet or a hanging plant directly above. If there is inadequate sunlight, use bushy silk plants to represent this important function.

PROSPERITY JOURNAL:
"THE ESSENCE OF WEALTH IN MY BATHROOM"

Since the bathroom is often the most luxurious area in the home, you should definitely apply your three adjectives for wealth in this room. Write a few notes about how you will do this, and note the top feng shui adjustments you would like to make this week.

Dirt

Since the 1960s, we have come to think of dirt as an indication that we are more "natural," more "down-to-earth," more truly ourselves. In reality, the opposite is true. Examine the ways that animals care for themselves and their dwellings. They may live close to the earth, but most species spend a good deal of their time grooming and cleaning themselves. How many birds' nests or beehives have you seen that are filled with clutter?

By fouling our nest, we are acting out a rebellion that started when our parents first told us to clean our rooms. "It's my room," you probably wanted to yell, "and I will keep it any way I want!" Dirt and mess spell freedom, while organization and maintenance reek of primal defeat.

But by cultivating an "I don't care" attitude in our homes, we affect not only our space, but the way we feel about ourselves. In the end, a dirty home reflects anger that we have turned against ourselves.

When I was in college, I worked each summer at a wonderful, liberal summer camp in Vermont. One summer, the director told a story I will always remember. She was very interested in psychology, and she owned a white lab rat. One time, the rat escaped from its cage and was not found for weeks. When the rat was finally discovered, it seemed neurotic and anxious, and was so grimy and blackened with dirt that it was barely recognizable. The rat was returned to its cage, and something very interesting happened. As soon as it settled into its home and started to feel secure again, the rat took the time to thoroughly clean itself and once again regained its shiny white coat.

This lesson has stayed with me: dirt is a sign of insecurity and distress. When feeling good, one of the first things you may want to do is clean your space, so it reflects your positive energy. Just like the lost lab rat, our dirt is a sign of anguish. Unlike the rat, we are able to create a sense of safety anytime we want.

Bagua Sector of the Week: Chyan

If you don't feel supported in your career, you are having a problem with Chyan, the mentor section in your space.

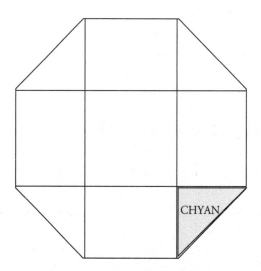

Bagua sector of the week: Chyan.

Located on the front line of the floor plan, in the bottom right-hand area, Chyan represents the energy of all helpful people in our lives. It is no accident that this section of the bagua is directly opposite Hsun, the area related to prosperity. The accumulation of wealth depends upon good teachers and mentors.

The Chyan position is also associated with travel, since we all need help when venturing into foreign territories. If you travel a lot for business and rely on this for your money, it is especially important that you cultivate the energy in this sector of your home.

The element associated with Chyan is metal. This represents the tenacity of support we need in our lives. The expression "a will of iron" is associated with this gua, and it's no mistake that our financial support comes as metal coins stamped with the faces of our country's leaders.

PROSPERITY JOURNAL: "HELPFUL INFLUENCES"

1. Write a few notes to describe how the mentors and helpful people have been in your life. You may want to include how you feel about traveling and how other people have influenced your experience of these trips.

2. Now, go to the Chyan corner of your home, which is at the bottom right of the bagua, and get a sense of how this area feels right now. Write a few words to describe this energy. Compare these conditions with the way helpful people have been in your life so far.

3. Consider how you would like your experience of mentors and helpful people to be in your life, and put a few notes in your journal. You can refer to this when you are creating the right vibration in this area of your home.

Feng Shui Applications for Financial Development in Chyan

Because Chyan is associated with metal, this is the perfect location for the kitchen, garage, or tool shed, where you can proudly display your shiny metal tools, pots, pans, or luxury vehicle. In the living room or bedroom, you might favor chrome furniture, brass lamps, or your shiny bowling trophies.

When I was living in New York, I was actually missing the Chyan section in my apartment, so I decided to "wallpaper" the inside of two closets with aluminum foil (no kidding), and the results were amazing. I then became truly blessed with wonderful teachers and mentors in my life.

Metal wind chimes are always good for sparking Chyan energy, as are bells attached to moving doors. Mirrors are also especially auspicious in Chyan, since metal "produces" water. Try to avoid the color red and anything associated with fire in this sector, since fire melts metal.

The color associated with Chyan is gray, like the color of pewter, but you can also use a combination of white and black, since these colors are on either side of this sector. Black-and-white photographs are perfect, especially if they are of your favorite teachers, supporters, and historical figures. Books by favorite scholars are also appropriate. You should definitely plan to hang your bagua of Your Sacred Circle, described later in this chapter, somewhere in this sector, and empower it to feed you advice at times when you need it most.

Because of the association with travel, you can store your luggage, maps, and raincoats in this area. Decorating the walls with travel photos and maps will give the perfect tone for the Chyan energy in your life.

If you are missing any parts of the Chyan position in your home, you are welcome to try my aluminum foil trick. Large mirrors, or nine crystals hung in a row along the walls, will also work.

PROSPERITY JOURNAL: "THE FENG SHUI OF CHYAN"

Review the adjectives you chose for the Chyan area of your life, and make a list of two or three things you can do this week to manifest the desired feeling in this sector of your home. Try to include at least one of the traditional feng shui cures, and don't forget to do the Three Secret Reinforcements every time you make a change.

Speaking of Helpful People . . . Get a Maid!

The more you give to the world, the more you need the assistance of mentors and helpful people. This week, start putting some important support systems in place.

Most people wouldn't dream of baking all their own bread or of making soups from scratch. It takes a lot of energy, when it is just as easy to pick it up from the store, ready-made. The same is true for housecleaning. Sure, you could probably scrub your own floors, polish the furniture, and even do the windows, if you really wanted—but do you? If not, it's time to enlist some help.

Even in the "olden days," when women were expected to keep up the home, few wives did all the tasks themselves. Hired help was a common fixture in many households, and extended families worked together. In modern society, with most women commuting to demanding full-time jobs, hiring help for the home is not a luxury—it is a requirement.

It is amazing, really: We may pay between 20 and 50 percent of our income for our homes, and then might balk at an (extra) fee for a cleaner to keep it livable. Taking care of a home is, at least, a part-time job. If you are working full-time and want to increase your income even more, you need to delegate some of the work.

I know that all married women are going to highlight this section and force their spouses to read it!

How do you feel when you walk into a home that is bright, shiny, and crystal clean? I feel energized and excited and ready to do something productive with my time. As you take better care of your space, it will affect your energy and your life in ways that you haven't yet imagined.

The Still Water Cure

If you are feeling lost and overwhelmed with your professional life, this ancient ritual will help you find a new direction. It takes at least thirty-six days to fulfill the sequence, but the results of this transcendental cure can be illuminating. To perform the ritual, you will need the following materials:

1. A round mirror, three inches in diameter
2. A new, white handkerchief
3. Access to the outdoors, or at least an open window, each night before you go to sleep

This cure is done for a total of thirty-six days. It is best initiated on an auspicious day, which is determined by checking *The Classic Chinese Almanac*, referenced in appendix D, Bibliography.

On the night you begin the ritual, gather the mirror and the handkerchief and chant the Calming Heart Sutra nine times. To further empower yourself before initiating the cure, you may want to "borrow the Buddha's chi," the meditation that is taught in week 5.

Take the mirror in one hand, and with the other, wipe the mirror nine times in a clockwise direction to clear any old energy. Men should use the left hand to wipe the mirror, and women the right hand.

Perform the Three Secret Reinforcements and empower the mirror with the mission of providing you with a clear vision for a happy future. If there are any unresolved questions that you have about your career, set the intention that these will be answered in the course of this ritual.

Place the mirror face up between your mattress and box spring/bed frame, in the area where you lay your head, and leave it there for nine days. During this time, imagine that the mirror is absorbing the chi of your dreams and integrating them into a new life vision.

After nine days, take out the mirror before you go to sleep, and wipe the mirror nine times in a clockwise direction to clear any stagnant chi. Take the mirror outdoors, or at least extend it out an open window, and expose it to the sky. Imagine the mirror is soaking up the energy of the moon and mixing it with your own chi. As you do this, you should say a prayer something like this: "I extend this mirror to the sky and ask that the Great Universal Being illuminate the path of my career, for the greatest fulfillment of myself and all others." Format the prayer according to your personal religious orientation.

After completing the prayer, return to your bedside, and this time, put the mirror under the mattress at the foot of your bed, where your feet generally rest. From this position, the mirror will start to illuminate the path under your feet and lead you in the right direction.

For a total of twenty-seven nights, take out the mirror each night, wipe it nine times, expose it to the sky, and ask that your path be revealed to you. After it has been under your feet for twenty-seven days, you can either leave it under your mattress or wrap it in the white cloth and store it in the self-knowledge corner of your bedroom. The mirror should not be used for any other purpose once it has been used for this ritual.

If you forget to do the ritual one night, you will need to start the process again—from the beginning. So, write yourself a note! Part of the benefit of this process is learning to commit solidly to something for thirty-six days. Once you master this, undertaking the path of success will seem that much easier!

The first time I tried this ritual, I would get to the tenth or eleventh day and then forget to do it. I had to restart a number of times, until finally I made it to the end of the cycle. I even took the mirror with me on vacation, so I could complete the ritual. And then, on the twenty-seventh day, the mirror broke! In feng shui, if something breaks, it just means it absorbed a lot of negative chi, which had to be released. So, with that, I had to start all over again.

FINANCIAL FENG SHUI—YOUR FINANCIAL KARMA

When you hear the word "karma," you may think of reincarnation; some people believe that if you are facing hard times now, it must because you did something really awful to someone in a distant lifetime.

From my perspective, karma is not fixed punishment for unknown past deeds. It is a fluid relationship between the energy that you put out in the world and the energy that comes back. It is a basic spiritual principle: "What you reap is what you sow." How you act toward others becomes the standard for how they treat you. This makes you stop and think, doesn't it? At least, it should!

Discovering Your Mission

Everything that happens to you has seeds in your own behavior. If there is anything in your life that is displeasing you, ask yourself, "In what way am I doing this to others?" This puts the mettle in the Golden Rule, "Do unto others as you would have them do unto you." Until you clean the ill will from your own system, how can you expect others to do the same?

Since money represents our energy in the world, financial karma is simply the way we give and receive energy. As the tide goes out, so it comes back in. When you understand this basic principle, there is really no mystery to life. You can literally predict what is going to happen to you, based on the energy that you are putting out.

This principle became agonizingly clear to me recently. I had a situation in which a corporate client owed me a sizeable payment. I called, sent emails, and felt so frustrated that I even considered legal action, but nothing happened. I would rant and rave to my friends about how angry I was, but I did not know what to do.

After I got off my pedestal, I considered the law of karma. I explored how this could be a reflection of the energy I was giving out. Even if the error of my ways was only 1 percent as negative as that of the company, I had to be doing something to incite this event. And sure enough, I was.

I realized that I had been putting off filing some insurance claims for a therapy client, and he must have felt I was withholding my help. In addition, I had become nonchalant with some of my utility bills and would sometimes toss them in a drawer until receiving a reminder. Was I innocent of withholding energy and payments? No way! This incident with the company was simply reminding me how bad it feels to be on the receiving end. Life is educational; it treats us to the error, or benefit, of our ways.

If you are not making enough money to support your dreams, it is because you are withholding your contributions in the world. That's it, pure and simple. There is no need to feel sorry for yourself or to see yourself as the victim of the economy. Every time you have financial difficulties, ask yourself, "In what way am I withholding my gifts?" There will always be an answer.

Please note that money is a reflection of the *quality* of the energy that you are putting out. You may be working hard, but are you giving from the deepest parts of yourself? Are you tapping into your unique talents and giving what is most special about your contributions? If not, the money that comes to you will not be very deep. A "job" is never going to make you enough money, no matter how hard you work; your career will.

In an even bigger picture, the law of karma takes another turn, so get ready. The way others treat you is also a reflection of the way that you treat *yourself.* Our self-care sets the standard for how others perceive and behave toward us. This is why clothing is very important: it represents how we value ourselves and what sort of treatment we expect.

Looking again at the problem with my corporate client, I asked myself: in what way was I withholding from myself? The answer, sorely, was across the board. The way I was rushing through life, not listening to my needs, sleeping too little, eating too fast, not respecting my feelings . . . this had become a theme in my daily life. No wonder I was so irritated by this company's withholding; it was a sore reminder of how I treated myself!

If you want to develop good karma, start with yourself. Look seriously at the way that you treat your life energy. Then, you can start to understand why you treat others the way that you do and why they respond to you in kind. You can always find someone to mirror your behavior. The only question now is what you want that reflection to look like.

PROSPERITY JOURNAL: "MY KARMA"

Examine a few incidents in your life that are bothering you, and choose one as the focus for this exercise. Consider your energetic role in the dilemma with the following questions:

1. How is someone treating me in a way I do not like?
2. In what way have I been doing this to others?
3. In what way am I doing this to myself?

Now, choose one way that you can clean up your karma with this situation.

The Tao of Money: Giving and Receiving

In feng shui, money is a spiritual issue, and the exchange of it is considered a sacred ritual. Every time we give or receive money, we create a flow of energy in the universe that can affect the rest of the world.

The next time you buy something, notice how you feel about making the payment. Do you give freely, with pleasure in contributing to the person or company? Or do you do it because it is expected of you and because you would be arrested if you walked off without paying? Some people, when getting the bill at a restaurant, will inquire, "What's the damage?" Imagine how this mindset affects their attitudes about money!

If you do not agree with a company or its product, you have an *obligation* not to support it financially. Money is empowerment, and every dollar spent promotes the person's influence in the world. This is part of embracing your financial integrity.

Likewise, if there is a company or organization that is doing work that you value, you have an obligation to dedicate your money to its activities. It doesn't matter if the organization is feeding the homeless or producing your favorite video game; if you really believe in what they are doing, it is your right and responsibility to show your support. This is capitalism at its best: letting people vote, with their money, for the goods and services that they value most.

From this perspective, every purchase is a spiritual "tithe." When you pay your electric bill, you are "tithing" to the people who bring light and warmth into the world. Do they make the world a better place to live? I think so. But if you disagree, it is your responsibility not to support them—not by withholding payments, but by seeking other options that seem preferable to you.

This same principle applies to the work you do for others. If you believe it is valuable, you have a spiritual responsibility to be paid at a level commensurate with its importance. If you do not charge adequately, you not only undermine the support you receive, you devalue the perception of that work in the world. It is not "being generous" or spiritual to consistently undervalue yourself and the work you deliver.

When you start to see the exchange of money as a series of contributions, not obligations, you release yourself from poverty consciousness. Recognize yourself as an important investor in the company, not just a harried bill payer. Without people like you, these products and services would not exist at all.

Red Envelopes

Originally, feng shui masters did not set a fee for their services. They expected the client to assess the importance of the work and to bestow a donation that was appropriate. In modern times, however, we have become disconnected from our true sense of value. We haggle and moan about prices, instead of esteeming each product and service for the contribution it brings us. For this reason, feng shui consultants now need to set a standard fee!

Whenever we break the *Tao* cycle of giving and receiving—by trying to give without receiving or taking without giving—we disrupt the natural flow of life and create an imbalance. For this reason, feng shui consultants are required to charge for their services; if there is no payment for the session, it is considered very bad luck. Even if the session is for a friend or family member (which is usually not a good idea, anyway), there has to be some sort of formal exchange, usually in the form of money.

Clients usually make the payment in cash, because the energetic association with cash is much stronger than a check. With a check, you are giving a voucher that can be exchanged for money, but it is not money itself.

The payment for a session is traditionally presented in one or more envelopes that are red in color. In Chinese culture, these envelopes are often used at the New Year for gifts of money. By placing money in red envelopes, you seal the sacred quality of the payment. The client divides the money among one or more envelopes, often according to the number of issues that were addressed by the session, or perhaps by the number of rooms that were evaluated. Often, people like to give red envelopes in quantities of nine, which is the number of wholeness: nine, eighteen, twenty-seven, and so forth.

Many consultants do one more step at the end of the day to take in the energy of the money. Before going to sleep, a feng shui practitioner might take all of the red envelopes received that day and place them under the pillow for the night. In this way, the energy of the money is absorbed while sleeping. Then, in the morning, the consultant can take the money to the bank and make a deposit, or use it for purchases.

I like to accumulate all of the red envelopes that I receive during the year and collect them in a special area of my desk. Then, at the Chinese New Year, I burn the envelopes and release the old energy into the universe, creating the space for new clients—and new wealth—to come into my life.

The Sacred Exchange of Money

Consider bringing the philosophy and practice of the Chinese red envelopes into your financial life. The sacred exchange of money should not be limited to feng shui consultations. To begin, consider paying only in cash during the last three weeks of this program, and perhaps beyond that point. Paying every transaction in cash does two things: it reminds us of the value that we are exchanging, and it prevents us from buying on credit.

When you write a check or use a credit or debit card, the cost of an item becomes blurred. The only difference between writing a check for $10 and one for $100 is the speck of a decimal point, and we tend to forget how much the transaction is for. When you take the bills from your wallet, count them, and physically hand them to another person, the value of the transaction is clear, and it makes you think twice.

Paying in cash is not easy. On a practical level, it involves trips to the bank, displaying money in public, and having to deal with change. On a psychological level, it makes us confront our feelings about money. It's a lot easier to be in denial about your money when you don't have to look at it.

Paying in cash forces us to "pay as we go." No more bounced checks, no interest accrued on credit cards, and no questions about what we are spending. It's all right there, in green and white (or in a variety of colors, if you live abroad!)

'Tis Better to Give *and* Receive

When you give, do it consciously and with conviction. Visualize the money going directly to the recipient's benefit. If the payment is to a company, visualize people in the organization prospering directly from your money.

Make each payment as a blessing, and notice how this affects the way you feel about money. You might even do the Three Secret Reinforcements on your payments. Here is a blessing I like to use: "I offer you this money with gratitude. May it bring you many benefits." Try saying this, at least in your mind, every time you offer a payment.

When you receive a payment, take in the blessing. With each payment, you can say, "I receive this money with gratitude, that it may bring me many benefits." This blessing has completely changed my feelings about money.

Since people are often paid by check, bank transfer, online banking, or direct deposit, we become disconnected from the cycle of financial giving and receiving. When it is payday, you might choose to withdraw the cash that you receive and follow some sort of ritual to denote its acceptance. Hold the cash equivalent of your paycheck in your hands, and say a blessing over it. You may want to place the sum in a red envelope (hopefully a *large* red envelope!) and place the envelope under your pillow to absorb the energy. If anything could make you feel more prosperous about your job, this should do it.

Nourishing the Ones Who Feed Us

By tithing 10 percent to yourself, you can begin manifesting your ideal life right away. Taking yourself on weekly Prosperity Dates also creates momentum for this to happen. Have you been doing this? If not, ask yourself why you would starve your dreams, just when they are most important. The path to greater wealth is only going to happen when you take a weekly stand for what you want.

There is one more area of tithing to suggest, which supports the spiritual mentors in your life. Each week, as you assess your income, no matter how large or small, put aside at least 1 percent to give freely to the person or organization that is your "spiritual food." This does not need to go to a religious person, and even if you are already tithing to a church or other organization, consider this as a separate blessing, and be very specific about its destination. It doesn't have to be a large amount of money to be important.

To sanctify this blessing, put the bill(s) in one or more red envelopes, and attach a note that explains its purpose. You might write something like this:

> Dear _____,
>
> I want to thank you for the positive ways you contribute to my life. Your influence is spiritual food to me. I am enclosing a few Chinese red envelopes, which are a traditional way to extend appreciation. I hope this brings you health, prosperity, and happiness, just as you have done for me.

You can sign the note, or send it anonymously. Do the Three Secret Reinforcements on the envelopes before sending them or delivering them in person.

Because money represents pure energy, it is generally preferred for tithing. You can, however, decide how you want to communicate your blessings. You might tithe material gifts in some form, but also examine why you may be shy about giving money. The law of karma says that you will get back what you give. Money begets money; chocolates and flowers attract the same!

Helpers Anonymous

If you really want to bring joy into your life, try this experiment: every day, find a small way to do something positive for another person. It can be for someone you know or for a complete stranger, but the offering must be made freely and without any strings attached. And it must be anonymous!

Just a simple deed can brighten someone's day. It doesn't have to be expensive or cost any money at all. But if the person finds out who did it, you need to do another good deed that day.

There are lots of fun ways you can touch a person's life. One man regularly paid for the car behind him whenever he went through a tollbooth. When I was in college, I left a message on the bulletin board of my Hall Monitor that said, "Thank you for what you said yesterday—it really made a difference!" I scribbled the signature so he would not know who wrote it—and I know that he walked around with a smile on his face all day, knowing that he had helped someone.

Bit by bit, day by day, you can make the world a better place to live by giving freely of yourself. Recognize your true nature as a source of joy. Start today, and by the end of this program, you will have an entirely different outlook on the impact of your energy.

INNER FENG SHUI—EXPOSING YOUR GIFTS TO THE WORLD

The reason we hold back in our careers is not because we have nothing to offer, but because we are probably afraid to expose our real talents to the world. Ideally, our unique gifts would have been celebrated by our family, friends, and teachers as we were growing up, but this is too rarely the case. Most of us had to fight for our self-expression, and after years of criticism and humiliation, we became resentful, withdrawn, apathetic, and cold. And, oh yes, impoverished.

I am thinking now of Nancy, a very talented artist who suffers from the identity cloak of "the struggling artist." She gets tremendous acclaim for the originality of her work, but she never seems to sell many pieces or get any energy back for the work that she does.

Talking with Nancy revealed that she has two negative forces working against her. First, she feels very scared of criticism and hesitates to really get her work out there. The child of critical and even competitive parents, she learned to keep her gifts to herself. By avoiding public feedback, she is preventing her work from moving to the next level.

The second negative force in Nancy's professional life is her desire to feel "special." In the face of negative parents, and the resulting difficulty in making friends, Nancy tries to use her artwork to put herself on an emotional and spiritual pedestal. Her talents reign supreme . . . as long as she keeps them to herself.

The key to Nancy's prosperity is the realization that she may be special, but she is not that different from everyone else in the world. She has talents, but she also has needs like everyone else and is just as vulnerable as the real estate agent who needs to fill a quota or the baker responsible for delivering fresh bread. Nancy's gift is her artwork, and her responsibility is to bring it to the world in every way that she can.

Just as our bodies need a certain number of breaths every day, the financial world requires that we make certain contributions in exchange for our livelihood. If you are having money problems, one thing is certain: you are withholding your gifts. And anything you withhold will be reflected in your bank accounts.

Your Unique Talents

"But wait a second," you may cry, "I really don't feel valuable, and I don't know what I want to become!" And my answer to that: "I am not convinced." And do you know why? Because I've been there—taken stupid jobs and told everyone, "I still don't know what I want to be when I grow up." But please note, this is not a question about what you want to be, this is a question about what contributions you would enjoy making. Ease off on the self-definition; you are already who you are. The questions now are about what you like to do and whether you believe it's important.

"But what if I just want to stay home and bake cookies?" Talk to Famous Amos, the guy who made a fortune off his cookie recipes. Ice cream? Ben and Jerry. Funky clothes? Norma Kamali. They all did what they loved and what they considered exciting. What's the world without a great cookie? A sorrier place to live, in my opinion. No one is asking you to save the world—the world is just asking you to do your thing, whatever that is. Your job is to fulfill your small part of the whole.

In our heart of hearts, each of us is a uniquely special human being, with a gift or talent that is uniquely our own. This is not just a pleasant New Age thought—it's the foundation of good business. People work better when they like what they are doing. What you like to do is what you should be doing. I believe that God made sex enjoyable so that we would produce children without having to be reminded! It is the same with your contribution to the world: if you love doing it, you have found your calling.

What is it about *you* that you feel is important? Maybe you really love working with children. Do you believe that's important? Probably so. Do others believe that it's important? Maybe, maybe not. But if you really believe in it, and want others to share your enthusiasm, I am sure that you will find a way to communicate your inspiration.

If your plan for making a fortune rests on a lottery ticket, it's like you are saying, "My only important talent is in buying tickets. That is really all there is of me." If you believe that's true, I feel sad just thinking about it. And I don't believe you. Because if you had the gumption to buy this book, and the tenacity to read this far, I feel sure there is more to you than just being a ticket buyer. At least you're a book buyer, and that's an upgrade, in my opinion! Perhaps this is why you haven't made a fortune with the lottery yet; the universe is trying to remind you that you have more important work to do.

So how do you know if you are doing the right work? Well, ask yourself, "Is the work important to me?" If you answer "yes," you are in a good profession. It's that simple. Then ask, "Is it fun?" If you feel your work is important, but it's not fun, maybe you are doing the right work but not doing it the right way. Experiment: how can you make it fun for yourself? In this way, you bring *more* of your unique self into the work, and uniqueness just makes you more interesting in the market-place, leading to bigger profits.

Before you set off into the woods for thirty days to find your unique talent, I have an easier path: go back to chapter 6, and review your Dream Clusters. In particular, look at the things that you said that you want to *do*. Ask yourself, "Which of these things would I enjoy doing on at least a part-time basis in exchange for money?"

Volunteering is not enough; we are looking for your dream *job*. The answer is probably sitting there in the middle of your primary cluster. If not, go over your lists more closely. With a bit of creative strategizing, I am sure that you can find at least one thing that you would enjoy doing, for which people would be willing to pay.

Ideally, you should be looking for not just one thing you want to do, but two or three. When you combine your interests, your uniqueness puts you at the head of the pack. For example, feng shui is an amalgamation of my background in psychotherapy, design, and spirituality. When I first started studying feng shui, it made sense to me right away. When I added my interest in writing, this book became a natural next step.

In the space below, list three of your top interests that you would like to pursue professionally in the next six months. Consider how you might combine them into one unique career. For instance, if you love photography, working with ani-mals, and designing clothing, you could make T-shirts with pictures of people's pets. That's an original idea. Or you could make goofy holiday costumes for pets and sell their photos. Once again, an original idea that sets you apart from the pack. Try this below:

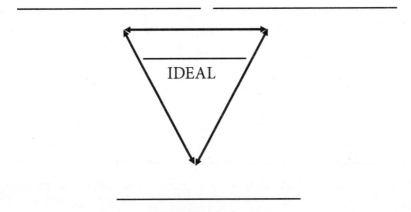

Creating the ideal career.

I know one woman who is a teacher, and in her spare time, she loves doing theater and baking. Her unique talent, she has learned, is baking special cakes and providing entertainment for children's birthday parties. There is a huge demand for this service, and she is on her way to a great career. I know another person who loves travel, writing, and teaching in small groups. She is now a famous writer who lectures on the cruise ship circuit. Define *your* unique talent, and get it out to the world. It's time to make some money!

Your Sacred Circle

Most of us learned, like our artist friend Nancy, to shut down our talents to protect ourselves. In the fragile periods of our youth, we either kept our gifts to ourselves or got ripped to shreds.

Unfortunately, there are people in this world who derive pleasure from tearing other people to bits. Frustrated with their own talents, they try to gain solace by preventing others from treading where they are afraid to go. It is a sad, destructive dance without a happy ending.

The way out is not to hide, but to disown any obligation to these critics. There will always be critics, just as there will always be viruses in the air. The key to staying healthy is not to stop breathing, but to fortify ourselves from minor attacks.

There is not a single great artist who has not been criticized or condemned by her peers, just as there is probably no political figure who has received 100 percent of the votes. Learn to see your mission as more sacred than the critics could ever understand.

As you develop your professional gifts and present them in the marketplace, you must surround yourself with a circle of well-wishers who only see the merits and importance of your work. If your associates do not see the value of your work, even before you can prove it with financial returns, they do not belong in your inner circle. It doesn't matter if they have positive intentions, if they mean well. Anyone who does not *automatically* see the value and importance of your work does not deserve to have an influence in the tender, formative stages of your development.

Your success is not strengthened by or dependent upon naysayers and critical "friends." If you truly respect your gifts and your life mission, you will only seek support from those people who want to give it.

In feng shui, we often place a wooden version of the bagua on our front door to deflect negative energy and protect the interior of our homes. On a metaphorical level, you need to do the same thing with your inner world. In the outline of the bagua below, there is an inner space and an outer space. Inside the bagua, write the names of the people you can really trust to give you unconditional support for the work you want do, even if you are not sure what it is! Then, outside the bagua, write the names of the people who have been critical in word or action and who cannot be trusted to be positive influences in your professional development.

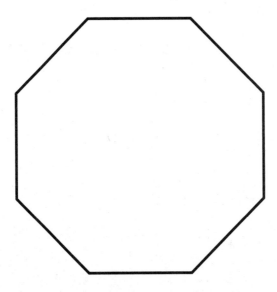

Bagua of your Inner Circle.

If you find that the inner portion of your bagua is vacant or sparse, remember that this is a reflection of the people you have drawn into your life so far. Now that you are more conscious about your needs, you can seek support more judiciously.

Prosperity Dates: Millionaire for the Day

Christmas may come but once a year, but the experience of prosperity should be part of your life all the time. In the last chapter, you learned how to define what you want and visualize it as your reality. Now, it's time for you to live it!

Once a week, for at least one hour, you will be going out in the field and living your dream life. This does not have to cost a lot of money, but it does require a bit of diligence and ingenuity. Just go to your Dream

Clusters, and ask yourself which aspect you want most to pursue. If you feel unsure, you can put this question into your daily meditation: "What would make me feel really wealthy this week?" Think about it, and explore it in your Prosperity Journal. Make sure that you come up with a definite idea, no matter how extreme or wacky. Then, think of a way to get as close to this goal as possible. Remember, getting 1 percent of your dream is the only way you are going to get 2 percent, and 3 percent, and more.

If your answer is "scuba diving," find a way to pursue it, to any degree you can. Even if you live in the frozen fields of Idaho, there must be *some way* that you can get one iota closer to your dream. Humor yourself: as you go about your week, consider the various ways that you could make that dream a reality. If you can hop a plane for Belize and get the real thing, more power to you! But if funds are just a bit limited this week, you need to develop further options. The goal is not to duplicate the full package, but to aspire to its essence.

Ask yourself a key question: What does a scuba diving adventure really mean to you? Is it the undersea exploration, swimming in warm water, margaritas on the beach, or showing off your new tan? Whatever it is, take note of the specific aspect that intrigues that millionaire in your heart, and figure out ways to pursue it now.

If it really is the tropical fish that excite you, perhaps you can take a trip to a nearby aquarium or buy a starter set at the local pet store. If it's the feel of warm tropical water you desire, search out a hot tub for an afternoon, or at least invest in some tropical-smelling bubble bath, for an afternoon soak with a South Seas romance novel. Remember, your inner millionaire is connected to your inner child. The final package is not as important as the essence of the adventure and the spirit with which you enjoy it.

For an hour or more each week, these Prosperity Dates should become regular events. Once you begin, you will start finding options in your local area to take you closer to your dreams. This weekly exercise will open your eyes to the abundance that, heretofore, you had been ignoring.

Oh, and one other thing. There is another requirement: you need to do these Prosperity Dates *alone*. That's right, just you with you. This rule is not meant to support the image that wealthy people are reclusive loners; rather, it's an appeal for you to build a relationship with your inner self. When you first start connecting to this side of yourself, it may seem vague and hard to find; that's because this part of you feels very vulnerable and afraid of criticism. If you make your Prosperity Dates contingent upon the agreement of another person, you may scare your inner self into the usual defenses of inhibition, false agreement, or bipartisan behavior.

Discovering Your Mission

A wealthy person needs to know what they want and be willing to expand their own frontiers. Here is your chance.

Whenever I teach this exercise, I find it is the hardest thing to get people to do. Adults are willing, and often eager, to subject themselves to endless personality tests, drills, and note taking, but when assigned the task of doing one fun thing a week, it's like inviting them for gum surgery. I've heard every excuse in the book: "I didn't feel well this week," "I was too tired," "I can't afford to do what I want," or our all-time favorite, "I DON'T HAVE THE TIME!"

If your dreams are falling prey to any of these insipid excuses, use the exercises in this book to get yourself on track. Tithe some money to yourself (ten dollars is often enough), cross at least one hour off your schedule, and get out of your own way. If you can't find a single hour a week to indulge your dreams, how on earth do you think you will shift your present reality into the one that you want? By embodying your inner millionaire for one hour a week, you will start to feel that way every day. But you have to start somewhere. So start.

Oh, and one more rule: Before you come back from your Prosperity Date, make sure that you pick up a souvenir to place on your Prosperity Altar at home, to remind you of your excursion and the experiences you enjoyed. You do not need to spend any money for a souvenir: it can be a ticket stub, a flyer, anything you like. Put them all on a piece of poster board, and hang them in the Hsun section of your home, bedroom, living room, or kitchen. If you have a family, perhaps each member would like to develop a display for the altar. Who knows: this week, the aquarium; next year, the Great Barrier Reef! This altar is a wonderful reminder of the progress that you are making toward your dreams.

ACTION STEPS ON THE JOURNEY TO WEALTH:
WEEK 7 SYNOPSIS

This chapter is a turning point in your journey to wealth. You might start to see that you are not a victim of circumstances, but a powerful messenger of universal energy with a mission to fulfill. What you want to do is what you are supposed to do. Check the boxes as you complete these tasks:

☐ Review the feng shui changes you would like to make in the bathroom, and do two this week.

☐ Review the goals you set for the Chyan section of your home, and implement at least two this week.

☐ Get a cleaning service. You won't regret it.

☐ The Still Water Cure: This is a long-term ritual. You don't need to do it this week, but do it when you can devote the focus to bringing in new opportunities.

☐ Purchase some red envelopes, and practice giving your gifts as a sacred exchange.

☐ Develop a benediction that works for you when you give and receive money, and practice this form of sacred exchange.

☐ Put aside at least 1 percent for your spiritual food, and offer it in red envelopes to those who deserve your gratitude.

☐ Join "Helpers Anonymous": Give, but give unnoticed. Find out how this can make your life blossom with excitement and promise!

☐ Develop your Sacred Circle diagram, and connect to the people who are central to your support.

☐ Okay, millionaire in the making—it's time for a vacation. Choose your destination, and take yourself on a Prosperity Date this week. Be sure to pick up a souvenir for your altar!

Getting Down to Business

With love, you become fearless.
With frugality, you become prosperous.
With humility, you become a leader in all affairs.
—The *Tao Te Ching*, Book 67

PRELUDE—MONEY MANAGEMENT

Building a dream life is not just about creating more recreation and glamour; it is about how you are going to participate in the world. There are few wealthy people who do not have a profession of one type or another. The important question now: what is your profession going to be?

It's time to get down to business. Whether you are aware of it or not, your life is a business, and your wealth depends on how well you are running it. Don't make the mistake of thinking you are working for anyone but yourself. Even the president of the United States is only in office for a maximum of eight years!

You might think being wealthy means that you don't have to think about your finances. But money is like any-  thing else in life: if you want to enjoy it, you need to take care of it. By deciding you want to be wealthy, you are hanging out your shingle and declaring you are "in business."

There are two common features I have observed about wealthy people. The first is that they care about every expense. Every single one. They take each expense personally and will fight for what they want. The second is that they enjoy managing money. If they didn't, they wouldn't spend so much time and energy with it.

When I was an acting teacher in New York, I was constantly confronted by young, talented actors who wanted to get into "the business." They would often ask if I thought they could "make it" as an actor, and I always had the same response: "If you love the *business* of acting, and truly enjoy making the rounds, you are going to make it. But if you don't like the business, you are going to fall out. It doesn't matter if you are talented, or good-looking, or even have an impressive résumé. If you don't love the business, you're not going to make it."

The same is true with wealth. If you love managing money and want to invest your time and energy into its care every day, you will become wealthy. But if you don't, your financial life will be limited. The dollars can't take care of themselves, and in the end, no one can do it for you but you.

Sure, you can hire accountants, stockbrokers, financial planners, and lawyers to care for your riches, and these helpers may be essential at some point, but if you are not the ultimate authority with your money, you will ultimately lose it. This is the sad story of too many rock stars, actors, and athletes who turned their financial futures over to "experts" and then lost everything.

You can affirm that you are serious about your money by finding a place in your home to dedicate to its purposes. The only tools you need are a calculator, notebooks for expenses, a calendar for noting payments due, and files for your papers. It's good to have a desk that can be "command central," but if one is not available, keep your tools on a shelf, and use a table when you sit down to work with your accounts.

The other tool you need is time. How much of your daily life are you willing to dedicate to the management of your wealth? Your financial condition reflects the time and energy you put into it. It's amazing—people may spend hours each day at the gym, but don't give a moment's attention to the financial energy fueling their life. Having a great body is one thing, but remember, being wealthy is sexy!

Finally, adopt your Beginner's Mind, and consider how much you really know about financial planning and investment. This program is just the beginning of your journey, and no single book can teach you everything you need you need to know about saving, investing, and financial planning. This is a lifelong learning process for building a life you love. With Beginner's Mind, anything is possible. Admit what you don't know, and take steps to fill in the gaps.

ENVIRONMENTAL FENG SHUI—FENG SHUI FOR THE OFFICE

In today's fluid business environment of virtual meetings and mobile communication, the stationary office building is becoming a thing of the past. Boundaries between "work" and "life" are getting blurrier by the second. Chats around the water cooler and two-hour commutes from the 'burbs are becoming extinct, and working from home has become a common option. But without that steady work environment, or even a steady job, we must take it upon ourselves to maintain the tranquil t'ai chi of our work life.

Your Office

Whether your desk is at home, in an office, or on your lap in transit, how you feel about your professional life has a lot to do with the feng shui of your work area. This is not just a superstitious view of furniture placement; it affects you every day at work.

The placement of your desk affects your feelings about interacting with the world. If your desk faces a wall, with your back to the entranceway, you may feel out of the flow of commerce.

Right now, while reading this chapter, go to the closest blank wall. Face the wall, stand there for a moment, and notice how this feels. When I do this, I tend to feel overpowered by the wall, unable to move ahead, and anxious. Then my thoughts tend to move inward, but underneath, there is a feeling of anxiety and limitation.

Now, turn and face the entire room. Feel your feet planted firmly underneath you, and take in the expanse in front of you. Notice how you feel. How does this new position affect your sense of potential and your desire to interact with the world? You may not want to stand there all day, but that's okay; most desks come with a chair.

As we discussed in the section on the bedroom, the Command Position is the point from which you can view the entranceway and the entire room. By placing your desk in the Command Position, you are in charge of the space. You should never sit with your back to the door or have your view obstructed.

Some people place their desk at a window, so they can admire the view. If you are a landscaper or professional birdwatcher, the outdoors may directly inspire your work; otherwise, this position actually diverts your focus. You may have lofty thoughts inspired by the view, but your energy is leaking away from the workplace. And if you work at night, the darkened windows will actually drain your energy.

Once your desk is in the Command Position, make sure there is nothing blocking your access at either side. With the advent of computers, many people set small side tables next to their desks. While this clears the bulky equipment from the desktop, a side table can divert your energy from the commanding view and obstruct access to one side of the desk.

If you feel boxed into a corner every time you go to your desk, this will translate into how you feel about your work. If you use a computer, consider working with a laptop, which can be moved aside when you have a meeting.

Your chair should be a comfortable height for the desk and able to move freely behind it. You might also choose the option of a desk with adjustable height, so you can stand up while working, which is much better for your health! Make sure electrical cables do not interfere with the movement of your chair and that you have adequate room between you and any wall behind you.

You should also place a chair at one side of your desk to receive clients or coworkers. Even if you work alone, this shows you are receptive to new opportunities. Consider putting a painting or photograph of a big mountain behind your desk, which gives you a commanding demeanor and supports the energy of your back.

Chinese coins, and other representations of money, are ideal for the office. You can hang a string of nine Chinese coins on a red string at the back of your chair for good money chi. Also, consider attaching one or three coins to your agenda book, important files, and even your telephone. Be sure to empower the coins with the Three Secret Reinforcements to ensure the prosperity of your business.

Office Clutter

Clutter on your desktop can be an instant drain on your energy. How exciting can it be to walk into the office each day and face the same piles of papers? Notice how long it takes to find the things you need. If you are suffering from disorganization at work, set aside time each day to proactively put things in their place. This is also a task that can also be delegated to an assistant.

Though I do enjoy a messy environment now and then, the top of my desk is one place where I draw the line. In fact, I go to the extreme, and I have even evolved a ritual about this.

At the end of each day, I clear everything from the top of my desk. (When I used a desktop computer, I allowed it to stay, but beyond that, everything came off the desk.) Then, I take a small cup of fresh water, and I sprinkle the top of the desk with a few drops nine times, to clear the old energy. I usually chant the Six True

Words, "Om Ma Ni Pad Me Hum," nine times as I do this. In the past, I have done this surreptitiously while coworkers are around. I mumble the words softly to myself, and so far, no one has accused me of desecrating any company furniture.

After clearing the energy of the desk, the only thing that I put on the desktop, besides a computer, is a small red Chinese cup in which I keep three coins. This rests in the Hsun position, at the top left corner of the desk. And that's it. Nothing more.

If you like, you can apply the bagua to the rest of the desk, just as you would to a floor plan; the "mouth of chi" is where you set your chair. You might place the photograph of a loved one in the Kun position at the top right corner and some symbol of recognition at the top center edge of the desk.

The other thing I do at the end of the day involves my ritual money cup. After sprinkling the desk with water to remove old energy, I pick up the cup and shuffle the coins nine times while repeating the Six True Words, and I visualize the financial accomplishments I want to achieve. This ritual concludes the affairs of the day and sets the intention for the next day's work.

By clearing the top of your desk, you may see it for the first time! You should avoid desktops that are black, since they absorb your energy. Glass-topped desks are also problematic, since you see right through them and they distort your focus on the work at hand. Try a blotter or mat that is brown, yellow, green, or red. Blotter papers are easily changed, so you can experiment with different colors to see how they affect your mood.

Shar Chi: Poison Arrows

If you feel that your boss or coworkers are staring daggers at you, the bad chi might not be coming from the people, but from the office building itself!

"Shar chi," or "poison arrow," is the Chinese term for any sharp corners or angles that cut into the space. Unfortunately, these angles are prevalent in modern architecture. By becoming aware of these influences and softening them with practical "cures," you can change a chaotic atmosphere into a place of tranquility and harmony.

Bookcases and filing cabinets are typical fixtures in an office. Make sure you do not have any shar chi from sharp corners pointing at your desk; this could be making you feel tired, irritable, and defensive. If you can't move your position from the line of attack, soften the corners with live or silk leafy plants. You can also hang cloth over the protruding corner or purchase a string of small Tibetan bells, which absorb the negative energy.

Be wary of bookcases that have the spines of books pointed directly at your workspace; this is like having dozens of knives pointing at you and can make you feel anxious, even paranoid, while working. I was once in an office that had a tall bookcase filled with books directly facing my desk. Though I liked the work and felt happy with what I was producing, I often felt nervous and even paranoid about my position in the company. I only lasted a year in that job, and I later learned how the energy in the office undermined my confidence.

Be wary of any shar chi from buildings outside your window. Placing a small bagua on the outside ledge can deflect negative energy from opposing structures. Obviously, shar chi does not just occur in the design of offices, and you should survey your home to diffuse any sharp angles that are facing beds, chairs, and dining areas.

PROSPERITY JOURNAL: "BACK TO WORK"

1. Take this book to work with you. If you are employed in a busy office, try to find time to be alone, when you can put on your private investigator hat. Go into your Beginner's Mind and do the Calming Heart Sutra to become centered.

2. Notice the condition of the work area. How does it feel? What sort of messages does this environment send, and what kinds of people would you imagine work here? How might they treat themselves and each other, and what are their values?

3. Refer to your three adjectives that describe your essence of wealth, and decide how to bring these qualities into your workspace. Even if you are only allotted a cubicle, there are ways to personalize and harmonize this space. This is where you spend many of your waking hours, so treat it with respect.

4. Finally, list feng shui changes you can make here, and prioritize the top cures you will implement this week.

Bagua Sector of the Week: Kan

The sector of the bagua called Kan ("kahn") connects to our life mission. Whether we are a laborer in the street or a physicist at a lab, the Kan energy invokes our skills and offers them in the banquet of life. Each of us is one of God's messengers, placed here for a special purpose that can be fulfilled by no one else.

The element associated with Kan is water. Just as water feeds the living plants, the Kan (career and mission) feeds the financial vibrations of Chen (family and

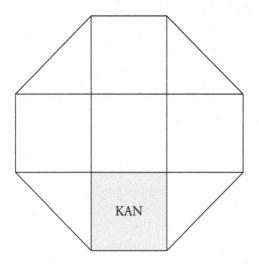

Bagua sector of the week: Kan.

households) and Hsun (wealth and luxury). As the currents of our gifts flow freely, they will naturally feed the growth of your wealth.

For some people, the very concept of a "career" may feel foreign, if not downright affronting. "What do you mean, my career? Don't you realize I have to work for a living?" In the face of daily expenses and an exhausting workload, the idea of sharing your inner gifts may sound like a fantasy. But once you unblock the Kan energy, you will start to flow with new potential.

PROSPERITY JOURNAL: "MY FEELINGS IN KAN"

1. Write a few notes about how you are feeling about your career. This is often a volatile question.
2. The Kan sector of your home is located at the bottom center of the bagua. Go to this area of your home, and use the Calming Heart Sutra to become sensitive to the energies. Write a few notes about how this part of the home feels to you. If you have been frustrated in your career, there is undoubtedly a problem with the feng shui in this area, and you will learn ways to improve the flow of chi energy.
3. Next, decide how you want this part of your life to feel. Write down three or four adjectives that describe the ideal expression of your true gifts, and begin to consider how you can bring these energies to this part of your home.

Feng Shui Applications for Financial Development in Kan

Mirrors are highly appropriate in the Kan gua, since they reflect you back to yourself and help you see your potential. They also represent the water element, to increase the flow of career opportunities. Tabletop fountains also fulfill this function.

If you install mirrors, make sure they are large enough to take in at least your full head and shoulders. Otherwise, you may end up running from one job to another, like a chicken with its head cut off! Mirrors are also the best solution if you have a missing section in Kan.

Finding a career path takes a lot of contemplation and insight. This gua is rightfully associated with the color black, which corresponds to mystery—the dark of night before the dawn. Using darker colors in your Kan sector makes it perfect for meditating on the mystery of your future.

Hanging a crystal in the Kan position, or above your desk, will help you to clarify your thoughts and gain insight about incoming opportunities. If there don't even seem to be any opportunities to consider, hanging a wind chime in these positions will ring in new possibilities.

PROSPERITY JOURNAL: "BRINGING THE DESIRED ESSENCE TO KAN"

Review the list of adjectives you provided as ideals for the Kan energy in your life, and decide how you can make this area of your home feel this way now. Also, choose at least one of the traditional feng shui cures for this area, and remember to do the Three Secret Reinforcements as you implement the cures to clarify your career path.

The Moving Water Cure

The Moving Water Cure actually does not use any water at all. Instead, it is based on the power of communication—it is an ancient form of networking. To do this ritual, all you need is a list of friends and contacts and your preferred means of communication with them: phone, email, texting, snail mail, or (Heaven forbid) good old-fashioned face-to-face connection. If you are without any contacts, and even without a friend in the world, you can still perform this ritual quite successfully—and build a whole new social life, as well!

This "cure" is especially helpful if you feel stuck in your career, need to bolster your self-esteem, or just want to create some new opportunities. It doesn't need to cost a thing, and you can use a time frame that best suits your needs.

Getting Down to Business

The basic ritual goes as follows: For nine days, contact at least one person with whom you have not spoken or corresponded in the past six months. These contacts do not have to be close friends or relatives, but they should be people with whom you really want to communicate. Your parole officer and the bully who beat you up when you were eight years old will probably not be included in this  list. Do not limit yourself to people who can further your career or financial goals. The idea is to overcome limited personal boundaries and establish your energy generously in the world.

Make sure the contact is positive in nature. With all of these communications, you are *not* allowed to ask for anything from the contacts—no harassing letters to ex-spouses asking for alimony, and not even a simple invitation for coffee. Just let them know that you are thinking of them and that you want to maintain positive communication.

If the person offers you something, however, you must accept to the fullest extent of your ability and morality. For instance, if you contact an old sweetheart, and this leads to a dinner invitation, you must say "yes"—but you might also need to bring your spouse with you! If your old college roommate enthusiastically takes your call, and then solicits you to join in a shady business deal, you are required to discuss this further, but warn him you may feel obligated to report all dealings to the IRS.

If you run out of people on your list, don't give up! You can initiate conversations with new people you meet at a street corner, restaurant, or local watering hole.

You should do this ritual for nine days, contacting one different person each day. Mass emails, fax "blasts," and conference calls do not count. However, if your life is a veritable dry bed of opportunity, the "cure" should be much more intense: Contact three people each day for nine days, or even nine people each day for nine days. You could also do the ritual for twenty-seven days, and contact one or three people each day throughout that period.

If, on any day, you fail to contact your quota, you have to start again, and you cannot recycle the people you have already contacted.

You may want to start this ritual on an auspicious day, as defined in *The Classic Chinese Almanac*. By practicing this ritual diligently, you will undoubtedly find your life flowing with all sorts of new opportunities, and you may get some invitations to free dinners as well!

FINANCIAL FENG SHUI—CHARTING YOUR COURSE

If you are unhappy about your salary, the next step is unavoidable: quit your job. It's that simple.

This is the part of the book where you will probably say, "Are you crazy? I just invested seven weeks or more of my life in this money program, and now you are telling me to quit my job? I can't do that—I have to bills to pay!" Well, it's due to these bills, and other financial goals, that you need to quit working for someone else. How else are you going to get ahead?

Before you toss this book on the shelf with the other 80 percent that have never been read to the end, let me clarify: I am not telling you to leave your job today, or even tomorrow. I am saying you need to quit the "worker mentality." From now on, cut the emotional ties with an employer, and do the work for yourself. Realize you are only in business for yourself—and perhaps getting health insurance benefits while you do it—and that your present job is just one more gig in your freelancing career.

Every job is temporary. The company you are working for is not your boss, but your client. Only you can be your boss. With that understanding intact, your career potential is unlimited.

The balance of power has returned to the proper perspective: you are hired by your client (your "boss") to use some of your specialized skills. When you do this, your client pays you. It's that simple. Now, you may not be using the skills that you really want to use, and it may not be for a cause that you value. If that's the case, you didn't market yourself very well, and you chose the wrong client. But this is an issue of how you run *your* business, not how your clients run theirs.

Refer back to your Dream Clusters: does your present "gig" reflect the values and interests that you identified for yourself? If you are unhappy, it is not a good match. But this is not the fault of your client (your "job"); this is the fault of how you have been defining and marketing yourself. If you like making birthday cakes, but you fall into catering for funerals, whose fault is that? The dead person's? You can't be recognized for traits that you don't express; that is a simple law of karma.

PROSPERITY JOURNAL: "NAME THAT GAME"

Here is your chance to define your ideal career:

1. List ten things that you *do not* like about your present employment. Be brutally honest—every business needs to undergo this type of evaluation. If you are unemployed, write down things that you do not like about not working.

2. Now, list the things that you *do* like about your present employment (or lack of a job, if that is the case). Be as specific as you can. Instead of writing "the people," you might put "talking about football at lunch" or "being appreciated during team meetings." Whatever you like about your present situation, put it here. If you are enjoying aspects of being unemployed, list what you like about it.

3. Next, go back to the first list, and for each negative characteristic, write its *opposite*. For instance, if you hate working in a noisy cubicle, you might write, "I have a spacious, serene office of my own, with a beautiful view." Make sure that you invert each of your negative items in detail.

4. You should now have a clear evaluation of your present situation. It's time to complete your vision of the future. Review the details of your primary Dream Cluster, and decide how you might integrate these into your present situation. Pursuing your dream does not mean leaving behind the things you like. If anything, it should emphasize them further.

5. Now, write a paragraph or two that describes your new, amalgamated vision of your career. Don't worry if it seems unreasonable or over the top; everything worth pursuing sounded that way before anyone did it. If we can put a man on the moon, we can get you into your ideal career. This is one of the main reasons you are on this planet in the first place!

The paragraphs that you wrote in this exercise are an indispensable map to your future. Make a few copies, and place at least one in your home (perhaps by your bed or by the bathroom mirror) and one at work, in your briefcase or on your computer or phone. Every day, review this description of your career purpose and find at least *one way* to manifest this in your present situation. Even discussing your interests with coworkers or volunteering for a new committee can put you on the right path. Even if your current job seems to have nothing to do with your real interests, find a way to move in the direction of your dreams. Don't wait for the ideal situation to stop you in your tracks. Create it for yourself. Remember, you are the boss.

What Is Your Time Worth?

It's time to do a little math, to see exactly how you are being valued in your current state of employment.

PROSPERITY JOURNAL: "MY HOURS AND WAGES"

1. Take out a recent pay stub, or use your ledger if you are self-employed, and note the exact net amount that you take home each week.

2. Next, figure the number of hours in your average workweek. Instead of stating the standard "four-oh," consider all your time obligations: commuting, prep time, business meals, trips, and all job-related concerns. Are you starting to see where your time has been going?

3. As a second calculation, tally any expenses that are in any way job-related, such as wardrobe, lunches and business meals, commuting, work supplies, career coaching, and so on. Deduct these expenses from your net income, and divide this amount by the number of work and work-related hours. This is your true hourly wage. Are you surprised? If you've wondered how a person can feel poor on a "decent" income, this may be your answer.

4. Now, take the total financial requirement of your monthly spending plan and divide this by your hourly wage. Write this number down. This tells you how many hours you need to work just to get by. No wonder it has been so hard to get wealthy, when all the hours that you are putting in barely help you break even.

If you feel shocked and angry by these calculations, good! We need to get outraged if our life energy is mercilessly sucked up by an economic system that does not promote both our wealth and health. It does not need to be this way, and it's time to calculate your future the way that you want it to be.

First, remember that no hourly wage will ever be enough if you don't feel your work is important or if you are not having fun. If that describes your present job, you need to start planning your exit, right away. Your life mission is one of the most important expressions of your self-nature, and life is too short to spend any time shortchanging that part of you.

By outlining your ideal career vision, you should have a solid idea of what you want to do and how you want to do it. If you do not, you *cannot* just skip to the next step—your life literally depends on it. Go back carefully over the exercises, or use any resources listed at the back of this book, until you have clear work goals that you can state in two sentences or less to everyone you meet.

Now it is time to assess your economic needs. Go back to your Prosperity Plan and assess exactly how much you need to make each month to get by. If you are surviving on your plan, and that is about all, there is not much margin for growth.

PROSPERITY JOURNAL:
"MY FINANCIAL GOALS AND COMFORT RANGE"

1. It is time to translate your dreams into financial terms. Money is not the only way to bring your desires into your life, but it is often the medium of exchange, and you need to prepare a financial base that will support your life's desires.

2. Go back to your Dream Clusters, and consider exactly how you want to be living at the end of the next twelve months. Define your top goals, and the revenue you will need to make them happen. Make the list as extensive as you like, but be sure these are goals that you will consistently pursue in the coming year with your time, money, energy, and focus. Remember: the more you put on your list, the more responsibilities you are adding to your life! Take anything off the list that does not measure up to this level of commitment.

3. Now, write down the amount you established on your Prosperity Journal for "getting by." This is your survival quotient. Add the total amount required for your financial goals, to establish your financial target for the coming year.

4. Finally, add an additional 20 percent to this target goal. We call this your "comfort range." No matter how carefully we may plan, our needs are often more extensive than we can imagine, and it is important to include a financial buffer. For whatever reason, no matter where you live or how much you make, your comfort level is usually 20 percent more than your expected budget. From now on, whenever we talk about your salary requirements, your financial target plus 20 percent will be the figure we will use.

5. Go back to your current hourly wage, and calculate how many hours you will need to work to fulfill your requirements. Write the following, replacing the blanks with the number you just calculated: "At my current salary, I will need to work _____ hours each week to fulfill my necessary plans."

6. Go back to your newly calculated comfort range, and calculate your required gross income by adding the percentage for your standard federal, state, and city taxes. If you do not know this exact percentage, add 25 percent, which is

probably what you can accomplish if you have a good accountant. Write down the amount and label it; this is your minimum required gross salary for the upcoming year.

7. Divide your new salary requirement by fifty-two (the number of weeks in the year), and note this as your weekly required gross income.

8. Divide this weekly rate by forty hours, which is considered a standard work week, and which, in my opinion, should include *all* job-related activities, including commuting, "homework," and travel. This is your new minimum hourly wage.

Now that you know your salary requirements, it is time for you to prepare your job description. But instead of talking about your present position, *this* résumé talks about your future.

PROSPERITY JOURNAL: "HERE'S MY JOB"

Refer to the ideal job description you created in the previous section, and write down the following:

My name is [*your name*]. I am a professional [*your ideal professional title*].
In my work, I enjoy [*list the primary activities that you envision doing for your dream job*].
I require a working environment that is [*write the descriptions you provided in the ideal career exercise*].
Including all job-related activities, I work no more than [*write "forty," unless you have other requirements*] hours a week.
In the year 20____ [*this year*] to 20____ [*next year*], I require a gross annual salary of at least [*write the gross annual salary defined by your comfort budget*], which breaks down to an hourly wage of at least [*write the hourly wage required by your comfort budget*].
I have excellent feng shui and karma, so I know that this statement is supported by the universe!

Sincerely, _____   Date: _____

This is your contract for your new life. Memorize it and repeat it, in some form, to everyone that you know and trust. Even if you don't know them, entrust them with this essential information about yourself. Try including these details when you do the Moving Water Cure, and you will really be putting your message out to the universe!

As you look at your new "lease on life," if you feel the financial terms are not possible in this lifetime, think again. In the next section, we will review how value is determined and ultimately reimbursed. This principle is essential if you are going to fulfill your dreams.

Marketing Yourself

If a tree falls in the forest, but no one hears it, will it make any money? Here is the basic principle of marketing: money is given according to the *perception* of value, and not necessarily because of any intrinsic value. Though fairly self-evident, this point is hard to swallow, especially if you are an English teacher in the ghetto or a social worker who qualifies for food stamps. But please note that the key word in this statement is "perception."

A lot of people associate salary with true value, which is ridiculous when you think of someone like Van Gogh, who died penniless. Make it clear to yourself: money is a statement of *perceived* value in society, not your intrinsic value. Is one soft drink really better than another? Only if you think so. Is one automobile really worth more than another? Ask the person buying it. Is a rock singer more important than a high school band teacher? Ask the culture that supports them. Your judgment is as good as mine.

The issue comes down to how we put ourselves out in the world. Once you realize that it is all about perception, not intrinsic value, it frees you up to be, and to charge, whatever you want. If you don't think that what you are doing is important, others will share your opinion, and don't expect to get paid a lot for it. But if you really see the value of your work, all you need to do is find a way to communicate this perception to the rest of the world.

Consider Jack Canfield, who started the *Chicken Soup for the Soul* series. Evidently, Jack really believed in his books, so much so that he shopped them around to over thirty different publishers. He was rejected at every turn. However, he believed so strongly in the value of his work that he felt sure that the world would eventually share his enthusiasm. And it did—oh, how it did!

Walt Disney once worked for the post office, but history will remember him for his animation and theme parks. Charles Schulz also loved cartooning. He made millions from his daily comic strips, and the day before his final *Peanuts* ran in the newspaper, he died. His work was done. Now, what will your work be?

If you are not making enough money with your chosen career, it is due to either of two factors: People don't think that it is very important (perception), or not enough people know about it (exposure). Usually, it is a combination of the two, and both are marketing issues. Your job is not just to offer your work to the world, but to teach the world just how important this work really is.

Please note the second part of the equation: exposure. If only one person agrees that your work is important, your cash flow if going to be limited. If a million people agree with you . . . well, you will get tired writing those deposit slips at the bank!

Setting Your Rates

If you want a rule of thumb about how much you can charge for your new services, this is what I recommend: call up at least three other people who are doing the same thing, take the average, and *double* it. Then, figure out why the services that you are offering are twice as good as what the other people do.

With this figure as your goal, you have a standard of quality you can aspire to. If you really think you are worth that rate, I am sure you can come up with at least ten viable reasons to support it. Pick your top three, and broadcast these reasons to every corner of your marketplace. Remember, we live in an electronic, global economy, and you now have potential customers across the planet.

Build incrementally toward your aspirational fee, so you feel comfortable and justified along the way. In my first feng shui consultation, I made $13 for an hour's work! Within weeks, I had tripled this fee, and a year later, I was making ten times that original amount.

Here's another simple formula for establishing rates. Ask yourself, "What would I be happy charging?" and then take the lowest amount that would be satisfactory. When that amount no longer feels right, move it to the next level. This way, you can move quickly up the scale in a way that is comfortable to you.

INNER FENG SHUI—TAKING YOUR PLACE IN THE WORLD

The desire for social acceptance often influences, and limits, how we pursue wealth. The supposed "need" to be liked often overrules our inclinations to do our own thing, pursue our own goals, and create the life we really want.

Most people continually face the dilemma of "What do I have to give up in order to be a member of this group?" We become so used to asking this question, we may not realize it is a dilemma at all. Self-sacrifice is seen more as a virtue than as the disguised self-defeat we are inflicting upon ourselves.

"I really wanted that job across the country," one client told me, "but I knew that my mother would never feel okay about it. How can I take a job that makes the rest of my family unhappy?" The intention on the part of the parents may not be consciously negative. They may feel that they are properly fulfilling their role, which is to preserve the "solidity" of the family in any way they can.

The same constriction often emerges in our peer groups and social circles. If we ever dare to challenge the unspoken norms—watch out! By challenging the group, it feels as if we are challenging each of its members.

Social groups are based on conformity, not self-expression. This affects every level of our lives, from the way that we talk, to the way we dress, to the way that we make and spend our money. Every time we express our truth, we challenge the members of the group to connect to that truth in themselves. They may be willing to make that connection, or they may not.

Social acceptance is not the same thing as agreement. Just because they can accept something about you doesn't mean that they have to like it! Without that acknowledgment of trust, it is difficult, if not impossible, to really feel like a member of a group at all.

We need to protect our new ventures as if our life depends upon it, because it does. This is not to say that it's always easy. You may get snide looks when you tell your friends you are taking a dance class. "At *your* age?" they may inquire, as if they are protecting you from some oncoming disaster. Or you may get looks of concern when planning to leave your job to start your own business. "Don't you know most new businesses fail?" they may implore. "Why can't you be happy just having a normal (miserable) life?"

I have a friend who always responds to the latest news about my feng shui business with the same reply: "Are you still doing *that*?" After years, he still says this as if he is waiting for me to come to my senses and get a "real job" at some soulless company. While I can still be friends with this individual, we may never be fully in agreement.

The implication is not that you should do your own thing at the expense of your social groups. Just do your own thing and adamantly represent it to everyone in your life. Love is based on self-expression and acknowledgment, not conformity. We must fight every day for this kind of love. Otherwise, we are depriving the world of our greatest gift: ourselves.

Your Inner Council

Wouldn't it be wonderful to be continually surrounded by a group of people who love, respect, and support everything that you do? A group that always sees the best in you, even on days when you cannot see this in yourself? Most people expect to have this experience in their families, which is why so many people are in therapy!

There is a traditional meditation in Black Sect feng shui that serves this desire. In this meditation, you visualize the bagua, and a Buddha from each of the eight guas approaches you and offers you a blessing.

I have adapted this meditation for modern readers. Instead of visualizing being approached by a Buddha, you will select some figure of fantasy that best represents that area of life for you. It may be someone you knew from childhood, a figure from history or literature, or maybe your favorite movie star. Yes, it can even be a favorite family member or relative. These are the people you will choose to honor and respect you and your ideas.

During the visualization, these figures will come to you to offer their advice and support your highest purpose. You do not need to censor yourself or your needs because they will be there for you, no matter what. And unlike your family and friends, these figures never sleep or have needs of their own. They are there for you at all times—all you need to do is ask.

In the journal assignment below, I have listed the eight areas of life that are addressed by feng shui. Each time you do this visualization, you will be asked to summon only one figure per area, but you are welcome to have more than one "on deck" to choose from. After a while, you will probably find that the right figures come to you each time to help you address the issues that are concerning you the most.

You may select figures that come from:

- Literature
- History
- Art
- Sports
- Movies and TV
- Religion
- Beloved friends and family members
- Teachers
- Your personal history
- Other

Just be sure to select people who seem best suited to specialize in each area of the bagua. For instance, Wolfgang Amadeus Mozart was a musical genius, and he would be a great advisor to have in the creativity, fame, or career areas of your bagua. He was not, evidently, so adept in his relationships, and he also died a pauper, so you might want someone else to advise you in the Kun and Hsun corners of your Inner Bagua!

PROSPERITY JOURNAL: "MY INNER COUNCIL"

1. List three personal advisors in Kan, the career gua. The color for this gua is black.
2. List three personal advisors in Ken, the self-knowledge and education gua. The color for this gua is dark blue.
3. List three personal advisors in Chen, the family and home life gua. The color for this gua is green.
4. List three personal advisors in Shun, the wealth and prosperity gua. The color for this gua is purple.
5. List three personal advisors in Li, the fame and recognition gua. The color for this gua is red.
6. List three personal advisors in Kun, the relationship and marriage gua. The color for this gua is pink.
7. List three personal advisors in Dui, the children and creativity gua. The color for this gua is white.
8. List three personal advisors in Chyan, the helpful people and mentor gua. The color for this gua is gray.

Now that you have selected the team from which you will construct the Inner Council, prepare for the meditation. Choose a time when you can sit undisturbed for about fifteen to twenty minutes. Ultimately, you will be able to consult your Inner Council at any moment, even in the midst of a crisis, but for right now, choose a time and place where you can sit undisturbed and really concentrate on the experience.

Before beginning the meditation, go over your list of Inner Council members, and select one for each gua. You might write the name of the person you have selected on the diagram that follows or on a separate piece of paper. Remember, you can always change your mind during the meditation, but try to complete the selection process before you begin.

Sit in an open position and close your eyes. Check in with your breath. Imagine you are breathing in relaxation and breathing out any tension. After a few relaxing breaths, chant the Calming Heart Sutra to yourself, nine times.

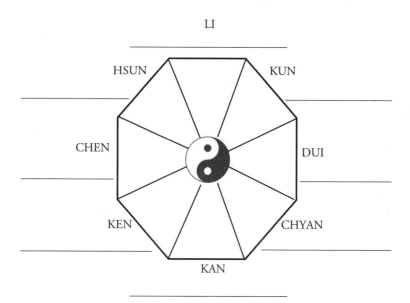

LI

HSUN

KUN

CHEN

DUI

KEN

CHYAN

KAN

Selection of your Inner Council.

Now, imagine you are standing in the t'ai chi center of your home or, if you prefer, your office. Sense the eight sides of the bagua shape all around you. Quietly, in your mind, see yourself turning to each of the areas of the bagua, starting with Kan at the lower center, and see yourself acknowledging each of the guas, stating the name of the gua quietly to yourself. If you need to, you can take quick glances at the list of the guas in your journal to get the names right.

Once you have gone to each gua, feel yourself standing in the middle of that powerful energy field, and sense the alignment and support it is offering you.

Now, turn back to the Kan (career) portion of the bagua, and imagine there is a mystical door superimposed over that area. On the door, see that the word "Kan" is written in big, black letters. Now, call the name of the person you selected to advise you in the career area of your life, and imagine that he or she is behind the door. When ready, this advisor will open the door and step toward you. You may want to imagine that the Kan advisor is wearing something black, to represent the color of this gua, or is perhaps holding some object or gift that demonstrates the purpose in visiting you.

After a while, see that the door opens, and the person you have selected for the Kan gua steps out. Notice how the advisor moves toward you and if anything is said in the approach.

See yourself greeting the advisor as he or she comes close to you, and then ask what advice is being brought to you in the area of your career. Take time to converse with your advisor briefly about this, and receive any gift or object that is offered you. Then, say goodbye for now, and see yourself turning to the next area of the bagua, which is Ken, the gua dedicated to self-knowledge and education.

At this next gua, see another door, but this time with the word "Ken" in big letters of dark blue. In a moment, the figure that you selected to advise you in this area will come from behind the door. This figure may be dressed in dark blue and may be holding a special object or gift to help you.

During the meditation, you will continue going to each area of the bagua in this way. Take time to speak with each of the eight representatives and to receive the wisdom offered you. If you are surprised by any of the things that happen during the meditation, try not to censor them. You can take time afterward to contemplate the meaning of these events.

Since the focus of the work in this book is on wealth and money, be sure to bring any problems of this nature to the representatives of your Inner Council. As you know, problems with money are not related solely to the Hsun, or wealth gua. Instead, they may be connected to any of the eight areas of the bagua, and you should receive advice from all selected members of your Inner Council.

Be wary: the first time I did an exercise like this, my Inner Council members were all vying for attention! Sometimes, you may have to act as the referee until you can establish a good working relationship between all the members. The way these representatives behave is an indication of the way each gua is integrated into your life. By bringing peace to your Inner Bagua, you are simultaneously working out your inner issues.

After you finish talking to your Inner Council, you can conclude this meeting of your board, and visualize each member going back through their respective doors (hopefully without slamming them). Feel yourself again in the center of your home or office, and sense your energy extending to all corners of that space. Feel the space receiving your energy and sending its energy back to you. Make a mental note of any feng shui adjustments that you might want to make in the space to mark the new growth or wisdom that you received in this meditation, and conclude by chanting the Six True Words nine times: "Om Ma Ni Pad Me Hum."

ACTION STEPS ON THE JOURNEY TO WEALTH:
WEEK 8 SYNOPSIS

You are making your mark on the world. This is not just about fortune and fame; it is about fulfilling your spiritual purpose and enjoying the rewards. Check the boxes as you complete these tasks:

☐ Review the goals you wrote for your office space, and choose at least two feng shui cures you can apply this week.

☐ Clear out the old office clutter and replace it with something enjoyable.

☐ Soften that pesky shar chi in your office and home this week.

☐ Review the goals you set for the Kan section of your home, and implement at least two this week.

☐ Get some action going. Start the Moving Water Cure this week, and see what waves you can cause!

☐ Outline the positive and negative circumstances of your present work situation, and integrate the details from your Dream Cluster to create a vision for your ideal career.

☐ Figure out what your time is worth.

☐ Complete your résumé for your ideal future, and tell everyone you meet about your new criteria.

☐ Try the Inner Council Meditation at least once this week, and gather your inner mentors to your side.

Celebrating the Spirituality of Money

> Only the Tao
> Is good at the beginning
> And also good at the end.
> —The *Tao Te Ching*, Book 41

PRELUDE—NATURAL ABUNDANCE

Wealth is a natural product of the way you really want to live. By doing the things you love to do and sharing them with others, you will naturally extend yourself in the world in a way that is meaningful and valuable. It's your individuality, and not your capacity for mindless labor, that makes you important in the world. Meaningful work is your gift to yourself and to others.

If you set off looking for a "job" to make you wealthy, you might be looking for a long time. But if you are open to the desires planted in your heart, every day is an opportunity for further riches. Feeling stuck financially indicates that you are blocking the expression of your gifts. Nothing can stand in the way of your self-expression except you. Money is just a way of keeping track of this spiritual rhythm.

Certainly, there will be exhausting days and situations that stretch you to the limits of your abilities. But by advancing confidently in the direction of your dreams, your life finally becomes your own. That is the essence of wealth.

Many years ago, I was directing a theater program for children, and I was unsure which play to produce. So I took a vote. I asked all the kids to rate which plays they liked the most, and then select the one they wanted to do. I chose to do the one that received the most votes, and do you know what? It was the worst play

I ever directed! (I won't say which one it was, in case any of the actors are now reading this book.) I had absolutely no feeling for the production and realized I was just going through the motions of directing it.

Since then, my attitude about art, and life in general, has changed a great deal. Making a contribution is not about doing what others want us to do. You can't please everyone anyway, so why try? Instead, the goal is to find the things that excite your spirit, and then share these experiences with others, in every way possible. This may feel riskier than trying to please the crowd, but it's much more satisfying.

I started writing this book because I was frustrated by the literature about money and feng shui already on the market. I felt there was a need for a book that could make these topics clear and understandable, so I created a format that I liked. I figured if I could understand it, perhaps others would as well. By contributing to myself, I developed something I could contribute to others.

A lot of people had opinions about how this book should be written. I'm sure that if I had diligently applied their advice, the book would never have happened! In the end, I wrote the book I most wanted to read, which means that there is, at least, one happy reader.

What's It All About?

The deep nature of feng shui asks us to thoroughly examine ourselves and to consider the very basis of our lives. Why are we born on this planet, anyway? Your answer to this question directly influences the way you pursue and use money. Let me explain.

If you believe you are on this planet to prove you are better than everyone else, you will use all your resources, including money, toward this goal. Fancy cars, designer labels, a super-platinum card . . . dress to impress. But on the other hand, if you believe you were put here to be "good," you will treat money according to your images of goodness: bequeathing it to the poor, or whatever else "good" people are supposed to do with it.

PROSPERITY JOURNAL: "ME"

Take a moment to meditate on your own self-nature. Inquire honestly of yourself, and write a paragraph: "What is the purpose of my birth? Is it just a big cosmic accident, or is there a spiritual meaning to my life?" Do not be rational about this question. It's your emotional reasoning, and not the scientific perspective, that is at the root of your behavior.

Now, write about how your answers to these questions affect the way you use and pursue money. Ask yourself: "If I met someone who had this purpose in life, how would I expect him or her to behave with money?"

I personally have some strong ideas on this subject. To come to a conclusion, I did a bit of empirical research and looked at the world around us, particularly the natural world before humanity had a chance to tamper with it. I always came to the same conclusion: the flowers in the field are working full-time to just be flowers in the field. Dogs aspire to be dogs. Babies commit themselves 24/7 to be babies. There is nothing that would be a better choice for them. Why are we any different?

I believe that it is our right and our responsibility to be exactly what we were created to be: ourselves. This may sound simple, but it's amazing that most people dedicate their lives to being everything but that! The goal is to become really good at being who we are. Once we stop the battle and embrace our self-nature, we succumb to the abundance of life within. This is the work of no work. So relax!

ENVIRONMENTAL FENG SHUI—WHEREVER YOU GO, THERE YOU ARE

As you expand your mission in the world, your path to wealth may take you to the far corners of the world and back again.

Whether it's for business or pleasure, travel can be exhausting, if not downright infuriating. It's no accident that the word "travel" comes from the French word "travail," which means "work" or "strive." Despite the streamlined methods of the modern "hospitality business," the impersonal nature of most hotels and lodgings can leave you feeling like you are staying in a hospital, or that you may need one!

The most important key to comfortable travel is to recognize your own needs. If you like to end each day with a hot soak in a tub, be sure a bathtub is part of the package. If you enjoy a breath of fresh air before going to sleep, choose a hotel in a neighborhood that can accommodate you. Be sure you request your preferences when making that reservation.

Decide what you need most in order to feel "at home" while you are away from home. Just as you use feng shui to enhance your home life, you need to carry that feeling with you when you travel. Some people take along pictures of relatives and friends so they will feel surrounded by the people they love. You might also bring pictures of your Inner Council to surround you on business trips. Collect a few small items that can bestow a sense of home—a beautiful scarf placed over a tabletop, a few pieces from your knickknack collection, whatever you like.

FENG SHUI AND MONEY

I have a small bag of pine needles I bought in a country store in Vermont, and years after the purchase, it still embodies that distinctive woodsy smell that reminds me of my childhood. Without taking up much space, that little souvenir is very soothing when placed under my pillow at night.

Now that you are adept at placing the bagua diagram over your home, do the same thing when you travel. When on a business trip, pay particular attention to the location of the Kan (career), Li (fame and recognition), and of course Hsun (wealth) positions in your room or hotel suite. If this is an important trip and the toilet is in the Hsun (wealth) position, do not hesitate to ask for a different room! In addition, pull that desk over to the Command Position if you need to do important work in your hotel room.

Once you have set up your money altar at home, you may want to assemble a portable altar to set up quickly when you travel. A Buddha or other spiritual figure, some candles, a bowl of Chinese or American coins, and perhaps some fresh flowers set in the Hsun gua of your hotel room will set the right tone for your trip. Remember to empower the altar with the Three Secret Reinforcements each time you set it up.

You needn't limit your horizons to your hometown, nor feel you have to leave your home behind. By taking feng shui with you, you can enjoy success and comfort wherever you go.

The Red Carpet Cure

As you set off on your journeys, make sure you are starting on the "right foot." Here is an ancient ritual for blessing your travels. You will need a long piece of red cloth, six feet long and about thirty-six to forty-five inches wide. Silk, wool, and cotton are good choices. You will be placing the cloth on the floor, so make sure it is sturdy enough to be walked upon.

When preparing to leave home for an important business engagement, place the cloth on the floor at your doorway, so that three feet are inside your home and three feet are outside the door.

Once you pass over the red carpet, you must leave the building without coming back inside to turn off lights, so be sure to use the toilet and check the stove before you go. Do these things first, and place your luggage outside the door.

Take a moment to meditate on the journey, and do the Calming Heart meditation to clear your mind. Spread the cloth out on the floor, and note the transition between the inside and outside of your home. Use the Three Secret Reinforcements, and visualize a safe and successful journey. Once the carpet is empowered, walk down your red carpet, and feel the protection that has been established underneath your feet.

194

Once you are outside the door, you have two choices. You can gather the cloth and toss it inside your house before closing the door, or you can refold it, put it in your suitcase, and take it to your first destination. If you take it with you, use the same ritual when you settle into your lodgings. Before entering the room, lay the cloth out over the threshold, and empower the cloth for a peaceful night's stay. Then, cross the threshold and gather up the cloth.

You can do this ritual at each step of your journey. If you have an extremely important business meeting, you can start the day this way as you leave your hotel room. In any case, the Red Carpet ritual should help you establish your intention for safe and happy travels.

Bagua Sector of the Week: Ken

The last section of the bagua we will address is called Ken (pronounced as it looks). This is the area of spirituality, self-knowledge, and education. The element associated with it is earth, like a huge mountain that reaches into the sky. Like the monks who seek solitude in a mountain cave or mountain climbers trying to approach the perspective of the stars, this gua invites us to be seekers, to step into the unknown and embrace the mysteries of life. Not a bad place to stop at the end of our book journey, don't you think?

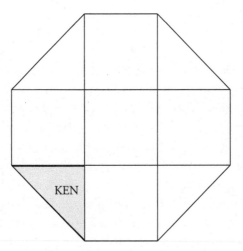

Bagua sector of the week: Ken.

If you are having trouble finding the right career or don't know the kind of life you want to create, the Ken gua is your refuge and your inspiration. How can you choose a lifestyle that pleases you if you don't know what you like?

In Native American cultures, young warriors undertook vision quests to discover their inner nature. In modern times, this has been replaced by going to the mall. But the need remains: to know ourselves deeply and to build our life on the knowledge of our true self.

Use your daily meditation to transcend your rational mind, open to the mystery of life, and ask for guidance. Each of us is a natural part of the universe. Call to the part of you that knows this connection, and be willing to receive its response.

PROSPERITY JOURNAL: "THE FENG SHUI OF KEN"

1. Consider how you are feeling about your spirituality and self-knowledge, and write about this in your journal.

2. Now, go to the Ken corner of your home; this sector is located in the bottom left area of your home. Do the Calming Heart Sutra to clear your mind. Get a sense of how this area feels right now, and write a few notes about the appearance and condition of this area.

3. Then, choose three or four adjectives that describe how you want your experience of spirituality and self-knowledge to feel in your life.

4. Consider how you might make this section of your home reflect these adjectives you have outlined and write down a few notes.

Feng Shui Applications for Financial Development in Ken

Since this is the area of your home aligned with spirituality and self-awareness, it is the perfect spot for an altar or sacred area devoted to your religious or spiritual orientation. Pictures of spiritual leaders, inspiring scenes from nature, and any objects or artifacts that remind you of the spiritual quality of life are important here. In addition, see if you can make this corner of your home a place to retreat, to contemplate your life's direction, and to find inspiration in certain books and teachings.

The element associated with this gua is "big earth," and it is an ideal place for heavy furniture, statues, and large earthen planters. If you feel you are "floating" in your life and can't seem to get your feet on the ground, consider placing nine large rocks, either inside or outside the home, to bring the necessary weightiness to your life.

The color associated with this gua is a deep midnight blue, which represents the vibration of the vast, unknown universe. You can use these darker colors to create a calming, nurturing space, which is ideal for meditation and contemplating the next phase of your journey.

"It is better to light a candle than to curse the darkness," as the adage goes. If you feel lost on your journey, try ceremoniously lighting a candle in this area of your home, and do the Three Secret Reinforcements to affirm the sacred intention of this light. Meditating on a candle flame is a traditional practice that helps to illuminate your mind.

If this gua is missing, you may suffer from a lack of focus or purpose. Try hanging nine crystals along the top of the inside wall, or use strong lights focused on the outside walls to illuminate the darker recesses of your home.

PROSPERITY JOURNAL:

"BRINGING THE DESIRED ESSENCE TO KEN"

Review the list of adjectives you noted for your desired spirituality and education, and decide how to apply this to the Ken gua of your home. Also, consider implementing some of the traditional feng shui cures, and remember to do the Three Secret Reinforcements with every change that you make.

FINANCIAL FENG SHUI—LIFE IS SUFFERING . . . OR IS IT?

One of the principle tenets of Buddhism is that life is suffering. We are caught in an endless cycle of life and death; we want something, we get it, and then we want something else. Round and round we go on the merry-go-round of life, continuously reaching for the golden ring, until finally we retire and fall comatose into a recliner. The ancient Buddhists predicted the American Dream.

If you think that a red convertible will make you sexy and desirable, you might pay anything to own one. Does this also mean that you will suddenly stop feeling that way as soon as you leave the driver's seat? If so, you had better never get out of that car!

As if we were being offered a magic pill, we are invited to "consume" material goods and services in the hopes that this consumption will bless us with the precious life qualities that we have been missing. But it is the very fact that the material goods *don't* fulfill us that keeps the businesses running. If we truly found the answer to our dreams, we would put away our wallets and spend the rest of our lives enjoying a feeling of bliss.

There will always be more things to buy, more advertisements that catch our eye, and something "new" that promises to make our lives complete. Dissatisfaction, satisfaction, dissatisfaction, satisfaction . . . the Wheel of Suffering never ends.

We call this the Rat Race. The problem with this race is that even if you win, you are still going to feel like a rat. Does this cycle of consumption make us feel wealthier? Happier? Not for long. It just makes us exhausted, feeling emptier than before we started.

The Kingdom of Heaven Is Within

The only way to love ourselves is to recognize that we are already complete, just the way we are. Can you imagine holding a child in your arms and saying, "I love you, but I would like you better if you were in a shiny red convertible stroller"? The child would probably start to cry! This is exactly what we do to ourselves, practically every moment of the day, as we push ourselves to do, be, and buy *more*.

In chapter 1, you were asked to come up with three adjectives to describe your ideal relationship with money. But why were you so attracted to those three adjectives in the first place? Why are *those* the qualities that make you feel fulfilled?

The material conditions we pursue are reflections of the qualities of our inner world. They are the feeling of your own self-nature. They are the Tao of You.

Is this to say that you should never pursue any material goals? Of course not. It's natural to want your environment to reflect how you are inside; in this way, we complete the connection between our inner and outer worlds. This is the creative act of life that keeps the Tao in motion.

The problem occurs only when we put a difficult, or even impossible, price tag on the essence we want to feel. If we do not already feel healthy, sexy, popular, or desirable, it may be because we are exhausting ourselves with forty- to sixty-hour workweeks in order to afford the placebos associated with these qualities.

Chasing illusions fuels our economy, but consider the price. Employment that lacks dignity and purpose is considered normal, even necessary. And then, when this starts to feel really bad, we run back to the mall for something that might make us feel better.

In the Buddhist perspective, the only way out of this Wheel of Suffering is to come back to the present and reconnect with the essence inside. Only then will the hunger be appeased. Only then will your journey be complete.

The Path to Financial Independence

In chapter 1, you were asked to write a definition of wealth. You may want to review your answer; your ideas may have changed greatly in the process of following this program.

Here is a vision of wealth to consider: "Wealth is money you don't have to work for." Sound shocking? Think about this: as long as you are working to get the money you need, you are a slave to the people who give it to you. You inhabit an invisible jail when you depend upon work to pay the bills. What will happen if you get downsized? Or become sick? If the clients get offended or your boss gets upset? These are not the thoughts of a wealthy person.

Consider your kitchen cabinets. How would you feel if, every time you wanted a meal, you had to run to the store, buy all the ingredients, and cook everything from scratch? That would be pretty exhausting and ultimately quite wasteful, don't you think?

The only way out is to never work again. That's right, quit this life of suffering forever. But without joining a cult or moving back in with our parents (which are usually the same thing), how is this possible?

There are basically two ways to be financially independent without working. One way is to do the things you love, whether you need money or not, and find a way to get paid really well for them. This was the focus of last week's program. While you still appear to be "working" in the traditional sense, the focus is not on making money, but on pursuing your mission. From this perspective, you are a servant only to your Higher Power, which is, I believe, the way it should be.

Of course, the only drawback is that you must still bring in enough money to support your costs. While your personal mission may ebb and flow, the need for income will remain steady. Many artists and creative types know this tension between inspiration and desperation, and it can be a hard row to hoe.

The alternative to constantly peddling your purpose is to grow your business large enough so that you don't perform the actual work, unless you want to. This way, you create financial independence while still doing your own thing. If you like to prepare birthday cakes, consider expanding the business by employing other creative bakers. You maintain the reputation and collect the money, while they do the work. Not a bad way to extend your mission even further into the world.

The downside of this approach: you still need to be at the helm. If problems come up, and they always will, your financial independence is once again at the mercy of the consumer. The Wheel of Suffering starts breathing down your neck once more. Is there no way out?

Beyond the Paycheck

No one can be rich without an income, but no one will remain rich by spending everything that comes in. Wealth is a reflection of your assets, not the rate of your spending. It doesn't matter if you travel first class or flash the biggest wad of bills in Vegas, your wealth comes down to the assets that you can liquidate to cash. And if that's not where you are putting your money, you will never be wealthy.

The only sure way to escape financial suffering is to accumulate enough capital so that you can live off the earnings. It's that simple. If you have $50 in a savings account earning 1 percent APR, your lifestyle as an independently wealthy person will consist of one plain bagel, without cream cheese, per year. But if you accumulate $200,000 and invest in a mutual fund averaging between 6 to 10 percent, the yearly growth will ultimately get you a decent cabana in Mexico with a hammock and a daily buffet of tropical fruits. And you will never have to do another stitch of work for the rest of your life. Getting the picture? Keep visualizing . . .

The goal of developing your assets is not just to have a "nest egg." Money is pure, potential energy in society, and it has the power to make things happen. Even when you are sleeping or on vacation, money that is properly invested can contribute to greater returns. With asset planning and development, your money will work *for* you, so you won't have to. This gives you the freedom to do whatever you want, whenever you want. That is true wealth.

Investing in Your Life

One of the greatest epidemics in modern culture is the annihilation of savings and the dependence on credit. This has infected all aspects of modern life. Anxiety, depression, lack of purpose, relationship problems, and general nihilism are all linked to this leeching of our finances. Think of this next time you get a "friendly" offer for a new card from a credit company.

The only way to take back our lives is to take back control of our money. It is exhausting to think that happiness, or even the experience of wealth, is linked to increased purchasing. The homes of many welfare recipients are packed with more features than most people could ever use. If you think that wealth is linked to buying and doing "more," you are setting yourself up for an endless journey on the Wheel of Suffering.

The daily experience of "wealth" does not have to be expensive. Wealth is an experience of how you take care of yourself and respond to your inner leanings. It doesn't reflect the amount of cash you are handling. By putting aside 10 percent of your salary to the stuff of your dreams and an additional 1 percent to your spiritual food, you should be feeling pretty happy inside. And that puts you in a great position to do some significant investing with the other 89 percent of your money. So let's get down to business.

Instead of giving your money away for other people to use, it's time to start investing in your own life. A Native American philosophy decrees never doing anything before considering how it will affect the next seven generations. Apply this perspective to how you use money: Figure out how old you will be in seven years, and ask yourself, "Will I feel the positive benefits of this  purchase seven years from now?" If the answer is "yes," you should make the purchase. But if not, put the money toward an investment that will really fulfill you. This is the nature of asset accumulation.

Now, you need to develop two types of accounts. First of all, you need a savings account for emergencies. The importance of this was discussed in chapter 4. Hopefully, you have been conscientiously following the Change Happens program and have accumulated a sizeable amount of loot over the past month!

The second type of asset accumulation is capital toward investment. The *only* true way to achieve financial independence is to accumulate enough capital so that you can live off the earnings.

This path, however, hits a detour if you are still in debt. The returns on most stocks *never* exceed the gouging that the credit card companies may be doing to you. If you still haven't taken action on this, it's not too late: cut the cards, lower your rates through a credit agency, and get on a reasonable plan for repayment. Don't sacrifice your six-month emergency fund to pay off the cards; the banks are not going to be interested in your plight if you lose your job.

The Tao of Spending and Investing

The yin/yang of the Tao represents the two currents of life: the active and the receptive. Ideally, our incomes would be feeding these two currents: the current of active spending for our daily desires, and receptive savings that will work for us so we do not have to do the work.

Most people develop some degree of capital, which they call their "retirement fund," but there is no reason why wealth has to wait until you are too old to enjoy it. By following the cycle of the Tao and simultaneously spending and investing each day, wealth can come a lot sooner than you think.

Ideally, we would follow this Tao to the exact percentile point, applying 50 percent of income to spending and 50 percent to savings and investments. Sound like an impossible idea? It is, if you are not willing to do it. I have actually had periods in my adult life when I applied this principle and put 50 percent of my net income into savings. At one time, I was even putting myself through graduate school, but I found inexpensive housing and reduced my expenses so that I could put aside half of my earnings. I know that it can be done, if you are truly committed to saving.

What if everyone handled money this way? Instead of living for fast food, fast sex, and transient lifestyles, people might feel their life energy was important and think carefully about the investment value of every action. We are trained to think that happiness comes from buying more things. As long as we believe it, we will never put our energy into the future, and we will shovel out the money as fast as it comes in.

Have you ever seen a billboard that said, "Put away your wallet! You have enough already"? What about a TV commercial that tells us to stay home with our friends and families, instead of going out shopping? What we see is generally what we do.

The Final Tithe: For Your Destiny

You do not have to observe a fifty-fifty prescription to follow the Tao of Money. Here is one way to bring these benefits into your life right now. Each week, you should be putting aside 10 percent of your income—Tithing to Yourself—for the immediate experience of wealth. To me, this is the "yang" of spending: luxury, pampering, and little adventures. Now, it is time to feed the "yin" side, the part that can get your money to grow. In addition to your luxury tithing, pull out another 10 percent from your monthly spending, and put it toward your savings and investments. Remember, without the accumulation of assets, your money will not have a chance to grow.

Two months ago, the idea of finding an additional 10 percent of available income might have seemed ludicrous and even impossible. You may have chosen this book because you couldn't make ends meet at all; excess income was not your problem! But by carefully following the principles and methods in this book, that extra 10 percent should not be so difficult to find.

Review your spending log, and question each item: "Will I really feel the benefits of this expense in seven years?" If not, you should devote little—or none—of your income to that purchase and put the money toward your investment tithe instead. Don't worry about how you might spend the money once it bears interest or how long it will take before you can retire. I can assure you, it will take a lot longer if you never invest it!

When you are in a store and you decide against a purchase, put the money in a separate section of your wallet, and write it down as "Savings" in your expenses book. A penny saved is a penny . . . earning interest! Then, at the end of the day, drop any money you have accumulated into your Hsun savings bank. If you accumulate funds like this every day, you may never have to think about tithing to savings at all. At the end of the month, if you saved less than 10 percent, just write yourself a check for the difference.

This way of accumulating savings is "hands-on" and can be a lot of fun. But if this seems to be complicated or involved, arrange for an automatic withdrawal from your checking account each month to go directly into your savings or investment account.

Start this investment tithe this week, no matter how much you are in debt or how much you really want that new television. Your bills and desires can wait, but your future cannot. How do you want to be living in twenty years? Your investment accounts hold the key.

If, after a week or two, you find that you still cannot manage an investment tithe of 10 percent, establish this as your goal, and set a solid date to achieve it. Then, create an incremental increase toward that date. If your goal is to invest 10 percent in six months, do 2 percent for the first two months and add an additional 2 percent each month thereafter. By setting a reasonable goal, your finances will start responding in ways that you never thought possible.

Here is a fun ritual that will help you appreciate the power of your capital. Don't plan to withdraw any of the interest you earn, but once a year, perhaps at the Chinese New Year, withdraw 1 percent of your fund and use it to *invest* in some material asset that you really want. Remember to use the seven-year rule when deciding what to purchase. You can do the Three Secret Reinforcements on this object and recognize it as a symbol of the wealth that you are accumulating. This can become a goal to inspire you to build your capital, and every time that you use it for these valued purchases, you will be reminded of the power of your wealth.

An Exercise on Investment

In chapter 4, we defined a simple, painless way to begin a savings account: Gather your change each day, and let the coins accumulate into a substantial monthly deposit. Hopefully, in the span of these four weeks, you have been able to evade the desire or need to spend that accumulation and now have a tidy sum in savings.

Once you have reached the equivalent of six months' net income in an interest-bearing account, it is time to shift your focus. What is a savings account, after all? It's basically dormant money, waiting to be spent. It is not much good to us while it sits in some account accruing 1 percent APR or less, and it won't be much good if we spend it either. The only other option is to put it to work. It's time to stop saving and start investing.

Investing your money is like sending your troops off to battle. If you select your battles wisely and minimize the risk of casualties as well as you can, you are assured some success. If you have never made an investment before, I recommend you start the process now.

Just by collecting your coins every day, you should now have a stack of coins worth between $50 and $100. Since this is basically "found money," I recommend that you use it as an important experiment in investing. Send those "troops" out into the field to see what they can do for you.

If you have never invested money before, consider using the $50 from your Change Happens account to plant the seed for your future wealth. By educating yourself enough to take this first step and actually investing "real money" for your future, you are opening up a new perspective on your life that could have huge ramifications.

There certainly isn't enough room in this book to cover all your investment options, but it's vital that you start to turn your mind toward the true earning potential of your dollars. A number of resources are outlined in the bibliography.

This week, decide to pursue a mutual fund or other investment with this first installment from your Change Happens savings account, and start to invest in a real future. You might also consider joining an investment club, either locally or online, to help you make educated decisions.

INNER FENG SHUI—TIME IS MONEY

Haste makes waste. The way we handle time is indicative of the way we handle money. Notice people who rush from one appointment to the next. When they pull out their wallets, their sense of disarray usually comes with it. If you want to start saving money, the best thing to do is slow down and become conscious of how you are using your energy.

Everyone on this planet has exactly the same amount of time each day: 1,440 minutes. What you do with those minutes is up to you. If you value time, you will invest it wisely. Or you can let it slip through your fingers.

The same experience is true of our money. If someone handed you $1,440, what would you do? Would you invest the money wisely, or would it disappear without a thought? Time is money. Your future is in your hands.

If you tend to invest your time poorly, after a while, you will start to resent time itself. How many times do you wake up in the morning and exclaim, "Oh boy, I have another sixteen waking hours to use as I please!"

Celebrating the Spirituality of Money

Just as we are learning to put aside money each week for both savings and luxuries, we need to make the same allotments with our time. Money conforms to fit the containers in which it is held. If it is not used in a focused way, it will flow without bringing many benefits. The same is true for time: it expands to fit the tasks at hand. If the only thing you absolutely had to do all day was brush your teeth, your entire day would revolve around this toothbrushing ritual!

In the following chart, write down the activities of your day, starting from the moment you open your eyes in the morning to the final moment when you turn out the lights. Be as detailed as you can. For instance, instead of blocking off an eight- to ten-hour period and writing one word, "Work," be specific. What do you do at work? What sorts of activities fill your workday?

Time	Activity	Rating	Action Step
8 A.M.			
9			
10			
11			
12 P.M.			
1			
2			
3			
4			
5			
6			
7			
8			
9			
10			
11			
12 A.M.			

Notice that the third column is headed "Rating." You are now going to rate the value of each of the activities, using the same criteria that you use with your financial expenses:

- One check if it is something you need to get done
- A second check if it is something that you love to do
- A third check if you did not waste time doing it, and it was the best use of your time

In the last column, note an action step for planning the best use of this time. If an activity received three checks, you don't need to change a thing. But if it got fewer than three, reconsider how you are spending your precious life chi!

For instance, here some things on a sample list:

Time	Activity	Rating	Action Step
7:30 A.M.	Drive to work (one hour).	Needed? Yes. Enjoyed? Yes, listened to audiobooks Best use of time? No, should take the train and get work done.	Get train schedule and commuter mug, decide how to use this time more wisely.
10:15 A.M.	Meeting with corporate "team" (one hour, fifteen minutes).	Needed? No, waste of time. Enjoyed? Hardly. Best use of time? No.	Speak with boss about emailing instead of meeting.
5 P.M.	Washed the dog (thirty minutes).	Needed? YES! Enjoyed? NO! Best use of time? NO!	Hire local kid to wash dog each week.
7 P.M.	Dinner out with gorgeous spouse (three hours).	Needed? Yes, to save marriage. Enjoyed? Very much. Best use of time? No, long drive and had to wait thirty minutes for a table.	Call ahead next time for reservation, and go to closer restaurant on work nights.

There are basically two ways to increase the value of your time: Say "no" to some activities and replace them with something more valuable, or learn to do two things at once. I know that this violates the old adage, "Do one thing at a time," but you can often increase both the value and pleasure of your time by combining activities. For example, the daily commute was made more pleasurable with audiobooks and even more valuable by getting work done on the train. Both of these are efficient uses of the "two-fer" rule.

If you need to do some task that is particularly unpleasant, try combining it with something pleasurable, or at least do it with another unenjoyable task, so you get more done faster and have time to do the things you enjoy.

The Time Bagua

Use the bagua diagram below to lay out how you use time. In each gua, there are up to twelve hours. Color in the number of hours that you spend in each of these areas of your life. If you spend more than twelve hours a day at work or in any other activity, you may need to break through the walls of the bagua to fit yourself in.

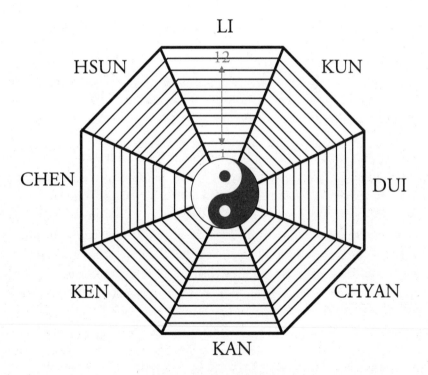

Bagua with time increments.

Notice how you feel as you look at this diagram. If you have been impoverished in any area of your life, this may provide you with the reason.

PROSPERITY JOURNAL: "IF I HAD MORE TIME, I WOULD . . ."

In your journal, list the nine sectors of the bagua, and answer this question for each: "If I had a bit more time, I would . . . ":

- Kan (career)
- Ken (self-knowledge)
- Chen (family and household)
- Hsun (wealth and luxury)
- Li (fame and recognition)
- Kun (relationships)
- Dui (children and creativity)
- Chyan (helpful people and travel)
- T'ai Chi (health)

Assign a simple pursuit to any sectors in your Time Bagua that are undeveloped.

Now we come to the hard part: how to address the problem. You may believe that you cannot use your time in any different way, but this is just not true. Even people in jail get free time, but hopefully, you will not need to be incarcerated in order to refocus your life!

After eight hours of blissful sleep, you are still left with 960 minutes in the day. Your mission, if you choose to accept it, is to allocate 10 percent of those minutes toward the areas of your life that have been deprived (see your Time Bagua, above). This is not just a luxury; it is an investment. How can you expect new developments to come into your life if you are not available to receive them?

If you really do not think that you can find the time, there is a blank copy of the Twenty-Four-Hour Time Rating Chart in appendix C. Use it every day to record, analyze, delegate, and combine your activities until the required ninety-six minutes are free for your better use. Here's a hint: most people stay longer at work than they really need to, because they don't know what else to do with their time. Now that you have listed what you really want to do with your time, leave work early (or at least on time), and get on with your life.

On the chart below, block off ninety-six minutes in each day for the fulfillment of your Time Bagua. These do not need to be consecutive minutes, but less

Celebrating the Spirituality of Money

than thirty minutes at a time is probably not enough to start a new activity. Then, write in the specific activity you will pursue. Do not leave it to chance. Your life energy is much too precious for that.

You may want to build a Sabbath ritual into your week and set aside one day for contemplation, rejuvenation, and other fulfilling activities. I like to use Sunday for this purpose, but you can choose any day of the week. You can use this time for your Prosperity Date, for fulfilling an area of your Time Bagua, or to do any of the meditations and rituals that we have covered in the book. Possess it as your own.

Time	Monday	Tuesday	Wednesday	Thursday	Friday	Saturday	Sunday
8 A.M.							
9							
10							
11							
12 P.M.							
1							
2							
3							
4							
5							
6							
7							
8							
9							
10							
11							
12 A.M.							

The Meditative Millionaire, Part 3: Your Inner Abundance

To end this week's program, this is an Abundance Meditation to help you connect to the abundance within. The world we see is a reflection of our inner world. If we experience poverty, it is because we feel poor inside. When we experience the wealth and beauty of our self-nature, the world reflects this vision.

1. Sit quietly, close your eyes, and connect to your breathing. Allow your breath to drop down into your belly, and follow its flow. Now, imagine your breath is dropping down even further to your feet, and then into the ground, so it feels as if your breath is ebbing and flowing from the ground itself.

2. As you focus on your breathing, imagine you are sitting on a large, pink lotus flower of a thousand petals that is floating in the middle of space. Visualize yourself resting on this blossom, feeling totally safe and secure. In this place of deep knowing, feel your connection to your inner spirit, which transcends the dualities of life.

3. Now, bring to mind an area in your life in which you often experience scarcity. Silently, with eyes still closed, allow yourself to experience this feeling of deprivation: physically, emotionally, mentally, and spiritually. If it feels uncomfortable, just allow it to be uncomfortable. You may feel vulnerable, angry, or bitter. Whatever your particular experience, allow yourself to have it. See if it feels familiar—perhaps recognize *how* familiar it is.

4. Now, imagine taking this experience of scarcity and mentally placing it on an imaginary altar in front of you. Notice that you are still connected, but now separated from it.

5. While still resting on the thousand-petal lotus, imagine an infinite number of Holy Figures and Buddhas surrounding you in space on all sides, to the furthest extension of the universe. Feel their presence supporting and comforting you, and imagine that their holy light is radiating toward you and filling every cell of your body.

6. As you are filled with this radiance, imagine that this light reaches your heart, contacting a beautiful closed lotus bud that

rests there. As the light touches this bud, the flower starts to open, until it spreads one thousand tiny little pink petals, and in the middle of the flower is a tiny Buddha, the essence of your own being.

7. The Buddha of your Heart's Blossom is filled with its own light, and this light starts to fill your body. As the light expands, the Buddha starts to grow, until it slowly fills every part of you. Your hands are now the Buddha's hands, your legs are the Buddha's legs, and so on. Feel how completely your body and the Buddha's body become one. Move your fingers, and you are moving the Buddha's fingers. *Here we experience ourselves as spaceless, timeless, joyful, and abundant.* From this place of connection, everything we do is an expression of this universal abundance.

8. Now, feel your Buddha light emanating out to all reaches of the universe. Send your light out to all the Buddhas and Holy Figures that are surrounding you. See how they receive your light, and that they then send their light back to you.

9. Send your light now to all the people you contact in your life: your teachers, spiritual leaders, family members, friends, children, animals, and so on. To all beings, those who suffer and those who release the suffering, send your light, see it received, and receive the light from them.

10. Now, send your light to the part of you that you placed on the imaginary altar, the part of you that suffers with feelings of scarcity and deprivation. Send your light with compassion and love, and allow yourself to understand this place of scarcity. Allow it to explain to you why it has been feeling as it did, and ask that the universe guide you in helping this portion of you that has suffered. Continue to send your light to this part of your being, see it released from suffering, and see it sending its light back to you.

11. Now, imagine standing at the entranceway of your home. Feel yourself filling your home with your light, and then feel the home sending its own light back to you.

12. Next, see yourself standing at the entranceway of your place of business. Fill this space with your light, giving it to all people who enter there, and then receive the light of this place.

13. Finally, make a wish for yourself, vocalize it softly, and release it to the universe. Imagine your wish coming to you in ways that make you happy and fulfilled on all levels of your being.

14. End this meditation with the Six True Words, "Om Ma Ni Pad Me Hum," and feel the presence of the divinity within you.

ACTION STEPS ON THE JOURNEY TO WEALTH:
WEEK 9 SYNOPSIS

Who have you become in the process of working through this book? Notice how your views on money, wealth, and even yourself have changed. Check off each task you fulfill, and enjoy the great feeling of accomplishment as you complete this program.

1. Discuss your feelings about your life purpose with someone close to you. Talk about how you came to your conclusions and how this affects your financial outlook.

2. If you travel for business or pleasure, find a way to implement a few of the feng shui tips on your next trip.

3. If you really want the royal treatment, try the Red Carpet Cure the next time you take an important trip or go to a big meeting.

4. Review the goals you set for the Ken section of your home, and implement at least two this week.

5. Your future is waiting, but not for long. If you haven't done it already, set up a savings account and decide the amount you will tithe to it each month.

6. Step into the market, and use $50 from your Change Happens account to make your first investment. Notice how your financial self-image has changed during these nine weeks.

7. Evaluate your current use of time, and identify the "time leaks."

8. Put your watch where your mouth is! Fight for those precious ninety-six minutes to expand your life and pursue your dreams.

9. Try the Abundance Meditation at least once this week, perhaps during a time you choose for your Sabbath.

Congratulations! The next step of this program is the rest of your life!

Commencement

You do not have to be a millionaire to be wealthy, and you do not have to be broke in order to feel poor. Feeling wealthy is based on how you feel about yourself, not the items you have collected.

If you are feeling pessimistic about your future, no amount of money can fill that hole. But if you feel bright about your prospects, the financial difficulties are just cracks in the sidewalk along your path.

There is a reason why we refer to graduation as commencement: it's the beginning of a whole new life. Imagine a college student working toward her degree. She may have to count nickels to pay the tuition each semester, yet she's building toward something bigger, and the inconvenience of any hardship seems minimal in the face of opportunities to come.

I wish all of us would take the perspective of the college student: to see each day as an investment in a brighter future, instead of looking at present circumstances as limiting statements of what we can become.

No matter what happened in the stock market today, the sun will rise tomorrow, and you will face a new blank canvas, ready for your signature. Take the challenge. Make the mark of your divine self-nature, in whatever way you can, before the sun sets on another page of your life.

Wealth is the feeling in your heart as you progress on the journey of your life. May you be blessed every step of the way.

APPENDIX A

Resources

FENG SHUI CONSULTING SERVICES AND TRAINING

E. J. Shaffert: Feng Shui Design Consulting
Director, The London School of Feng Shui
www.FengShuiandMoney.com

For information about feng shui classes/training, design services, and other resources connected to the material in this book, you can contact E. J. Shaffert directly through his website, *www.FengShuiandMoney.com*. His established feng shui design firm addresses the needs of a range of international residential and corporate clientele, specializing in design, financial feng shui, and transformational living.

Some of the services include:

- Free insights right to your email inbox: "Feng Shui Tips." In his popular newsletter, E. J. offers specific suggestions for creative, profitable feng shui approaches to living. Subscribe via the website: *www.FengShuiandMoney.com*
- The London School of Feng Shui offers extensive training programs, classes, and workshops at the London location and also online.
- Feng shui consultations for residences, businesses, and corporations are offered internationally. Clients can arrange on-site consultations to coincide with travel schedules, or you can arrange long-distance sessions via phone or Skype.
- Advisory consulting is also available for architects, landscape planners, interior designers, and real estate agents.
- Personal therapy/coaching is available internationally via phone or Skype or at the London office. For further information, please contact via the website *www.FengShuiandMoney.com*.

FINANCIAL ORGANIZATIONS

Debtors Anonymous
www.debtorsanonymous.org

Debt Repayment Plans

Check with your local Better Business Bureau before contracting with a debt consolidator. Here are some national groups to explore:

Consolidated Credit Counseling
www.consolidatedcredit.org
(800) 728–3632

National Foundation for Credit Counseling
www.nfcc.org
(800) 388–2227

For Information about Investing

National Association of Investors Corporation
www.better-investing.org
(248) 583–6242
Offers local investment clubs throughout the United States.

Alliance for Investor Education
www.investoreducation.org
Offers information on financial workshops and conferences.

Mutual Fund Education Alliance
(Creators of *The Investor's Guide to Low Cost Mutual Funds*)
www.mfea.com

Morningstar (mutual fund rating service)
(Publishes a directory that evaluates funds)
www.morningstar.com

APPENDIX B

Your Prosperity Plan

FENG SHUI AND MONEY **PROSPERITY PLAN**   Week: _____

Item	Estimated Costs	Mon	Tues	Wed	Thurs	Fri	Sat	Sun	Week Total	Balance

Twenty-Four-Hour Time Rating Chart

Use this chart every day, if necessary, until you can tithe 10 percent of your waking hours (approximately ninety minutes) to the development of your interests.

Time	Activity	Rating	Action Step
8 A.M.			
9			
10			
11			
12 P.M.			
1			
2			
3			
4			
5			
6			
7			
8			
9			
10			
11			
12 A.M.			

APPENDIX D

Bibliography

ENVIRONMENTAL FENG SHUI

Carter, Karen Rauch. *Move Your Stuff, Change Your Life*. New York: Fireside Books, 2000.

Emoto, Masaru. *The Hidden Messages of Water*. Hillsboro, OR: Beyond Words Publishing, 2005.

Kondo, Marie. *The Life-Changing Magic of Tidying Up*. Berkeley: Ten Speed Press, 2014.

Post, Steven. *The Modern Book of Feng Shui*. New York: Dell Publishing, 1998.

Ryan, Maxwell. *Apartment Therapy*. New York: Bantam Dell, 2006.

Stoddard, Alexandra. *Living a Beautiful Life*. New York: Avon Books, 1986.

Sung, Edgar, Ph.D. *The Classic Chinese Almanac*. San Francisco: MJE Publishing, 2017.

FINANCIAL FENG SHUI

Cameron, Julia, and Mark Bryan. *Money Drunk, Money Sober*. New York: Ballantine Publishing, 1992.

Chopra, Deepak. *The Seven Spiritual Laws of Success*. San Rafael, CA: Amber-Allen Publishing, 1995.

Dominguez, Joe, and Vicki Robin. *Your Money or Your Life*. New York: Penguin Books, 1992.

Kiyosaki, Robert T., and Sharon L. Lechter. *Rich Dad, Poor Dad*. New York: Warner Books, 1998.

Mundis, Jerrold. *How to Get out of Debt, Stay out of Debt, and Live Prosperously*. New York: Bantam Books, 1988.

Nemeth, Maria. *The Energy of Money*. New York: Ballantine Wellspring, 2000.

Ramsey, Dave. *The Total Money Makeover*. Nashville: Nelson Books. 2013.

INNER FENG SHUI

Beattie, Melody. *Journey to the Heart*. San Francisco: HarperSanFrancisco, 1996.

Cameron, Julia. *The Artist's Way*. New York: G. P. Putnam's Sons, 1992.

Gawain, Shakti. *Creative Visualization*. Novato, CA: New World Library, 1995.

Miedaner, Talane. *Coach Yourself to Success*. Chicago: Contemporary Books, 2000.

Pierrakos, Eva. *The Pathwork of Self-Transformation*. New York: Bantam Books, 1990.

Roberts, Jane. *The Nature of Personal Reality, a Seth Book*. New York: Prentice Hall, 1974.

———. *Seth Speaks: The Eternal Validity of the Soul*. New York: Bantam Books, 1972.

About the Author

E. J. Shaffert is a certified therapist and feng shui consultant, and director of the London School of Feng Shui. Combing ancient feng shui principles with a refreshingly modern perspective, his work enables individuals to deeply transform their lives by working with the energetic dynamics of their immediate environment.

Endorsed by His Holiness Professor Lin Yun, who brought this form of feng shui to the West, E. J. has worked as a feng shui design consultant and teacher for over eighteen years. He is a popular workshop and seminar leader and has offered his feng shui insights online and on television and radio.

At the London School of Feng Shui, E. J. directs an intensive two-year training in feng shui design and spiritual development. Some of these courses are also available online.

For individuals seeking therapy and coaching, E. J. also maintains a private practice in London and remotely by phone or Skype.

For further information about these and other services, visit his web site: *www.FengShuiandMoney.com.*

Index

Index

 **Books from Allworth Press**

Estate Planning for the Healthy, Wealthy Family
by Carla Garrity, Mitchell Baris, and Stanley Neeleman (6 × 9, 256 pages, ebook, $22.99)

Fund Your Dreams Like a Creative Genius™
by Brainard Carey (6⅛ × 6⅛, 160 pages, paperback, $12.99)

How to Plan and Settle Estates
by Edmund Fleming (6 × 9, 288 pages, paperback, $16.95)

How to Win Grants
by Alan Silver (5½ × 8¼, **140 pages, paperback, $12.95**)

Legal Forms for Everyone (Sixth Edition)
by Carl W. Battle (8½ × 11, 280 pages, paperback, $24.99)

Legal Guide to Social Media
by Kimberly A. Houser (6 × 9, 208 pages, paperback, $19.95)

Living Trusts for Everyone (Second Edition)
by Ronald Farrington Sharp (5½ × 8¼, 192 pages, paperback, $14.99)

Love & Money
by Ann-Margaret Carrozza (6 × 9, 240 pages, paperback, $19.99)

The Money Mentor
by Tad Crawford (6 × 9, 272 pages, paperback, $24.95)

Protecting Your Assets from Probate and Long-Term Care
by Evan H. Farr (5½ × 8¼, 208 pages, paperback, $14.99)

Scammed
by Gini Graham Scott, PhD (6 × 9, 256 pages, paperback, $14.99)

The Secret Life of Money
by Tad Crawford (5½ × 8½, 304 pages, paperback, $19.95)

The Smart Consumer's Guide to Good Credit
by John Ulzheimer (5¼ × 8¼, 216 pages, paperback, $14.95)

To see our complete catalog or to order online, please visit *www.allworth.com*.